Knowledge, Power and Educational Reform

Knowledge, Power and Educational Reform seeks to develop the field of educational policy and educational policy research by offering insights and examples of contemporary work which draws upon Basil Bernstein's sociology of pedagogy. The particular contribution of this collection is to demonstrate the power of Bernsteinian concepts to explore, analyse and engage with contemporary political reforms of education, contemporary pedagogic debates and the changing nature of professional knowledges, relationships and structures. There are contributions about the processes of schooling and higher education but also from a range of other educational settings which employ pedagogies and create professional identities. These contributions indicate another important aspect of Bernstein's project – that of its general reach and application. Taken together, these illustrate the scope of Bernstein's theory and its capacity to produce what he liked to call 'news' through the application of his ideas in research projects of remarkable variety. In this way, the book provides access to his theory by demonstrating the ideas in action. It is in this manner that Bernstein's work is perhaps unique amongst that of major social theorists.

Illustrating how contemporary pedagogic reforms can be analysed and understood in the context of social order and social change, individual chapters cover:

- the use of particular concepts such as voice research;
- the significance of social class in relation to the language, schooling and home cultures;
- the differences between official and pedagogic recontextualizing fields;
- the formation of different types of identities;
- the construction of the learner;
- the formation of teacher identities and use of pedagogic discourses; and
- the analysis of performance-based educational reforms and its impact on pedagogy.

Readers are encouraged to engage in a high level of scholarly discussion with Bernstein's sociology of pedagogy, spanning a range of international contexts and engaging at different levels with the implications of particular pedagogic forms.

Drawing together work by an international group of scholars, this book will appeal to those interested in the development of appropriate theoretical models for the study of educational policy and professional training including: sociologists of education, policy researchers, curriculum researchers, and those working within undergraduate, postgraduate and professional training contexts in professional education and social theory/sociology internationally.

Rob Moore is Senior Lecturer in Education at Cambridge University, UK. **Madeleine Arnot** is Professor of Sociology of Education at the University of Cambridge, UK. **John Beck** is Lecturer in Education at the University of Cambridge, UK. **Harry Daniels** is Professor of Education at the University of Bath, UK.

Knowledge, Power and Educational Reform

Applying the sociology of Basil Bernstein

Rob Moore, Madeleine Arnot, John Beck
and Harry Daniels

Routledge
Taylor & Francis Group

LONDON AND NEW YORK

First published 2006 by Routledge
2 Park Square, Milton Park,
Abingdon, Oxon OX14 4RN

Simultaneously published in the USA and Canada
by Routledge
270 Madison Ave, New York, NY 10016

Routledge is an imprint of the Taylor & Francis Group, an informa business

Transferred to Digital Printing 2009

Typeset in Garamond by
GreenGate Publishing Services, Tonbridge

British Library Cataloguing in Publication Data
A catalogue record for this book is available from the British Library

Library of Congress Cataloging in Publication Data
Knowledge, power and educational reform : applying the sociology of
basil bernstein / Rob Moore ... [et al].
    p. cm.
  Includes bibliographical references.
  ISBN 0-415-37914-8 (hardback)
1. Educational sociology. 2. Critical pedagogy. 3. Bernstein, Basil
B. I. Moore, Rob, 1946-
   LC191.K594 2006
   306.43–dc22

                                   2006009322

ISBN10: 0-415-37914-8 (hbk)
ISBN10: 0-415-55972-3 (pbk)

ISBN13: 978-0-415-37914-4 (hbk)
ISBN13: 978-0-415-55972-0 (pbk)

Contents

Illustrations

Figures

Tables

Contributors

Madeleine Arnot is Professor of Sociology of Education and Fellow of Jesus College at the University of Cambridge, UK. She has published extensively on the relevance of Bernstein's sociology for the study of gender relations (including gender code theory, feminist approaches to Bernsteinian theory, and invisible pedagogies). Her recent research with Diane Reay on pupil consultation in primary and secondary schools focuses on democratic pedagogic rights, the framing of social relations in pedagogic encounters and pupil voice in the context of performance pedagogies.

John Beck teaches sociology of education and curriculum, and professional studies. He is Education Team Chair in the University of Cambridge Faculty of Education and a Fellow of Homerton College. His research interests include citizenship, citizenship education, and personal and social education. Within the sociology of education, his most recent work has employed Bernsteinian approaches to analyse the changing structuring of identity and professionalism within education in Britain.

Andrew Brown is Head of the Doctoral School and Associate Dean of Research at the Institute of Education, University of London. His research focuses on the relationship between academic, professional and everyday discourse, knowledge and practice. He is co-author (with Paul Dowling) of *Doing Research/Reading Research: A Mode of Interrogation for Education* (London: RoutledgeFalmer, 1998) and (with David Scott, Ingrid Lunt and Lucy Thorne) *Professional Doctorates: Integrating Professional and Academic Knowledge* (Buckingham: Open University Press).

Harry Daniels is Director of the Centre for Sociocultural and Activity Theory Research at the University of Bath. His research is concerned with disadvantage and disability in a wide range of fields. He has published several books which are concerned with the development of post-Vygotskian theory and is concerned to further the case for a productive synthesis of the Vygotskian thesis with Bernstein's sociology of pedagogy.

Gerard Duveen is a Reader in Genetic Social Psychology in the Department of Social and Developmental Psychology at the University of Cambridge. His work is focused on studies of the development of social representations, and has included research on the emergence of gender identities in primary classrooms (*Gender Identities and Education*, with Barbara Lloyd, London: Harvester Wheatsheaf, 1990).

Ruqaiya Hasan is Emeritus Professor (linguistics) at Macquarie University, Australia. She did her Linguistics with Halliday, Mcintosh, Sinclair, Abercrombie, Catford and later with Sydney Lamb. Coming to linguistics from the teaching of literature, she has always been inclined to think in terms of text and social context. Her doctoral research concerned theoretical issues in linguistic stylistics, followed by work on Cohesion in English. Early in her career she worked with Basil Bernstein. In her major sociolinguistic research in the area of semantic variation, she made extensive use of Bernstein's code theory, providing a linguistic basis for code differentiation. Ruqaiya Hasan's collected works are currently being published in seven volumes, the first of which – dedicated to Bernstein – has just appeared (London: Equinox, 2005).

Wayne Hugo recently completed his doctoral thesis at Rhodes University (*Journeys of the Learning Soul: Plato to Descartes*). He has published in *Curriculum Studies, Philosophy* and *History of Education* and is currently a lecturer at the University of KwaZulu Natal.

Gabrielle Ivinson is a university lecturer in the Cardiff School of Social Sciences, Cardiff University. She is a social and developmental psychologist whose main interest is the way knowledge is socially constructed. Her doctoral thesis *The Construction of the Curriculum* (Cambridge University 1998) drew on Bernstein's sociology of pedagogy and Moscovici's theory of Social Representations. She worked on an ESRC project on cross-curricular themes in the national curriculum in the UK between 1991 and 1994 and an EU funded project 'Women as Citizens' between 1994 and 1998. She is writing a book on gender as an emergent social representation within pedagogic practice in single-sex classes with Patricia Murphy at the Open University.

Karl Maton recently completed his doctoral thesis at the University of Cambridge (*The Field of Higher Education: A Sociology of Reproduction, Transformation, Change and the Conditions of Emergence for Cultural Studies*), which develops Bernstein's approach to create a relational sociology of higher education (see http://www.KarlMaton.com). He has published in sociology, cultural studies, linguistics and education, and is currently Research Fellow in Sociology of Education at Wollongong University in Australia.

Rob Moore is Senior Lecturer in sociology of education in the Faculty of
Education of the University of Cambridge. He is a Fellow of Homerton
College. His work includes research into youth and the labour market,
educational decision-making and issues of citizenship amongst under-
graduates (with John Beck and John Ahier). His current work is
concerned with problems in the sociology of knowledge and the structuring of intellectual fields.

Ana M. Morais is Professor of Education and coordinator of the ESSA Group
– Sociological Studies of the Classroom – at the School of Science,
University of Lisbon, Portugal. Her recent research includes a number of
projects centred particularly on the primary and secondary classroom and
on curriculum, in the sciences.

Johan Muller is Professor of Education, Deputy Dean for Research and
Postgraduate Affairs and Director of the Graduate School in the Faculty
of Humanities at the University of Cape Town. In 2000 his book,
Reclaiming Knowledge (RoutledgeFalmer, London) was published, and in
2003, *Getting Schools Working* (with Nick Taylor and Penny Vinjevold,
Pearson Educational, Cape Town).

Isabel P. Neves is Associate Professor of Education and coordinator of the
ESSA Group at the School of Science, University of Lisbon, Portugal. Her
recent research includes a number of projects centred particularly on the
primary and secondary classroom and on curriculum, in the sciences.

Sally Power is a Professorial Fellow and Director of Research at the School of
Social Sciences, Cardiff University, and a Visiting Professorial Fellow at
the Institute of Education, University of London. She has a long-standing
interest in the empirical application of Bernstein's sociology of education
and, in recent years, its relevance for understanding middle-class differentiation and identity formation. Relevant publications in this area
include *Education and the Middle Class* (co-authored with Tony Edwards,
Geoff Whitty and Valerie Wigfall, published by Open University Press,
2003) and 'Bernstein and the Middle Class' (co-authored with Geoff
Whitty and published in the *British Journal of Sociology of Education*,
2002).

Diane Reay is Professor of Education at Cambridge University. She has published extensively in the area of social class and education, and has drawn
on Bernstein's sociology of education in order to understand class differences in involvement in schooling and students' pedagogic rights and
entitlements in classrooms. Her most recent research activities include
ESRC projects on children and social exclusion in urban settings, pupils'
identities and participation in learning, and the white middle classes and
inner-city comprehensives.

Alan Sadovnik is Professor of Education and Sociology, Director of the PhD Program in Urban Educational Policy and Associate Director of the Institute on Education Law and Policy at Rutgers University, Newark, New Jersey. Among his publications are *Equity and Excellence in Higher Education* (1995); *Exploring Education: An Introduction to the Foundations of Education* (1994, 2001, 2006); *Knowledge and Pedagogy: The Sociology of Basil Bernstein* (1995); *'Schools of Tomorrow', Schools of Today: What Happened to Progressive Education* (1999) and *Founding Mothers and Others: Women Educational Leaders During the Progressive Era* (2002). He received the Willard Waller Award in 1993 from the American Sociological Association's Sociology of Education Section for the outstanding article published in the field, and American Educational Studies Association Critics Choice Awards in 1995 for Knowledge and Pedagogy, in 2000 for *'Schools of Tomorrow'*, and in 2002 for *Founding Mothers and Others*.

Acknowledgements

We would like to thank Jan Oram for her hard work, efficiency and support in the organization of the Third International Basil Bernstein Symposium that took place at Clare College, Cambridge, England in July 2004. The papers in this volume were originally presented at that symposium.

Introduction

Rob Moore, Madeleine Arnot, John Beck and Harry Daniels

The chapters that comprise this book are a selection from papers presented at the Third International Basil Bernstein Symposium at Clare College, Cambridge, England in July 2004. The previous one was in Cape Town in 2002 (Muller *et al.* (eds) 2004) and the first in Lisbon in 2000 (Morais *et al.* (eds) 2001). It is instructive to register that, together, these volumes represent forty-one papers by a diverse group of Bernsteinian scholars and researchers operating globally, representing countries from five continents. Furthermore, each is a *selection* of papers from the symposia, which were attended, also, by others who did not present papers. This particular international symposium represents by no means all the work that is taking place within Bernstein's legacy – it is just one of a number of intersecting global networks. What we see here is an indicator of a remarkable, worldwide, wide-ranging and diverse set of activities taking place within the problematic that Bernstein constructed across his lifetime as a theorist, scholar and researcher. These facts beg a question: what was it about Bernstein's thinking and work that made possible such an exceptional proliferation of scholarship and of research programmes operating independently, in so many different places, within the framework of his problematic?

The question raised above is itself very much a Bernsteinian question. His broadest concern was with the relationship between the social division of labour and the symbolic division of labour. In a significant respect, his major effort was to flesh out these broad brush-stroke concepts – to fill in the detail, to 'close the discursive gap', as he put it, between any concept and the world. In a sense, the basic questions here are very simple, but also immensely demanding. Bernstein was exceptional as a major social theorist in that he confronted those demands head-on. It is in these terms that it is possible to describe what it is that the papers in this volume (and in the previous two) share in common. It is in doing the work of the theory and concepts that his thinking brought into being, in the continuing task of 'closing the discursive gap', of fleshing out concepts in such a way that they become refined as research instruments that can actively engage with data and create 'news'. To return to the question of what kind of theory Bernstein's theory is, then one answer is to say that it is a theory that *works* in the sense that it can be *put to work.* Part of what makes this possible is that Bernstein's system is not centred in any one particular approach (any one 'ism'), nor is it founded in any one category (such as class or gender), but rather it assembles approaches in ways that engage with the intricate interweaving of categories.

In order to understand the relationship between the papers in this volume, it might well be more appropriate to say that they are in the first instance located within Bernstein's *problematic* rather than within his *theory*, in that there is not *a* theory that defines Bernstein's intellectual system.

So, then, the papers represented in this volume are putting Bernsteinian concepts to work, but they are not all doing so in the same way. The authors represented are not all sociologists, but are located within a variety of disciplines and their concerns range across the philosophical and epistemological, address issues of identity and consciousness, social and educational policy and reform, and focus, also, on the organization and dynamics of schooling and of classroom interaction.

The volume is divided into four parts. In the first, the chapters by Muller, Moore, Maton and Hugo address issues relating to the distinctive features of Bernstein's problematic and the ways in which his work might enable us to theorize the structurings of intellectual fields and the conditions for their productivity. In part they do this through the exegesis, explication and further elaboration of Bernstein's work and concepts. Muller distinguishes between the ideas of 'verticality' and 'grammaticality' in Bernstein's later work. The former has to do with the capacity of theory to progressively integrate knowledge at increasing levels of generality and abstraction and the latter with the capacity of a theory, through its concepts, to engage with the world – to produce an 'external language of description' that specifies the manner in which we would recognize in the world the kinds of things the theory posits as existing there. It is precisely through its capacity to become increasingly concrete in terms of engaging with the mundane through the elaboration of ever more refined concepts that theory can accomplish the task of abstraction and integration – can achieve *verticality*. Where this interplay between verticality and grammaticality (between 'internal' and 'external' 'languages of description') is most effective, then knowledge structures assume what Bernstein described as a 'hierarchical' form, but where it is least successful the field assumes a 'horizontal' or segmented structure with numerous competing and supposedly incommensurable approaches. Muller locates Bernstein's contribution within broader historical and philosophical debates concerning the possibility of progress in knowledge. He also raises a crucial issue: does the character of the way in which knowledge is produced have implications for the manner in which it is reproduced – for pedagogy?

Moore's chapter explores similar themes, but in relation to the distinction that Bernstein makes between sociology of education that treats education as a 'relay' for things outside it (class, gender, ethnicity, etc.) and an approach that takes as its focus something that is internal to education – the *structure of pedagogic discourse*. Moore's concern is to show how this distinction relates not simply to competing approaches, but to theory operating in different modes. He shows how Bernstein's theory makes visible an 'object' that remains unseen in relay theories and how that 'object' can be systematically conceptualized in ways that generate external languages of description that in research work can close the 'discursive gap' between concept and data. He describes Bernstein's mode of theorizing as 'generative theory' and points out how this is distinctive of scientific theory more generally.

The generative capacity of Bernstein's theory is effectively illustrated in Maton's chapter. He places alongside Bernstein's concepts of 'knowledge code', 'pedagogic device' and 'knowledge structures' those of 'legitimation codes', 'epistemic device' and 'knower structures'. These latter concepts are underpinned by the distinction he draws between whether knowledge and knowers are specialized in terms of what is known or who is knowing it (essentially the latter corresponds to Bernstein's 'relay' approaches where knowledge comes to be characterized as 'middle-class', 'male', 'white', etc.). This distinction is conceptually elaborated in terms of how individuals are positioned within intellectual fields in terms of two dimensions: an 'epistemic relation' to the knowledge structure and a 'social relation' to the knower structure, and these two relations can vary independently in terms of stronger or weaker classification and framing. These distinctions enable Maton to generate a set of 'legitimation codes' in terms of the various ways in which knowledge is legitimated as in some manner worthwhile or valid as regulated by the 'epistemic device'. He applies this model to the historical case of the 'two cultures' debate in Britain in the late 1950s where the rise of science was seen as precipitating a 'crisis in the humanities', and then to a contemporary empirical study of how pupils in English schools perceive music as an examination subject in the upper school curriculum.

Hugo's chapter addresses a fundamental issue: that of *hierarchy*. For Bernstein, hierarchy in the form of verticality represents a knowledge structure operating in its most effective mode. Hugo explores verticality in terms of the pedagogic relationship between teacher and pupil. Within the philosophical poetic of his exposition of the relationship between Socrates and his (female) teacher and his (male) pupils in classical Greece, Hugo examines the manner in which the verticality of knowledge translates as a relation between teacher and taught – in that case as an embodied *relationship* that could be expressed in love, erotic desire and intimacy (a very particular form of a relationship between a social and a symbolic division of labour). Crucially, as the title of his chapter suggests, the distance between teacher and taught is measured in terms of their relative positions on the ladder of knowledge and this, in turn, is understood in terms of the distance between that which is restricted to what is immediate, circumscribed and restricted in time and space – that which already is – and that which could or is yet to be: what Bernstein liked to call the 'yet to be thought'. The verticality of hierarchical knowledge structures in this manner corresponds to Durkheim's sense of the 'sacred' as he employed that concept in *The Elementary Forms of Religious Life*

(Durkheim 1995). Hugo is, however, sensitive to the problems of employing the very term 'hierarchy' and the knee-jerk reactions that it might provoke given the ideological default settings of much established educational discourse. He explores different modes of hierarchy and emphasizes the key point that the verticality of hierarchical knowledge structures does not merely reflect the social division of labour but, in the structuring of pedagogic discourse, has the power to disrupt and move beyond it.

Part II focuses on three particular Bernsteinian 'building blocks' in his theory of pedagogy: the concepts of voice, identity and pedagogic discourses. All three concepts imply a mediation of power relations that are relayed through the pedagogic device – a device which Bernstein describes as equivalent to the grammar of the educational system. The pedagogic device creates the conditions for the realization of the message, but always in a recognizable form. Power relations define for Bernstein the nature of the social order, any social order. Although never neatly defined, they are indicative of social class relations. As Sally Power argues, definitions of the concept of social class are less a feature of Bernstein's opus than the notion of change in social class locations. His analysis of social class differentiates between those in the symbolic fields and those in the production fields. Of interest to educational policy researchers is how these fields are transformed, how particularly the middle classes are differentially positioned within these fields in different eras, and how those positionings are deeply connected to the forms of knowledge, pedagogy and identities relayed through schooling.

Power relations, as seen in Arnot and Reay's chapter, provide the conditions for specialized voices. These voices, however, are not as sociologists often have it, simply reflective of social identities such as class, gender and race. 'Voice', for Bernstein, is the mechanism which distributes social privileges in the educational context. Voice uniquely represents the *relation* between the school and the social structure. It is a pedagogic voice, the voice of the pedagogy. Arnot and Reay's chapter, therefore, makes the case for a sociology of *pedagogic voices,* rather than voice research which focuses, in a reductively essentialist way, on social identities and identifications. The sociology of pedagogic voices attempts to make explicit, empirically, the forms of recognition and the possibilities of realization of the principles which govern educational transmission.

Empirically, it is only the latter – the forms of realization expressed through talk – that sociologists can collect and analyse, but the analysis, if it is to be fruitful, would need to understand that the message and the text it generates are the product of a complex interface between pedagogic device and the social positioning of the pupil.

Social change comes through this analysis of voice, revealing the power of 'realizations' to introduce change in specialized voices and, indeed, power relations. However, Bernstein was quick to recognize that power relations, boundaries and insulations quickly re-establish themselves if threatened by new messages/realizations. What is revealed in this focused analysis of voice is the complexity of the subject, framed in Bernsteinian theory, as a 'symbolic space for the realization of power positions that fragment voice into voices internal to the individual ... Power establishes difference, and difference creates identity' (Diaz 2001: 85–6).

Bernstein's thoughts on the variety of different 'retrospective' and 'prospective' identities are the focus of Sally Power's chapter. Here we see how these concepts touch upon the complex interface between educational reforms, social positioning, identities and identifications with time and space. Young people are described as engaging with the politics of today whilst drawing on the past or future to make sense of their lives. Their pedagogic identities, shaped by the need to aim for 'success', are reflective of the new and old fractions of the middle classes, their educational trajectories and their very different political understandings. What is not clear, as Power comments, is the relationship between identity and class fractions. Here, there are tensions between social and pedagogic identities which Bernstein might have moved on to clarify.

These themes resonate with Gabrielle Ivinson and Gerard Duveen's study of the recontextualization of knowledge through different types of pedagogic practice. Bernstein's distinction between 'competence' and 'performance' modes is demonstrative of the strength of his analytic distinctions. Both models represent different forms of power and social control, moving, as Ivinson and Duveen put it, from 'the surface structure of classroom organization to models of social relations'. Each model, they argue, creates an 'imaginary subject' – the learner who is expected to recognize boundaries, regularities and difference and articulate the rules which govern regulation of their learning and realizations of appropriate knowledge forms and representations of knowledge.

Drawing on Kelly's repertory grid technique to analyse children's utterances, Ivinson and Duveen apply distinctions between 'feature talk', 'function talk', 'structure talk' and 'other talk'. These distinctions, although different from those of Arnot and Reay who highlight what they call 'classroom talk', 'subject talk', 'identity talk' and 'code talk', likewise suggest ways in which the pupil messages (realizations) can be collected, analysed and understood theoretically. As with Power's experiment with Bernstein's identity models, so more work is needed to bring these various classifications together.

In all three articles, the theme of educational reform, the variety of different types of pedagogic practice found in schools and the notion of the 'yet to be voiced' engage the reader in thinking about how, despite extensive regulation, the learner or, indeed, the teacher can attempt to transform the rules which shape the pedagogic device and, by extension, the social order. These glimpses are conceptualized briefly, momentarily, but are important indicators of the work of the school. Although performance-led, although marketized and choice-based, schools are not represented, here, in Bernsteinian language, as static organizations. They are understood as pivotal sites for the interplay of social inequalities through complex processes of recognition and realization.

In the third part of the book, the papers by Brown and by Morais and Neves both engage with questions of professional preparation. Brown examines preparation for the work of a researcher and Morais considers professional development of teachers involved in in-service teacher training programmes. In the final paper, Daniels' concern is with the development of tools for studying pedagogic change.

Brown invokes Bernstein's (1996: 134–44) paper 'Research and Languages of Description' in which he elaborated the notion of research as the development of 'languages of description'. He opens with an account of Bernstein's pessimism about the economics of detailed engagement with some of his ideas in the course of doctoral work and moves to consider the opportunities that are presented in recent developments in researcher education. He argues that:

> Bernstein's notion of analysis as the development of languages of description establishes a dynamic relationship between theory, empirical research and practice and fosters an openness and transparency in presentation of the analysis of data that facilitates both induction into the practices of analysis and critical engagement with processes and products of research.

Brown illustrates these points by reference to research of his own.

In Chapter 9, Morais and Neves direct their attention to the acquisition of coding orientations in the context of preparation for specific forms of pedagogic practice. Thus, the focus is on the acquisition of recognition and realization rules for a given context. With Bernstein, they argue that the acquisition of the specific coding orientation is fundamental to the success of acquirers in that context. They remind us that Bernstein insists that, in order for the subject to produce legitimate text in a given context, s/he should also have aspirations, motivations, values and attitudes commensurate to the production of that text. Their work entails a discussion of the acquisition of specific coding orientations and socio-affective characteristics. Morais and Neves developed data-gathering instruments that allowed them to analyse teacher performance in terms of specific coding orientation. Through very fine-grained work they were able to identify the components of performance with which teachers experienced greatest difficulties. Through the deployment of Bernstein's theory Morais and Neves were able to study professional development in terms of the acquisition by teachers of recognition and realization rules. They suggest that this work provides the basis for a methodological approach which gives the possibility of discriminating between specific components of teacher performance and thus could make a significant contribution to the study of the development of the acquisition of professional knowledge.

In the final chapter in this section, Daniels seeks to synthesize the tools of analysis that Bernstein developed with those of the 'activity theorists'. He seeks to identify strengths and limitations in both fields of endeavour and makes proposals for the future development of a theoretical account which benefits from their shared assumptions and complementary repositories of analytical power.

The chapters in the fourth and final part all combine macro-level policy analysis with trenchant policy critique. Those by Beck and Hasan focus primarily on policy *discourse,* while that of Sadovnik examines the impact of the 'No Child Left Behind' (NCLB) legislation in the United States. All three chapters are informed by Bernstein's analysis of the shifting balance of power in many countries between the pedagogic and the official recontextualizing fields (PRF and ORF), itself resulting from a weakening of the strength of classification between the spheres of economic production and education, in the wider context of a re-organizing and expansive global capitalism, with its associated pressures towards intensified marketization and managerialization.

Hasan focuses on certain *linguistic* concomitants of these developments, extending well beyond pedagogy, notably the proliferation of what she terms 'glib-speak' across a broad range of policy as well as political discourse, and manifested in mystificatory usages by neo-liberals of terms such as 'democracy', 'accountability' or 'the liberalization of trade'. The key discursive strategy involved what she calls 're-semanticization', which maintains conformity with normal grammatical usage whilst weaving 'a perfect web of lexical camouflage by ... subverting meaning'. Within this wider context of distorting representation, Beck, Hasan and Sadovnik all, in rather different ways, draw attention to a *temporal* dimension of the policy developments they analyse – what might be termed an 'agenda of urgency', evident pervasively in what Hasan calls 'an *acceleration* in the re-semanticization of language', in what Beck identifies as the 'acceleration of the standards agenda' of New Labour education policy in England, and in what Sadovnik sees as the unrelenting pressure for rapid, measurable results associated with the 'high-stakes testing' approach which informs NCLB initiatives. All three of these writers also highlight the significance of (and the importance of combating) various 'agendas of *necessity*', in the form of demands that educators and educational institutions simply accommodate government-led policy change which is in turn represented as unarguably requisite for national economic survival in a globalizing world. Such discourses, as well as the policies in which they are embedded, as Sadovnik points out, have the additional consequence of paving the way for further erosion of public sector provision, as private sector organizations become increasingly aware of the opportunities for profit that can be opened up in education – including what Colin Crouch has recently called 'contract winning as the new core education business' (Crouch 2003: 50). Discursively, both these agendas are evident in the titles of a range of government initiatives in these countries, going back as far as *A Nation at Risk* which inaugurated the standards agenda in the US in 1983.

These chapters are representative of only some of the work that continues to be done within the framework of Bernstein's problematic. Readers should not expect these chapters to click neatly together like the pieces of a jigsaw to form some seamless whole that is 'Bernstein's theory'. Though each chapter has its own well-defined focus, they are, relative to each other, 'fuzzy' at the edges. Collectively, they do not aspire or presume to represent a closure to Bernstein's system. Rather, they celebrate its continuing and open-ended capacity to lead from what he thought, through the endeavours of others, to the yet-to-be thought.

Part I

Knowledge structures and epistemology

1 On the shoulders of giants

Verticality of knowledge and the school curriculum

Johan Muller

This paper will explore the question of knowledge specialization or 'depth'. It will proceed by addressing the question: how does knowledge grow? The paper asks further: what does this mean for what, and how, children learn at school?

The first issue to be clarified concerns whether all knowledge ensembles are structurally alike, and whether they all grow in the same fashion. A dominant strain in the social theory literature holds that there is a principled distinction to be drawn, and various thinkers have at different times advanced a map of the territory. As shown in Table 1.1, Paul Dowling (1999) has usefully summarized some principal efforts that have, across the past two centuries, tried to delineate the continuum of knowledge organization and growth.

What is most striking about Table 1.1 is the lack of specificity of the distinctions drawn. Most social thinkers, if not quite all, have delineated the universe of symbolic differentiation by naming linearly opposed poles.

Table 1.1 Distinguishing knowledge continua

Author	Abstract *Context-independent*	Concrete *Context-dependent*
Bourdieu	Theoretical logic	Practical logic
Foucault	Programmes	Technologies
Freud	Ego	Id
Levi-Strauss	Science	Bricolage
Levy-Bruhl	Modern thinking	Primitive thinking
Lotman	Rule-governed	Exemplary texts
Luria	Abstract thinking	Situational thinking
Piaget	Science/effective thought	Technique/sensori-motor
Sohn-Rethel	Intellectual	Manual
Vygotsky	Conceptual thinking	Complex thinking
Walkerdine	Formal reasoning	Practical reasoning

Questions remain about the logic of the distinction being made. Are there only two knowledge categories, with all ensembles forming sub-types of one or other pole, which would make the distinction a strictly dichotomous one? Or do the poles name a continuum, with all ensembles differing in terms of a single, or perhaps multiple, classificatory dimensions?

There are at least two kinds of problem with these dichotomies. The first forms the point of departure for Basil Bernstein's (2000) magisterial intervention in the discussion: 'To my mind much of the work generating these oppositions, homogenizes these discursive forms so that they take on stereotypical forms where their differences or similarities are emphasized.' In other words, as Moore and Muller (2002) have observed, much of the discussion, instead of elaborating the dichotomous distinction, perpetually collapses the terms of discussion back into the crude simples, which simultaneously distorts the discussion and keeps it mired in ideology. Bernstein's analysis explicitly sets out to break this vicious circle as we will see below. But a second tendency has also been responsible for retarding development of the issues in the past, which is a pervasive one in nearly all these discussions, namely, to treat the terms of the distinction as delineating differences of activity or practice, rather than differences of symbolic organization, casting the discussion in *knower* rather than *knowledge* terms (Moore and Maton, 2001). This reluctance to speak directly about symbolic systems is an old one, and below I will trace its origins to the terms of a debate that began in the eighteenth century at the advent of the age of science (or was it perhaps of much older provenance?), continuing to the present. This debate is about the idea of progress in general, and the idea of progress in knowledge in particular. We are, it would seem, exceedingly reluctant to speak about the social dimensions of knowledge variation, not only in terms of relations between different knowledge forms, but particularly in terms of relations within knowledge forms. The idea of progress haunts us, nowhere more so than in regard to the question of knowledge progression and growth.

Bernstein has, as I have said, intervened decisively in the discussion about the form of symbolic systems, setting out to delineate the 'internal principles of their construction and their social base' (Bernstein, 2000: 155). As is by now well known, he distinguishes between two forms of discourse: horizontal and vertical. Since, in his view, only vertical discourse can be said to contain knowledge structures, strictly speaking, this paper will not discuss further the question of discourses and will concentrate on the question of variation between knowledge structures within vertical discourse. Here Bernstein distinguishes between two kinds of knowledge structure: hierarchical and horizontal. It is in this latter distinction that he stakes his claim to go beyond the homogenizing form of account mentioned above (ibid. 161).

For Bernstein, knowledge structures differ in two ways. The first is in terms of what may be called *verticality*. Verticality is concerned with how theory develops. In hierarchical knowledge structures it develops through integration towards ever more integrative or general propositions, the trajectory of development of which lends hierarchical knowledge structures a unitary convergent shape. Horizontal knowledge structures, on the other hand, are not unitary but plural, consisting of a series of parallel incommensurable languages. Progress in horizontal knowledge structures occurs not through theory integration (or at least not primarily) but rather through the introduction of a new language which constructs a 'fresh perspective, a new set of questions, a new set of connections, and an apparently new problematic, and most importantly a new set of speakers' (ibid. 162). Because these languages are incommensurable, they defy incorporation. The level of integration, and the possibility for knowledge progress in the sense of greater generality and hence explanatory reach, is thus strictly pegged.

Before I proceed to discuss the second form of knowledge form variation, it is worth making a few observations on verticality. The first observation is that it artfully incorporates and recapitulates the fierce dispute in the philosophy and sociology of science between the logical positivists and the non-realists, a dispute I shall selectively re-visit below. Bernstein is implicitly asserting that the logical positivists (or realists) were right, but only in respect of hierarchical knowledge structures; the non-realists (Kuhn and after) were likewise right, but only in respect of horizontal knowledge structures. In other words, encoded into Bernstein's principle of verticality are the terms of debate in the philosophy of science since the romantic revolt of the eighteenth century. Second, though, we should note that the category of horizontal knowledge structures spans a very broad range, from mathematics to sociology and the humanities. Although there is more than one mathematical language, and mathematics is in this sense a 'horizontal' knowledge structure, this example makes clear that verticality is certainly possible within discrete languages, verticality of an order perhaps equivalent to that obtained in hierarchical knowledge structures. The germane question then becomes not so much what constrains progression in all horizontal knowledge structures, but rather what internal characteristics constrain it in those that proliferate languages rather than in those where language proliferation is constrained. It was in search of a sociological answer to this question that Bernstein initially began, setting out to provide an alternative to Bourdieu's sociological reductionism (see Bernstein, 1996).

This brings me to the second form of knowledge variation: *grammaticality*. If verticality has to do with how theory develops internally, with what Bernstein later called the *internal* language of description, grammaticality has to do with how theory deals with the world, or how theoretical statements deal with their empirical predicates, the *external* language of description (Bernstein, 2000). The stronger the grammaticality of a language, the more stably it is able to generate empirical correlates and the more unambiguous because more restricted the field of referents. The weaker it is, the weaker is its capacity to stably identify empirical correlates and the more ambiguous because much broader is the field of referents, thus depriving such weak grammar knowledge structures of a principal means of generating progress, namely empirical disconfirmation: 'Weak powers of empirical descriptions removes a crucial resource for either development or rejection of a particular language and so contribute to its stability as a frozen form' (Bernstein, 2000, 167–168). In other words, grammaticality determines the capacity of a theory or language to progress through worldly corroboration; verticality determines the capacity of a theory or language to progress integratively through explanatory sophistication. Together, we may say that these two criteria determine the capacity of a particular knowledge structure to progress.

But for all its richness, this analysis merely starts the ball rolling, so to speak. What it provides is a survey of features of variation, but even the charitable must admit that the poles remain clearer than the intermediate zones of the range. This is partly because the precise nature of and relation between verticality and grammaticality is unclear. A plausible surmise could be the following: that verticality is a categorical principle, consigning knowledge structures to either a theory-integrating or a theory-proliferating category (in turn broken down into a constrained proliferation or an unconstrained proliferation category), while grammaticality is an ordinal principle, constructing a continuum of grammaticality within each category, or perhaps across the entire spectrum.[1] But this does not help us understand the more striking differences between knowledge structures, for example temporal extension, as displayed by Moore and Maton (2001) in the story of the proof of Fermat's last theorem:

> What is so striking about this story is its sheer *scale* in historical time and in geographical and cultural space. It tells a story of a mathematician in late-twentieth century England effectively communicating with a French judge at the court of Louis XIV, and through him with Babylonians from three millennia ago. It represents an epistemic community with an *extended* existence in time and space, a community where the past is present, one in which, when living members die, will be in turn the living concern of future members ...
>
> (Ibid. 172)

As I will show in the next section, this sense of extension in time and space is the hallmark of the modern idea of knowledge progression. The point here though is that things could not look more different in sociology, which barely dates back as far as the nineteenth century. On the other hand, mathematics shares this feature with literature. Gyorgy Markus (2003) has remarked that the 'tradition' in the arts is 'ever expanding' and 'of great depth in time' (p. 15), a feature he contrasts to science which has a 'short-term' tradition, because it is ever 'evolving' (that is, progressing) (ibid.). Which knowledge form is nearer to which? The fact is, which forms comprise the middle of the knowledge range is not clear at all. Is geography closer to physics than to biology, for example, and how would we know? Would we count their respective numbers of languages? Could we create an index of theory integratedness? It is certainly the case that empirical study would help to shed light on the theory, but it is also the case that the theory stands in need of some elaboration. This paper is a ground-clearing digression preparatory to that task. In what follows, I will concentrate mainly, though not exclusively, on verticality – on the internal characteristics of the internal language of description.

Why would one want to elaborate a theory of knowledge forms? After all, we seem to have coped reasonably well without one for a long time. Bernstein only turned to the issue towards the end of his work. The contention here is that this lacuna in the study of knowledge and education was not accidental. Rather, I hope to show, it was produced by the failure of social thought to deal with the dilemma of progress. The failure to reckon with the material structural differences in knowledge forms has become something of an obstacle in educational thinking. This can briefly be illustrated in two domains of education practice, namely, curriculum planning and research administration.

Curriculum planning has been thrust into the limelight by global learner performance comparisons, most vividly displayed by the Trends in International Mathematics and Science Study (TIMSS). A central tenet of assessment is that the instrument measuring performance is valid to the degree that it assesses what has been made available for acquisition. TIMSS has made visible the fact that not all children of the same age cohort across the globe learn the same things in the same order at the same level of cognitive demand. This has put a spotlight on the stipulation, sequence and progression requirements of curricula and has begun to suggest that not all subjects in the curriculum have the same requirements. Could this be because their parent knowledge forms are different? To answer this seriously requires greater clarity than we have at present.

As for the question of research administration: research assessments of individuals and bodies of work have made possible comparisons between individuals, faculties, universities and countries. As more and more comes to depend on assessments of innovation and novelty ('Is this paper really a contribution to new knowledge, or a re-hash of the known?'), the question arises as to what exactly constitutes innovation in different areas of research endeavour, and whether they are all the same. This is only the tip of the iceberg: it soon becomes clear that there are different epistemic cultures, different kinds of collaboration, different publishing traditions, and so on. In short, the globally emergent audit culture compels us to reflect on our knowledge practices, at the centre of which sits the question of their likeness, their comparability, and their compatibility. Once again, we realize how little we really know about how they may be alike or different, and what difference this might make. At the centre of this conundrum lies the question of knowledge progression.

Progress: the very idea, and its sceptics

The foundation of the Cartesian revolution in the seventeenth century was an axiom that appeared to be radically new, namely, that 'true' knowledge was characterized by knowledge progression, that that 'which had once been established did not need to be proved again, that is to say, in which scientific progress, universally recognized as such by rational thinkers, was possible' (Berlin, 2000a: 28). The conventional account depicts this as the decisive moment in the emergence from the closed tautological world of antiquity, and the birth of the modern (Shapin, 1996).

There are a number of entailments to this view. First, Descartes believed that only in a bona fide branch of knowledge can we find 'clear and distinct ideas' (Berlin, 2000a: 28):

> The paradigm of true knowledge, according to the Cartesian school, consisted in beginning from truths so clear and distinct that they could be contradicted only on pain of falling into absurdities; and in proceeding thence, by strict deductive rules, to conclusions whose truth was guaranteed by the unbreakable rules of deduction ...
>
> (Ibid.)

This was indeed a lofty aim for knowledge in the seventeenth century, and it meant that Descartes viewed the knowledge array then available in a particular way. For example, the human sciences might generate edification and improvement, but were otherwise of little enduring social value because they could not produce 'strict deductive rules'. Here lies the foundation of the distinction between science and all other symbolic ensembles, and it rests on the notion of what may be called *strong progression*.

No-one today is a thorough-going Cartesian; no-one today believes in strong progression. Challenges to Cartesian rationalism have come from both within and outside of science. One challenge to this idea of strong progression from within science has culminated in the generally accepted position in science today of what may be called *weak progression*, or what Haack (2003) would call progress 'within reason', which I will return to below. This is a revision which accepts the postulate of progression (and hence of the division of the field of representations into 'true' or progressive knowledge, and belief or mere narrative), but recognizing at the same time that the 'true' in true knowledge did not equal absolute knowledge, and that progress in knowledge, if in the long run ineluctable, could always and in principle be revised – hence, weak progression.

The dominant challenge to strong progression from outside science has sought to overturn the distinction between knowledge that progresses ('science') and knowledge that does not. The first brilliantly original formulation can be traced back to Giambattista Vico who, with his seventh inaugural lecture in 1708, and later with the publication of the first edition of *Scienza nuova (New Science)* in 1725, rejected the fundamental premise of Cartesian rationalism, the distinction between the true (*verum*) and the artificial (*factum*). Vico begins by arguing their essential unity: 'We demonstrate geometry because we make it' (Berlin, 2000a: 31). What he meant by this was that we can be said to fully know something not only because we know what it is (i.e. through rational reconstruction) but because we know how it came to be (i.e. through historical or genetic reconstruction), which he called *per caussas*. By this logic, we only know what we create. If we did not create it, we cannot know it, because it then has no human history. 'The true (*verum*) and the made (*factum*) are convertible' (ibid. 35), or, 'The criterion of truth is to have made it' (ibid. 36). In other words, with this argument, truth becomes a human artefact, and Vico becomes the first constructivist.

Incidentally, this form of the argument yields a hierarchy of knowledges with mathematics at its head (the most artificial of knowledge systems for Vico), leading with arithmetic, algebra and geometry, then mechanics, physics (contra the Cartesians who put this at the head), down to psychology, morality and history (here Vico and Descartes are at one). The hierarchy is one of 'make-ability', with the least made knowledge the most opaque to our minds. Although far from Vico's intent, this reasoning buttresses that of the humanists of the Trivium, who sought to keep the humanities and hermeneutics sovereign, against the claims of physics and the Quadrivium as the paramount font of knowledge (Durkheim, 1977). How things have changed.

This brief survey may be summed up by saying that whereas Descartes with his criterion of 'clear and distinct ideas' fundamentally sundered *verum* from *factum*, Vico fundamentally subverts this criterion by re-uniting them. The 'demarcation debate' in the philosophy of science, as to whether there is or is not a significant distinction between 'science' and other knowledge forms, begins here.

Vico's careful revolt has come to be a mere dress rehearsal for the more thoroughgoing romantic revolt of the nineteenth century, and the anti-realist one of our own time. The European romantics took up Vico's anti-demarcatory premise of the make-ability of truth and of the world:

> the common assumption of the romantics that runs counter to the *philosophia perennis* is that the answers to the great questions are not to be discovered so much as to be invented. They are not something found; they are something literally made.
>
> (Berlin, 2000b: 202, 203)

Amongst the romantics and their contemporary successors there are strong and weak traditions of make-ability. Common to all, however, is the following:

> Hence that new emphasis on the subjective [the maker] and ideal rather than the objective and the real, on the process of creation rather than its effects, on motives rather than consequences; and, as a necessary corollary of this, on the quality of the vision, the state of mind or soul of the acting

agent – purity of heart, innocence of intention, sincerity of purpose rather than getting the answer right, that is, accurate correspondence to the 'given'.

(Ibid. 203)

It is this tradition of 'make-ability' that I will trace below, first as it snakes its way through the debates on knowledge and then, in a homologous way, through the debates on curriculum. As we will see, the tradition of 'make-ability' translates into a 'knower' as opposed to a 'knowledge' perspective on curriculum (Moore and Maton, 2001).

On the shoulders of giants

What the scientific revolution of the seventeenth century accomplished was a decisive challenge by the self-styled Moderns to the 'human-centred universe' (Shapin, 1996: 20) of the Ancients, as consecrated by Aristotelianism, which had become a hermetic dogma of a priori truth. The cultural shock should not be underestimated. By 1611, the clerical poet John Donne could write: 'And New Philosophy calls all in doubt', ending with:

'Tis all in pieces, all coherence gone;
All just supply, and all Relation.

(Donne, 1611, cited in Shapin, 1996: 28)

A century before Vico, Donne was registering a commonly felt shock at the cultural displacement of a deeply cherished world-view. What was gone was the measure of man, man as the measure of nature, and with it, the dominance of the Trivium over the Quadrivium was decisively broken (Durkheim, 1977; Bernstein, 2000). At the heart of it was the entirely novel notion of progression towards a not-yet-attained truth that was not determined by man, but could be discovered by him through rational methods and intellectual daring. With the future and man's fate loosed from the comforting embrace of classical-Christian teleology, the classicists, Christians and humanists of every stripe discerned a cultural abyss. The threat was felt to every form of social authority that depended on that world-view. The humanist counter-revolution would be only a matter of time.

In the meantime, the intoxication of the expanded temporal horizon that the idea of progress suddenly constituted can be graphically seen in drawings and sayings of the time. In the frontispiece to his 1620 *Instauration magna (The Great Instauration)*, an already provocative title, Francis Bacon depicted a ship boldly sailing out beyond the Pillars of Hercules, symbolizing the traditional limits of knowledge, below which was written the biblical text from Daniel: 'Many shall pass to and fro, and science shall be increased' (cited in Shapin, 1996: 21). But if the forward horizon was extended, so too was the horizon backwards into the past in like manner re-constituted.

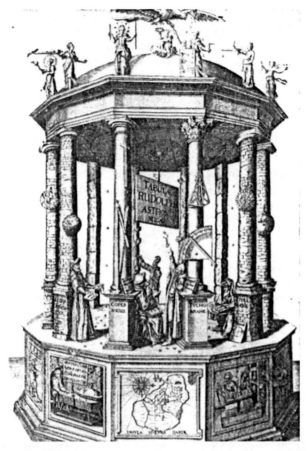

Figure 1.1 The *Astro-poecilo-pyrgium* (the variegated star tower) from the title page of Johannes Kepler's *Tabulae Rudolphinae* (1627) (Shapin, 1996)

This expanded retrospect is given iconographical expression in Johannes Kepler's tower, shown in Figure 1.1. At the front of the tower are two modern columns named for Copernicus and Tycho Brahe. Further back are more rough-hewn columns representing the earlier knowledge of Ptolemy and Agrippa; at the back are crude columns representing ancient astronomy. Right at the front, seated, is Kepler himself: the more recent, hence, the more sophisticated. The Moderns are thus separated from the Ancients by two dimensions. The first is clearly time. But in order to express progress across time, a second dimension is crucial to the first, namely, greater differentiation. In order to express this, then, the further towers are less differentiated, the nearer ones more so. What evolves, or progresses, is differentiation. The condition of that progression is a progressive capitulation and building on previous knowledge, a greater differentiality of knowledge. This compound and quintessentially 'modern' idea, progressive differentiation and dual temporality, is embodied in

Newton's famous aphorism, 'if I have seen farther, it is by standing on the shoulders of giants' (Merton, 1993: 1).

In one of the richest ironies in the history of science, it turns out that the aphorism, everywhere attributed to Newton and hence taken as emblematic of the modern view of progress, does not originate with him at all. Indeed, it appears to have been common currency in knowledge circles since at least Bernard of Chartres in 1126, who probably got it from his Priscian predecessors, and was used in various forms, at regular intervals. Merton (1993: 268, 269) records at least 27 usages in print before Newton. The aphorism continues to be used today in a wide variety of more or less appropriate contexts. The original point of the aphorism was to highlight inter-generational cooperation as the ground for scientific progress, usually expressed in humble, or mock-humble, terms: 'A dwarf standing on the shoulders of a giant may see farther than a giant himself' (ibid. 4). Or as Merton himself puts it:

> When you come right down to it, the essential point is that the dwarfs-on-the-shoulders-of-giants aphorism is a rough equivalent to the twentieth-century sociological conception that scientific discoveries emerge from the existing social base and consequently become, under conditions that can be reasonably well defined, practically inevitable.
>
> (Ibid. 267)

What we learn from this pithy story is that scientists probably had a pragmatic view of themselves and the process of science from relatively early on – they certainly didn't have to wait for social studies of science to discover messiness and serendipity in the twentieth century – but it was only in the seventeenth century that the threat to social order, until then clearly contained by the hegemonic view, provoked the first in a series of backlashes that have continued with greater and greater sophistication to this day. The debate is variously figured, but it is probably fair to say that it has been between various kinds of realism and irrealism, those for a more or less strong view of progress in science (called by Haack, 2003, the 'Old Deferentialists'), and those against (the 'New Cynics'). Before being sucked irretrievably into the complexities of contemporary philosophy of science, I should immediately declare that my aim in what follows is solely to get a grip on the way that knowledge systems are internally differentiated, or are said to progress, and to answer the question: 'What is it that progresses when they do progress?' And is it only science that progresses? The philosophy of science debate detracts from asking the question about the non-science disciplines. Yet the point must hold for the non-science disciplines too, at least in one form or another, if these disciplines are not to surrender all claims to relevance in an information or knowledge age.

Kinds of verticality

In answer to the question, 'What is it that accumulates when knowledge progresses?' the logical positivists gave an unequivocal answer: it was the piled-up structure of laws related to one another by strict definition, in strict order of explanatory integratedness, that is, in strict order of their approximation to the truth. Here is to be found the definition of Basil Bernstein's verticality, namely, *the degree of integratedness and 'subsume-ability' of theory.*

The logical positivist idea of progression has come under universal attack. The debate has been intricate and technical, a far cry from the 'village or tabloid' scapegoat of positivism (Matthews, 2004a: 2) that has taken centre stage in the social sciences. The principal objection has been to the founding idea of progression, to the idea of a single convergent system of knowledge. There was no single progression path, said one criticism, not least because the explanatory reach and range of application of most covering laws was much more modest, leading to a notion of a cluster of 'languages' rather than a single converged-upon structure, an idea conceded already by leading logical positivist Otto Neurath, he of the modest title of 'Director of the Agency for Full Social Planning' in ante-bellum socialist Vienna (Cartwright, 2001). Nor is it a matter simply of 'inductive scepticism', of asserting the messiness of discovery against the seeming imperialism of the subsumptive structure: after all, the 'Old Deferentialists', following Reichenbach in the early twentieth century, maintained a distinction between the 'context of discovery' as distinct from the 'context of justification' to deal with just this objection (Phillips, 2004), though the distinction proved difficult to sustain. The contemporary disavowal of progress by the 'New Cynics' cuts far deeper, against the heart of the impersonality of this vision of progress (Popper's 'epistemology without a knowing subject'), against the notion of a knowledge about the world that exists without man at the centre, in its most extreme reduction, against the idea that there is a real independent world to be known at all, a disavowal that eliminates progress by disavowing the world and the possibility of real knowledge about it (Moore and Muller, 1999).

Just as all forms of realism have built into them some form of progress, thus all forms of the 'New Cynicism' have built into them the idea that knowledge progress is incoherent. While there are many alternative accounts (meaning holism and constructive empiricism to name but two), the landmark account belongs to Thomas Kuhn and his account of innovation by 'revolution' or paradigm change (Kuhn, 1962). This can be grasped by seeing that Kuhn turns the tables on the imperialism of the 'Old Deferentialists' who depicted all knowledge in the image of science, by depicting all knowledge, science included, as behaving like Basil Bernstein's horizontal knowledge structure, advancing up to a point, only to break off into an alternative theoretical language.

One of Bernstein's great contributions, as I suggested above, is to have recapitulated realism's loss of innocence, as staged in the literature of the philosophy of science, and recast the terms of debate into a taxonomy of knowledge forms, with verticality, or 'subsume-ability', as one principal criterion. In the introduction I suggested that verticality was a categorical principle. In the discussion above it is apparent that though this criterion has been considerably weakened, and though it is now conceded that knowledge grows by virtue of different kinds and paths of conceptual change, these are still categorically distinguished as to whether they are commensurable or not.

The discussion may be summed up as follows. As far as the internal structure of internal languages of description is concerned, that is, as regards their verticality, languages vary as to:

- their capacity to subsume statements into logical types (syntactic/semantic axis); therefore
- their relative expressibility in terms of general and particular statements (general/particular axis); and therefore
- their relative expressibility in terms of propositional content and stylistic content (content/form axis).

One could go on. The question now for this paper is: how are different powers of subsumption, of verticality, expressed by pedagogy?

The knowledge structure/pedagogic structure link

Does knowledge structure constrain pedagogic structure. Does it place any onus on the way that the 'what is to be learnt' is written and taught? Do these internal characteristics of knowledge structures place limits on the form their curricular offspring optimally could and should take? We know that pedagogic structure has distributive potential, but does knowledge structure come with an already encoded distributive potential, placing structural limits on pedagogic form? We know that it takes a specialized language to specialize consciousness: but can we determine what kind of specialization a pedagogy must encode to effectively realize a specialized consciousness in a specialized language? All these different ways of posing the question presuppose answering the question one way or another.

One affirmative response to these questions is given in the Review Committee's (2000) report on a review of the South African grade 1 to 9 national curriculum, known as Curriculum 2005 (C2005). The Review found that the curricular form of C2005 was under-stipulated, under-sequenced and its pacing requirements under-signalled. It was a form of invisible or competence pedagogy (Bernstein, 2000) which provided minimal markers as to what should be learnt or evaluated at what level. Unsurprisingly, the Review found that poorly trained teachers, teaching largely disadvantaged children, fared worst with this pedagogy: they had not covered what the curriculum expected them to cover by the end of each grade. Consequently, children entered the next grade with knowledge gaps, elements of knowledge presupposed by the curriculum of the next grade. These knowledge gaps had more serious consequences in what the Review called 'content-rich' subjects (maths, science and language) than in more skills-based subjects like life skills, because the former had content, sequence and progression requirements deriving from their parent disciplines.

How does Bernstein answer the question? Equivocally, it turns out. In the paper on the pedagogic device, the answer is negative:

> As physics is appropriated by the recontextualizing agents, the results cannot formally be derived from the logic of that discourse. Irrespective of the intrinsic logic which constitutes the specialized discourse and activities called physics, the recontextualizing agents will select from the totality of practices which is called physics ... But these selections cannot be derived from the logic of the discourse of physics ...
>
> (Bernstein, 2000: 34)

Here Bernstein appears to contradict the Review, but we should note the context, where Bernstein is asserting the theoretical priority of the regulative over the instructional, meaning that the internal order of school physics is wholly derived from normative social order. In one sense this is undoubtedly correct. Any social order can, on the basis of its ideology, decide what pedagogic modality to impose. It can even appear to choose a de-specializing pedagogy in defiance or denial of the requirements of its specialized division of labour, at least for a while. This is indeed what happened in South Africa. But in another sense, this is quite misleading. Indeed, the argument can be made that Bernstein came to the view, late in his career, that the instructional domain – or knowledge – has an internal determinative logic of its own, one which cannot simply be reduced to subordination to the regulative order. The strongest evidence for this view is Bernstein's 'vertical and horizontal discourse' paper (Bernstein, 2000).

The principal reason Bernstein opposed the idea of a link in his early work is because he maintained that the recontextualized discourse (e.g. school physics) was a wholly separate discourse to that of research-based physics. It was necessary to maintain this position in order to stay true to the postulate that all symbolic formations were specific to a context with its specializing practices. But if recontextualization totally severs any relation, then how are specialized knowledges ever reproduced? After all, school maths performance predicts (imperfectly, to be sure) university maths performance; and that predicts in turn proper maths adeptness. The only way this can be intelligible is by conceiving that school maths competence 'precurses' (Gee, 2001) university maths competence, which 'precurses' real maths adeptness. There has to be some form of specialization of consciousness continuum in play; this could be called a founding assumption of modern education. After all, this idea of the interpenetration of symbolic competence is built into Bernstein's explanation of how the middle-class home code precurses its young into the school code better than does the working-class home code. So, a relation there must be. One might pursue the exact nature of the relation. A more interesting question in my view is: What *effects* the relation? What activates it?

There are two typical answers: let us call them a *knowledge/curricular* answer, and a *knower/transmission* answer. A knowledge approach is epitomized by TIMSS and their principal intellectual construct: 'opportunity to learn' (OTL). OTL in its simplest form is defined as coverage of the curriculum, and the original TIMSS project defined coverage in terms of a serial list of topics only (Porter, 2002). But is that sufficient to map coverage in a vertical curriculum? It certainly wasn't adequate in TIMSS. A syntactical view will say: list the principal propositional steps in the knowledge hierarchy. Each propositional step will function like a rule with rules of combination, each cluster of which can generate an indefinite number of possibilities; for example, 'odd numbers' in arithmetic (see Pinker, 1999: 318). A complete list will describe the internal grammar of the internal language of the subject. Table 1.2 shows one way of representing this, drawn from Reeves and Muller's (2005) investigation into the coverage requirements of the grade 6 maths curriculum.

This table provides a finite list of content presumed to be learnt in grade 6 under the rubric of 'representing numbers', listed in order of cognitive complexity. It tells us that, in Reeves and Muller's sample, the grade 6 classes spent far less time on the grade 6 items proper, and far more time on grades 5 and 4, that is, on 'easier' items.

But here a question arises. Does a list of topics in order of complexity, in other words in order of disciplinary progression, constitute an optimal learning path? The reconstituted logic of a discipline and the optimal pedagogical learning sequence might overlap only by default. The reason for this lies with the way subsumption works: the same semantic topics (the same particulars) play different roles in different generals. The upshot is that particular topics, even for the most hierarchical of subjects, are repeated across learning levels, but differently. In short, *imperfect subsumption* has so far stymied the linear representation of content in a curriculum, and the relation of curricular structure to disciplinary structure has remained an open, more usually an avoided, question.

All in all, it is not too surprising that by far the most common way of representing verticality in the literature has been distilled from what teachers do, in terms of an index of 'cognitive demand', usually depicted as a scale from 'memorization', through 'routine procedures', communication of understanding', 'problem solving', to 'conjecture/generalize/prove' (Porter, 2002: 4). Each listed topic is given a 'cognitive demand' rating. Proportion of coverage by degree of demand yields a proportion of instructional time spent. This temporal proportion becomes a proxy for 'opportunity to learn verticality'. There are clearly other ways of compiling a demand index (see Morais *et al.*, 2004, for a good example). All of them, as far as I can see, shift the focus from the knowledge itself to the knower-actors, from a knowledge approach to a knower approach.

Table 1.2 Extract of aggregated results for grade 6 content coverage and emphasis

Section 1: Number, operation and relationships				
1.1 Recognizing, classifying and representing numbers	*% of learners that covered task*	*Ideal time for grade 6 content* Number of single 30 min. periods	*Estimated average number of lessons spent on content* Less than one	If one or more, estimated average no. single periods
Counting including:				
Counting forwards and backwards in				
2s (g4,5)	82		X	
3s (g4,5)	76		X	
5s (g4,5)	76		X	
10s (g4,5)	79			1
25s (g4,5)	71			1
50s (g4,5)	68			1
100s (g4,5)	74			1
a variety of whole number intervals between 0 and 10 000 (g4,5)	50			1
fractions (g5)	45			2
decimals (g6)	26	2–4		2
Representing and comparing whole numbers including zero and fractions including:				
Whole numbers to				
4-digit numbers (g4)	84			3
6-digit numbers (g5)	76			3
9-digit numbers (g6)	21	4–6	X	

(from Reeves and Muller, 2005)

In the wake of the demise of logical positivism, and the discrediting of the distinction between the contexts of discovery and justification, a new orthodoxy under the aegis of the 'New Cynics' and their pedagogical confrères the educational progressives took hold, to the effect that sequence and progression in pedagogy simply didn't matter, that there was no one royal road to learning, and that only the most minimal stipulations were necessary to signal the learning end points as measured by common assessment instruments (Muller, 2002; Labaree, 2004). This turned out to be wrong, in South Africa and elsewhere. Such radically invisible pedagogies can work, but only for middle-class pupils, and exactly how they do that is still being unearthed. For the majority of poorer children, the evidence increasingly suggests, clear and explicit articulation of evaluation criteria is sine qua non (see the various papers in Muller *et al.*, 2004).

What are the evaluation criteria evaluations of? It is hard to avoid the conclusion that they are evaluations of the knowledge steps to be traversed. To be sure, there is not only one set of steps per discipline, nor need we assume that these steps are always to be traversed in the same order. Nevertheless, insofar as the idea of theory integration means anything at all, it does, qua hierarchy, specify the formal minimal grammatical steps to be acquired in order for sense to be made at all. So, making concessions to messiness and agreeing that we cannot stipulate a once-and-for-all path, we would still have to concede, retrospectively considered, that there is a specifiable necessary minimum set of steps that must be pedagogically traversed.

The question then arises; does this argument do away with the necessity of the teacher? Not at all. What it does is emphasize the knowledge dimension of what makes a teacher a teacher. The condition for a teacher being an authoritative pedagogical agent is, at the minimum, an internalized map of the grammar of the subject, acquired through disciplinary training (this is perhaps why Morais *et al.*, 2004, dub the index of the *what* 'teacher competence' in their study). In other words, the condition for teachers to be able to induct pupils into strong grammar subjects is that they themselves already stand on the shoulders of giants – in other words, that they can speak with the disciplinary grammar. But if they can't? I am inclined to say: let us then train them so that they can. The difficulty is, it is often not clear what they don't know. Two things stand out in the global literature on effective learning. The first is that teacher competence is by far the most important factor in learner attainment; the second is that in-service teacher training has had almost no effect. I fear this will continue unless we pay as much attention in future to knowledge as we have to knowers.

Conclusion

I have proceeded in this paper on the hunch that the contemporary avoidance of knowledge structure, principally of the question of progress or verticality, lies at the heart of many current pedagogical dilemmas, in particular those concerned with providing to poor children access to the tools of powerful knowledge. I have not kept that in the foreground of the discussion, but it nevertheless remains a principal motive force. Why verticality, and what is its sociological significance? It remains plausible, perhaps even likely, that knowledge structure has distributional implications, which interact with distributional alignments of pedagogy. It has proved easier discussing verticality in hierarchical disciplines than in those with horizontal knowledge structures. This remains a task to be done, not least because it seems likely to me that the exceptionalism that the social sciences and humanities have claimed for so long will progressively dissolve in the global networks of the knowledge society. When that happens, I fear that the 'New Cynicism' and its pedagogical analogues will be about as effective a cloak against the cold winds of global comparability as fashionable decadence was for the artistic fringe in ante-bellum Berlin.

Note

1   Though Bernstein (2000) depicts grammaticality as a feature only of horizontal knowledge structures in the diagram on p. 168, he refers to physics as having a 'strong grammar' on p. 163.

2 Knowledge structures and intellectual fields

Basil Bernstein and the sociology of knowledge

Rob Moore

In some of his later papers, Bernstein began to develop a theoretical language through which to examine the organization of intellectual fields and the conditions for their productivity. This language is that of 'hierarchical and horizontal knowledge structures' and of 'internal and external languages of description' (Bernstein 2000, Chs 7, 9). In keeping with his more general approach, it is assumed that there is a relationship between the *structures* of fields and the character of the knowledge (the symbolic forms) that they produce. These ideas can be traced back to a paper from the early 1970s, 'The Sociology of Education: a brief account' (Bernstein 1977, Ch. 7) and represent a long-standing concern on his part. The broader issues can be related also to the distinction that Bernstein made between sociology that treats education as no more than a 'relay' for forces outside of it (class, gender, race, etc.) and that which is concerned with relations *within* – with the 'structure of pedagogic discourse' (Bernstein 1990, Ch. 5). The type of distinction that Bernstein is pointing to is not simply that between yet one more perspective and others in an already extensive array, but between fields operating in different *modes* with different principles of knowledge production and which assume different forms. These forms themselves can become objects of analysis within a revivified sociology of knowledge concerned with the structuring of the social relations of symbolic production (Moore 2004a, Ch. 6; Moore and Maton 2001). The key issue is the *production* of knowledge and the capacity of fields organized in different ways to produce knowledge of different types.

The purpose of this paper is to examine Bernstein's thinking on the structuring of fields and the distinction between sociology of education that has the structure of pedagogic discourse as its foundational theoretical object and that which treats education as a relay for things outside it.

Relations *to* and relations *within*

It is first necessary to distinguish between approaches concerned with relations 'within' education and those concerned with relations 'to' education. The 'within' of education is the *structure of pedagogic discourse* that constitutes, for Bernstein, the theoretical object of the sociology of education (see below). The main difference between fields organized around different principles of production is in the character of the knowledge that they produce and what counts as legitimate issues, questions, modes of inquiry and answers. In Bernstein's view, the sociology of education has for a long time assumed the form of a 'horizontal knowledge structure with a weak grammar' (2000). Knowledge structures of this type have a limited capacity to produce empirical knowledge in a way that is cumulative and progressively integrated within theoretical systems of increasing generality and abstraction. He contrasts such knowledge structures with those of the 'hierarchical' type exemplified by physics and other horizontal knowledge structures such as mathematics. In Bernstein's later language, this difference is referred to in terms of strength of 'grammar' (see Muller, this volume). Elucidating these differences clarifies the distinctive features of Bernstein's problematic.

An initial sense of the distinction that Bernstein is describing can be provided by contrasting two different ways of conceptualizing educational relationships. One very familiar way of doing this (Bowles and Gintis' *Schooling in Capitalist America* (1976) would be a famous example) takes an established view of education and through a process of reinterpretation *re-presents* it in a different way whilst arguing that this is supported by empirical evidence. Official liberal educational philosophy, for instance, declares that the purpose of education is to develop the potential of all pupils irrespective of background and to provide them with equality of opportunity in an open meritocratic society. A reinterpretation of this official view from a class analysis approach argues that, in fact, what education does is to prepare children of different classes for predestined positions within the capitalist occupational structure and to reproduce the unequal class relations of capitalism in a way that is accepted as legitimate. This reinterpretation is achieved through a process or 'switch' (Moore and Maton 2001) that translates the description of education from one language into another – in this case the translator is a form of Marxist theory. The same kind of 'critical' deconstruction/reconstruction can be presented in terms of gender and race relations or in terms of sexualities or post-colonial/indigenous identities, etc. Such approaches are primarily concerned with education and the reproduction of social inequalities and power, and usually operate within a reductive standpoint analysis perspective.

Although in one respect the two languages produced (that of the account of the official discourse and that of its critically deconstructed, demystified form) are radically different, in another respect they are the same in that both have the form of descriptions at the *empirical level*. The two languages relate to each other rather in the manner of the alternative pictures associated with optical illusions such as the duck/rabbit hand picture – we thought we were looking at a duck, whereas in fact, we find, we are looking at a rabbit. Liberal educationalists see a duck; Marxist correspondence theorists see a rabbit. Both descriptions, however, though giving radically different *meanings* to the same

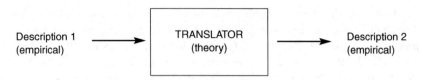

Figure 2.1 'Relations to'

object, are generated by the same type of syntax: in both cases the descriptions are given at the empirical level. This can be represented as shown in Figure 2.1.

In respect to theory of this type, Bernstein observes that:

> General theories of cultural reproduction ... appear to be more concerned with an analysis of what is reproduced in, and by, education than with an analysis of the medium of reproduction, the nature of the specialized discourse. It is as if the specialized discourse of education is only a voice through which others speak (class, gender, religion, race, region). It is as if pedagogic discourse is itself no more than a relay for power relations external to itself; a relay whose form has no consequences for what is relayed.
>
> (Bernstein 1990: 166)

Immediately prior to this, Bernstein observed that the New Sociology of Education (NSE) (Young 1971) 'took as its focus *the problematic nature of knowledge and the manner of its transmission, acquisition, and evaluation in schools*' (Bernstein 1990: 166, my emphasis). But he then adds that, 'this programme, whatever else it produced, did not produce what it called for'. Hence, Bernstein believed that there was a different kind of sociology of education immanent within the NSE, but one that remains largely unrealized because unrecognized. What is this other sociology that Bernstein, at least, saw the NSE as calling for?

The pedagogic device, relations 'within' and the theoretic object

Bernstein contrasts 'relay' theories (concerned with 'relations *to*') and a sociology of education (concerned with relations *within*) that takes as its object 'the specialized discourse of education', 'the *medium* of reproduction' that is associated with 'knowledge and the manner of its transmission, acquisition, and evaluation'. He refers to this as the 'voice' of pedagogy (1990: 190 *et passim*) that is constituted by the 'pedagogic device' (ibid.):

> the pedagogic device is a grammar for producing specialized messages, realizations, a grammar which regulates what it processes: a grammar which orders and positions and yet contains the potential of its own transformation. Any sociology of education should have a theory of the

pedagogic device. Indeed, such a theory could well be its *necessary foundation and provide the theoretical object of the discipline.*

(Bernstein 1990: 190, my emphasis)

The issues, then, are fundamental. The 'theoretical object' of the sociology of
education is unavailable to 'relay' theories because by their nature as theories
they cannot make such an object *visible* (see Moore and Maton 2001:
153–154). Bernstein says of this situation that:

> Thus we have theories of cultural reproduction/resistance and pedagogic
> discourse critique which cannot *generate the principles of description* of the
> agencies of their concern. And the answer is clear why they cannot do
> this. For those theories and approaches are not really concerned with such
> descriptions. They are concerned only to understand how external power
> relations are *carried* by the system, they are not concerned with the
> *description of the carrier,* only with a diagnosis of its pathology. Their con-
> cepts specify what is to be described, they call for a description, but are
> unable to provide *the principles for that description.*
>
> (Bernstein 1990: 171–172, my emphases)

More precisely, the 'theoretical object', the 'pedagogic device', is associated
with '*the principles of description*' of the agencies concerned – with something
internal to them rather than something having its source outside them. The
crucial difference that Bernstein is pointing to lies in that between the languages at points 1 and 2 (in Figure 2.1) and that difference is the product of
the translator (the theory) and this, in turn, relates to two quite different ways
of understanding the language of theory.

Consider, for instance, the manner in which Bernstein goes about describing progressive pedagogy as weak classification/weak framing (⁻C⁻F)
(Bernstein 1977, Ch. 6). In the first instance he provides an empirical
description of the key characteristics of a progressive infant classroom condensed into six effective features (see ibid. 116). He then theorizes the
structuring of transmission codes in terms of the relations between *hierarchy,
sequencing rules,* and *criteria* (ibid. 117–120) and condenses those relations in
terms of the distinction between 'visible' and 'invisible' pedagogies that are
themselves understood in terms of the possibilities of classification and framing. In this case the representation is as shown in Figure 2.2.

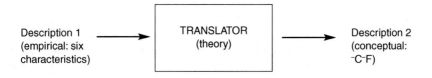

Figure 2.2 'Relations within'

Here, the translator (the theory) generates a language of a different *type,* a language *of* theory. The switch from language 1 to language 2 is a switch between languages of a qualitatively different type, from empirical description to theoretic conceptualization. As will be developed below, the difference between these languages is in their generative powers in modelling social relations and integrating empirical data.

Generative theory

The character of this difference between the languages can be initially indicated in the following way: although we can 'see' the progressive classroom in Description 1 terms (these terms have a commonsense, though culturally specialized, set of referents), we cannot 'see' $^{-}C^{-}F$. We can only know it via the theory that produces it as a systematic product of the conceptualization of educational transmission codes. This is the language of theory and of science. To say that it is a *systematic conceptualization* is to understand it as a realization of a *set* of possibilities given by a particular generative principle.

This way of representing pedagogic relations operates with two qualitatively different languages of description. First, we know that $^{-}C^{-}F$ is a possibility given by the theory that produces the principles whereby educational transmission codes can be written as: $^{+}C^{+}F$, $^{+}C^{-}F$, $^{-}C^{+}F$ and $^{-}C^{-}F$. These are theoretic 'objects' in the sense that they are the product of the principles of classification and framing that *generate* them as possibilities – the products of a *generative* theory of educational transmission codes. But, second, we also know that $^{-}C^{-}F$ can be rewritten in terms of empirical descriptors – things we can experience in consciousness and that are recognizable to us in the world. Although in the case being considered here Bernstein begins with the empirical characteristics and moves on to $^{-}C^{-}F$ and 'invisible' pedagogy', it is clear that if we understand the principles, we can equally well move in the other direction.[1] We could begin with $^{-}C^{-}F$ and generate a description of the empirical characteristics. We could ask the question: what would a $^{-}C^{-}F$ look like if we came across it in the world? This, indeed, is fundamental to all of Bernstein's theory in application – the methodological production of *recognition and realization rules.* How does a theory recognize itself in encounters with the world (e.g. Bernstein 2000: 132–134; Moore 2004a, Ch. 5)?

The logic of inquiry: theory and research

Imagine a world that had only ever, in practice, known pedagogy in its $^{-}C^{-}F$ form, as 'invisible' pedagogy. A Bernsteinian theorist in that world could, on producing the theory of classification and framing, announce that things could in fact be done differently – he or she could generate a description, for instance, of a $^{+}C^{+}F$ transmission code, a blueprint of a possible alternative way of doing education that could be put into practice. What begins as an object in theory could become an object in experience, a possibility both of consciousness and of experience – it could be realized in the world. The difference is between the ways in which things are given in consciousness as aspects of experience and the manner in which the principle of their possibility is represented (modelled) isomorphically in theory as the set of the forms of the realizations of that principle (whether or not experienced).

In our imaginary one-pedagogy world, the Bernsteinian researcher would be required to specify in advance what would count as an empirical instance of a ⁻C⁻F pedagogy; what are the effective characteristics in terms of which such a thing could be recognized? To put this into a broader context, what Bernstein is describing is a central feature of the logic of scientific inquiry. To provide one classic illustration, consider the invention of the periodic table. Very briefly, in the middle of the nineteenth century two main things were known about elements: (1) that they could be grouped into families according to similar characteristics, and (2) that they differed by atomic weight. Dmitri Mendeleev realized that there was a distinctive pattern to the differences and similarities between the elements. Essentially, they could be arranged in order of atomic weight in a series of vertical columns, the rows of which comprise the families of related elements. Atomic weight and family resemblances articulated in a consistent, structured way. In effect, Mendeleev had discovered a principle or rule that generated a matrix of positions across which the elements were distributed in a systematic fashion. Crucially, however, at that time only sixty-three of the ninety-two elements were recognized – there were 'holes' in the matrix. Mendeleev's genius was to realize that the empty places in his matrix were indeed *unknown* (unexperienced or experienced but *untheorized*) elements whose characteristics could be correctly deduced prior to their discovery. He was able to predict, for example, the properties of eka-silicon (*germanium*) twenty-five years before its discovery. Mendeleev's periodic table not only made sense of what was already known, but produced objects yet to be known – things first posited in theory as putative objects, but not yet given in experience. The theory was able to specify in advance the characteristics whereby those objects could be recognized should they become available to experience.[2]

It can be noted that the periodic table not only solved problems, it also created one very big one: how to account for these systematic differences in elements in terms of atomic weight. The problem being that if atoms are indivisible, as believed at the time, in terms of what could they differ? It was this problem that eventually resulted in the recognition that atoms themselves have structures and that the periodic table reflects the differences between the structures of atoms (atomic number replaced atomic weight). We recognize here the logic of advance that drove science (and especially physics) forward across the twentieth century.[3] This capacity of theory embeds within the field the capacity for progressive self-transformation (paradigm change).

Bernstein has described these characteristics of his mode of theorizing in this way:

It is often said that the theory works by producing opposing dichotomies in which each side functions as an ideal type: elaborated/restricted, positional/personal, stratified/differentiated, open/closed, visible/invisible, collection or serial/integrated. That these are opposing forms (models) I certainly agree. That they are ideal types I certainly disagree. Classically the ideal type is constructed by assembling in a model *a number of features* abstracted from a phenomenon in such a way as to provide a means of analyzing the presence or absence of the phenomenon, and a means of analyzing the 'workings' of the phenomenon from an analysis of the assembly of its features. Ideal types constructed in this way cannot *generate* other than themselves. They are not constructed by a principle that generates sets of relations of which any one form may be only *one of the forms* the principle may regulate.

(Bernstein 1996: 126)

The final sentence above summarizes the approach that this paper has examined so far. The language of this approach moves between that of theory and description and between that which already is and that which is possible.

What is at issue here is effectively represented in Bernstein's observation concerning the use of the concept of *habitus* in the work of Bourdieu:

The formation of the internal structure of the particular habitus, the mode of its specific acquisition, which gives it its specificity, is not described. How it comes to be is not part of the description, only what it does. There is no description of its specific formation. *We cannot replace habitus by X, that is by the description of its internal relation.* Habitus is known by its output, not by its input. Putting it crudely, there is no necessity between the concept or what counts as its realization. This means that once an illustration is challenged or a correlation, or an alternative interpretation given, there are problems.

(Bernstein 2000: 133, my emphasis)

Here is the fundamental difference between the two theories: whereas Bernstein can rewrite progressive pedagogy as ⁻C⁻F, Bourdieu can represent *habitus* only in terms of those things assumed (axiomatically) to be the realization of *habiti* of different types. Essentially, despite the centrality of the concept of *habitus* to Bourdieu's theory, he has no theory of *habitus* itself (as opposed to numerous extended definitions that are simply long ways of saying '*habitus*').[4] He provides no specification of the 'internal relation' of *habitus* as distinct from descriptions of the (culturally arbitrary) relations that structure fields as the realization of the necessities of objective probability structures configured within given moments of the social formation (Moore 2004b).

Hence, Bernstein's mode of theorizing has the following features:

- It provides principles whereby empirical instances can be understood as instances of a set of possibilities represented by a generative rule.
- These rules systematically generate sets of instances of particular types that can be provided with empirical referents or indices.
- It is historically contingent which of these possibilities is realized in practice and, hence, might be present to us in experience.
- It is sociologically contingent as to how these realizations (or their absences) occur and are distributed and how they are open to change. It is within that distribution that power comes into play and positions are socially and politically valorized within particular historical configurations.[5]

The theory contains experienced types, but also has a capacity to point beyond what is to what is possible, but as yet unrealized. It engages with the world by acknowledging what is absent from it through a modelling of what is present. In this respect, its powers as a generative theory carry a surplus element that points beyond that which is known only on the basis of experience. In this fundamental respect this approach differs from both positivism and constructionism,[6] each of which, in its own manner, reduces knowledge to experience (or *knowing*); to empirically given sense data or the subjectivities of identity. Bernstein's type of theory recovers that:

> *particular order* of meaning which establishes the particular relation between the material and the immaterial, so relating one world to another, the mundane to the transcendental. This relation always, by definition, transcends the local and the discrete. It is not that this order of relation is abstract; it is more a question of the form taken by the abstraction. It is a form whereby there is an indirect relation between meanings and a specific material base (a given social division of labour and its social relations). Under these conditions there is a potential discursive 'gap', a 'space' which can become the site of alternative possibilities, for alternative realizations of the relation between the material and the immaterial. This potential 'gap', 'space', the site of the 'unthinkable', the 'impossible', can be beneficial and dangerous at the same time. It is the meeting point of order and disorder, of coherence and incoherence; it is the crucial site of the 'yet to be thought'.
>
> (Bernstein 1990: 182)

It is sometimes presented as a complaint that Bernstein's theory is 'abstract', but it is the particular 'form taken by the abstraction' that is important and this form is that which enables the abstract to be made concrete in the manner represented in the impressive and varied body of empirical research that has arisen from the theory. It works simultaneously with two languages: an *internal* language of theory and an *external* one that specifies how things in the world must be if we are to be able to recognize them as possibilities given by the theory. 'A language of description, from this point of view, consists of rules for the unambiguous recognition of what is to count as a relevant empirical relation, and rules (realization rules) for reading the manifest contingent enactments of those empirical relations' (Bernstein 2000: 133).

The discursive gap

To a considerable extent Bernsteinian research is concerned with closing the gap between concepts given in theory and things as they are in the world through the production of research devices sufficiently both so robust and so precise as to enable an engagement between the internal language of the theory and the language of that which is outside the theory.

Consider, for instance, how he presents Morais *et al.* and the designing of 'three pedagogic practices in terms of variations in their $\pm C^{ie}/F^{ie}$ values' (Bernstein 2000: 101).[7] He says that 'Morais' remarkable study shows uniquely the intimate relationship between the theory, principles of description and the research' (ibid.). We have, then, three terms or moments: 'theory', 'principles of description' and 'research'. Essentially the research unpacks what is condensed into the expression $\pm C^{ie}/F^{ie}$ (or more usually a particular term within the expression) and translates it into a realization device such that it can be recognized and actualized as a pedagogic practice. The research produces empirical descriptions of the set of relations that is generated by $\pm C^{ie}/F^{ie}$ values and these descriptions are realized in the form of 'a very explicit and detailed teaching protocol' (ibid.).[8] This process involves a series of steps whereby terms are successively subdivided into smaller and smaller and more substantively concrete elements whereby the concept comes into an ever closer (less approximate and ambiguous) relationship to the phenomenon with which it seeks to engage. For any concept the question is asked: 'what does this *mean?*', 'what does it *look like?*', 'how do we *know* it when we see it?' (e.g. 'recognition rules'). Through a series of descriptive steps a theoretical term is translated into a process in the world ('realization rules'), e.g. into teaching a science lesson in a particular way:

$$\frac{\pm C^{ie}/F^{ie} \qquad\qquad \longrightarrow \qquad\qquad \text{teaching protocol}}{\text{theory} \qquad \text{principles of description} \qquad \text{research/practice}}$$

or the other way around, from the empirical descriptors to the code values:

$$\frac{\text{teaching protocol} \qquad\qquad \longrightarrow \qquad\qquad \pm C^{ie}/F^{ie}}{\text{research/practice} \quad \text{principles of description} \qquad \text{theory}}$$

(This form of representation is derived from Boudon (1971) – see note 1.)

The power of the theory, through its principles of description, lies in its capacity to systematically generate a nuanced set of transmission codes.

Bernstein says, 'In other words we could *design* pedagogic practices on a rational basis and evaluate their outcomes' (2000: 101). In this respect it far exceeds the possibilities of external 'relay' theories that can do little more than diagnose the pathologies of educational relations as 'capitalist', 'male', 'white', 'eurocentric', etc.

A good example of this process is represented in the diagram of the rationale 'subsystem networks' in the Appendix to Bernstein 2000, ch. 7: 140–141 (see also Moore and Muller 2002: 632) where the concern of the study in question was to model the types of responses that mothers of different classes could give to questions relating to the behaviour of their young children. Bernstein says that, 'Analysis of the choices in the network can create a very differentiated picture and in this way the *description respects the responses*' (ibid. 141, my emphasis). Again, if we understand the principles underlying the model, we could produce exemplar sentences of the actual types produced by the mothers in their natural speech in the research context. We could use the theory to generate, as it were, a virtual version of the speech that the theory predicts would be produced in the natural sentences. This process of successive unpacking, or 'translation' of concepts, attempts to shorten as far as possible the 'discursive gap' (Bernstein 2000: 125–126) between the theory and the world. It is this that Bernstein is pointing to in the earlier extract referring to Bourdieu's concept of *habitus* and the need for 'necessity between the concept or what counts as its realization'.

This complexity is represented in the following description of the 'pedagogic device':

> We consider that this device provides the intrinsic grammar of pedagogic discourse through *distributive rules, recontextualization rules, and rules of evaluation.* These rules are themselves hierarchically related in the sense that the nature of the distributive rules regulates the recontextualizing rules, which in turn regulate the rules of evaluation. These distributive rules regulate the fundamental relation between power, social groups, forms of consciousness and practice, and their reproductions and productions. The recontextualizing rules regulate the constitution of specific pedagogic discourse. The rules of evaluation are constituted in pedagogic practice. The pedagogic device generates a symbolic ruler of consciousness. The question becomes: whose ruler, what consciousness?
>
> (Bernstein 1990: 180)

Each of the terms in this description can be further refined in such a way that eventually it produces a language of description that approximates the language of the data through which the theory engages with the world. Typically in Bernstein's writing a description of this type can be represented as a diagram or model (see Bernstein 2000, Ch. 11) and, also, in its most condensed form in an expression of this familiar type:

Pedagogic codes can now be written as:

$$\frac{E}{\pm C^{ie}/\pm F^{ie}}$$

Where E refers to the orientation of the discourse (elaborated): $\pm C^{ie}/\pm F^{ie}$ refers to the embedding of this orientation in classification and framing values. Thus variations in the strength of classification and framing values generate different modalities of pedagogic practice.

(Bernstein 1990: 100)

If this expression were to be successively unpacked it would undergo the process of fractal elaboration whereby its terms would acquire increasingly concrete forms as it closes the discursive gap between concept and data. Bernstein's diagrams can be read as expanded or 'unpacked' versions of such expressions. They can be read both up and down and from side to side through the process whereby terms are successively transformed between levels and sites.[9] In the conclusion to his seminal paper on classification and framing Bernstein (1977) says that,

> It then becomes possible in one framework to derive a typology of educational codes, to show the inter-relationships between organizational and knowledge properties, to move from macro- to micro-levels of analysis, to relate the patterns internal to educational institutions to the external social antecedents of such patterns, and to consider questions of maintenance and change. At the same time, it is hoped that the analysis makes explicit tacit assumptions underlying various educational transmission codes. It attempts to show at a *theoretical* level, the relationships between a particular symbolic order and the structuring of experience.
>
> (Bernstein 1977: 111–112)

It is this quality of the translation of concepts between levels and sites within *one framework* that in the later paper on 'knowledge structures' is expressed in terms of the strength of 'grammar'. In this manner, Bernstein's sociology of the structure of pedagogic discourse constitutes a strong grammar in contrast to the weak grammar of relay theories (see below). Bernstein emphasizes the centrality of theory to research and the amount of theoretical work that is done prior to research (e.g. Bernstein 2000, Ch. 6). This work involves the placing of conceptual stepping-stones across the discursive gap between theory and data through the unpacking of concepts into successively more substantive elements.

Strong and weak grammars

It was stressed at the beginning of this paper that what is being considered here is not just how one more particular theoretical perspective operates relative to others. The perspective that is being outlined above is operating in a different epistemological mode from those that otherwise constitute the field of sociology of education. Having attempted to provide a representation of Bernstein's theoretical mode, the question now is: how did Bernstein represent the differences between theories operating in these different modes? In the first instance, what is at issue is the question of the strength and weakness of the 'grammars' of fields operating in different ways. In Bernstein 2000, Ch. 9, a contrast is made between what counts as 'development' in hierarchical and horizontal knowledge structures (pp.161–163). This is associated with a fundamental distinction that Bernstein describes as follows:

> *Horizontal Knowledge Structures,* unlike *Hierarchical Knowledge Structures* which are based on integrating codes, are based upon collection or serial codes; integration *of* language in one case and accumulation of *languages* in the other.
>
> (Bernstein 2000: 162)

The contrast is between integrating codes/integrating languages and serial codes/accumulation of languages. Essentially, the distinction is in terms of the strength of classification or boundary and how this affects the possibility of translation. Hierarchical knowledge structures (or horizontal ones with strong grammar) see development as 'the development of the theory which is more general, more integrating than previous theory' (ibid.) (with weak grammar languages, languages or approaches seek to displace rather than complement each other) . Bernstein makes clear that he hopes that his own concepts will contribute to such a situation in the understanding of intellectual fields rather than being just 'yet another language' (ibid. 156). Translation (integration of language) depends upon weak boundaries between knowledge and the capacity for terms in one area to be seen as commensurable with those in another (see Moore and Maton 2000, esp. pp. 162–164). For horizontal knowledge structures with a weak grammar, translation is not possible because:

> the set of languages which constitute any one *Horizontal Knowledge Structure* are not translatable, since they make different and often opposing assumptions, with each language having its own criteria for legitimate texts, what counts as evidence and what counts as legitimate questions or a legitimate problematic. Indeed the speakers of each language become as specialized as the language. Their capital is bound up with the language and therefore defence of and challenge of other languages is intrinsic to a *Horizontal Knowledge Structure*. A particular field is constructed by the internal characteristics of a *Horizontal Knowledge Structure*. Thus the internal characteristics and external field amplify the serial character of a *Horizontal Knowledge Structure*.
>
> (Bernstein 2000: 162)

Hence, in distinguishing between the strength of grammars in horizontal knowledge structures, it is the question of translation that is crucial and this in turn relates to the strength of classification. In the case of hierarchical knowledge structures, Bernstein argues,

> opposition between theories ... is played out in attempts to refute positions where possible, or to incorporate them in more general propositions. At some time, sometimes later than sooner, because of special investments, a choice is possible provided the issue can be settled by empirical procedures.
>
> (Bernstein 2000: 162)

The same principle applies to horizontal knowledge structures with relatively strong grammar. Theories are *open* to each other: 'The strong grammar visibly announces what it is. For the acquirer the passage from one theory to another *does not signal a break in the language*. It is simply an extension of its explanatory/descriptive powers' (Bernstein 2000: 164–163, my emphasis). Strong grammar enables translation because it aims at the *integration of language* rather than the *accumulation of languages* (as in the case of the proliferation of hyphenated identities in post-structuralism). The problem with weak grammar is that knowledge is held to be intrinsically inseparable from selves, from experience and the experience of selves as specialized categories of knowers and their exclusive (i.e. strongly classified) languages. On this condition, Bernstein wrote as follows:

> Because a *Horizontal Knowledge Structure* consists of an array of languages any one transmission necessarily entails some selection, and some privileging within the set recontextualized for the transmission of the *Horizontal Knowledge Structure*. The social basis of the principle of this recontextualization indicates whose 'social' is speaking. The social basis of the principle of the recontextualizing constructs the perspective of the *Horizontal Knowledge Structure*. Whose perspective is it? How is it generated and legitimated? I say that this principle is social in order to indicate that choice here is not rational in the sense that it is based on the 'truth' of one of the specialized languages. For each language reveals some 'truth', although to a great extent this partial 'truth' is incommensurate and language specific.
>
> (Bernstein 2000: 164)

This raises a crucial issue concerning the position of *theory* between strong and weak grammars. In a weak grammar horizontal knowledge structure, theory is underdeveloped. It functions through rules of *reinterpretation* of the empirical more than through theorization of objects. Indeed, theory might even be rejected as a form of subjugating elitism as when some radical phenomenologists in the 1970s or certain more recent versions of feminist method proclaim that the sociologists' meanings cannot go beyond members' meanings. But this should not be seen as implying a difference between more or less theory – any more than the distinction between visible and invisible pedagogy is that between more or fewer rules in the classroom. As Bernstein points out, 'transmission necessarily entails some selection, and some privileging within the set recontextualized for the transmission'. Although weak grammar approaches often legitimate themselves by the claim that their text reproduces an authentic 'voice' of a silenced or marginalized group (as with certain 'invisible pedagogies'), in reality such voices are always the product of the 'text within the text' (the theory that provides the tacit principle of selection and recontextualization), even when such a thing is being formally denied (see Moore and Muller 1999: 194; Bernstein 2000: 169–170). As Bernstein observed, weak grammar approaches in their 'voice' form (as with progressive pedagogies in the school) frequently assume a posture of 'popularism in the name of empowering or unsilencing voices to combat the alleged authoritarianism of *Vertical discourse*' (Bernstein 2000: 170 – see Arnot and Reay, this volume).

In epistemological terms, weak grammar is associated with the conflation of knowledge with knowing and the reduction of knowledge relations to the power relations between groups. Knowledge is reduced to experience and experience is determined by membership ('identity') within a structure of power relations, and this, in turn, is reduced to the binary (semiotic relational) form of dominant-hegemonic/subjugated-other. In the earlier 'brief account' of the sociology of education (Bernstein 1977, Ch. 7), Bernstein says:

> And this takes us to the heart of the matter. In a subject where theories and methods are weak, intellectual shifts are likely to arise out of conflict between *approaches* rather than conflict between explanations, for, by definition, most explanations will be weak and often non-comparable, because they are approach-specific. The weakness of explanation is likely to be attributed to the approach which is analyzed in terms of its ideological stance. Once the ideological stance is exposed, then all the work can be written off. Every new approach becomes a social movement or sect which immediately defines the nature of the subject by re-defining what is to be admitted and what is beyond the pale, so that with every new approach the subject almost starts from scratch. Old bibliographies are scrapped, the new references become more and more contemporary, new legitimations are 'socially constructed' and courses take on a different focus. What may be talked about and how it is to be talked about has changed.
>
> (Bernstein 1977: 167–168)

In this earlier paper Bernstein is describing the condition of a horizontal knowledge structure with a weak grammar before having developed the concept and the more formal analysis of intellectual fields presented in the later paper. What is remarkable about this piece from thirty years ago is how accurately it reflects *today's* condition. Within a postmodernist climate it is even more apt because now there is an account that explicitly endorses, through the recontextualizing device of 'identity', the condition of segmentation and fragmentation in the field. As observed in the extract on the preceding page, it is *approaches* (understood in terms of categories of knowers) rather than explanations that are the focus of concern. Who knows rather than what is known – approaches rather than explanations. As Bernstein says, 'The dangers of "approach paradigms" are that they tend to witch-hunting and heresy-spotting' (ibid. 158). 'Once the ideological stance is exposed, then all the work can be written off.' This is a major reason why so little knowledge is accumulated in such fields.

Conclusion

If we now return to the original question concerning the difference between sociology of education that treats education as a relay for things outside it (relations *to* education) and that which is concerned with relations *within,* with the 'medium that makes the relaying possible' (Bernstein 1990: 169), then it is clear that Bernstein's approach makes visible a 'theoretical object' (the structuring of pedagogic discourse) that is entirely invisible to the former. An 'object' of this type is distinctive in the following important respects.

First, it is *complex* (as opposed to the simple singulars of positivist logical atomism). This complexity resides in the power of the principles of the object to generate a range of possibilities (the pedagogic device is not a single thing, rather it is the principle of the systematic possibility of a number of things). Second (in contrast to the empiricist subjectivism of constructionism), it is an object of *theory* not of experience. As to when and how such possibilities are realized in the world and become available as objects of experience is a substantive issue for research within this problematic. In this respect it is as much concerned with absence as with what is present.

Third, it generates *two languages of description:* one that is internal to theory and one that specifies the empirical features of the phenomena with which the theory seeks to engage. These languages relate to each other as condensed and expanded versions and introduce a principle of necessity between concept and realization.

Put in this context, we can see Bernstein's mode of theorizing as consistent with a more general logic of critical–rational inquiry. It is unfamiliar to a horizontal field with a weak grammar that cannot make visible the 'theoretical object' of such an approach, but characteristic of fields with a strong grammar (whether hierarchical or horizontal). The oddity of a sociology of education as a horizontal knowledge structure with a weak grammar is that an approach such as Bernstein's should itself appear as the oddity.

Notes

1   See also Raymond Boudon (1971) *The Uses of Structuralism,* Ch. 3, especially pp. 72–78 and the expression on pages 73 and 76.

2   The experimental phase of scientific inquiry is concerned with devising the means whereby the conditions can be specified (and created) under which theoretical objects might become available in experience and in what unambiguously recognizable form.

3   It is important to stress, in order to avoid unnecessary complications and diversions, that what is being described here is not positivism, but a form of epistemological realism. Positivism, as an empiricist doctrine, precisely disallows theoretical objects not given in experience. It is for this reason that positivism fails to provide a satisfactory account of science.

4   This condition of Bourdieu's theory is the result of two things: first, the principle of *necessity* attributed to 'objective probability structures' such that their intuitive perception by members of social groups, by virtue of *habitus,* guarantees, through appropriate dispositions, the realization of those probabilities. Second, the principle of the *arbitrary* that governs his semiotic relational model of the field (Bernstein 2000: *xiv* fn 1). Together, these things constitute a determinism whereby it is taken for granted that things are as they are because they can be no other way. This dogmaticism removes the need for Bourdieu to ever consider the problem of rewriting *habitus* as X – he can never be anything other than right because the world he describes can never be other than it is (Moore 2004b).

5   The place of 'power' in Bernstein's theory is not addressed in this chapter. See, however, Arnot and Reay (this volume) and the distinction made between 'message' and 'voice'. As Arnot and Reay demonstrate, it is in 'voice' that message is valorized in terms of power.

6   Though he was himself dismissive of what he termed 'epistemological botany', Bernstein's theory is best understood as a form of critical realism.

7   The '*i*' and '*e*' refer to 'internal' and 'external'. For instance, a school might have weak classification within its own internal relations, but maintain a strong insulation, or classification, between itself and external, local community-based knowledge and relations.

8   An extended, well-illustrated example of the process whereby condensed theoretical terms are progressively unpacked and refined into descriptions of an increasingly substantive kind that can be effectively applied in the research process is provided in Bernstein 1990, Ch. 1, Appendix 1.5: 54–59.

9   See, here, the typical manner in which Bernstein (1990: 180) describes how 'relations to' and 'relations within', and the 'macro' and the 'micro' can be read across each other in the diagram (Figure 5.1: 173).

3　On knowledge structures and knower structures

Karl Maton

Basil Bernstein (1977, 1990, 1999) shows how structures of knowledge in intellectual and educational fields specialize discourses and actors in ways that have structuring significance for those discourses and actors as well as the fields of social and symbolic practice they inhabit. Using the concepts of educational knowledge codes, the pedagogic device and knowledge structures, Bernstein's framework helps reveal the effects of the structuring of pedagogic and intellectual discourse for social relations, organization, disciplinary and curricular change, and identities (Singh 2002, Moore 2004a). In this chapter I suggest that exploring *knower structures* develops these insights further, opening up new and fruitful possibilities for research. Using the concepts of legitimation codes, the epistemic device and knower structures, I shall build on Bernstein's framework to add a second dimension to understanding intellectual and educational fields.

My specific focus is how knowledge and knowers are specialized or, put another way, what makes some ideas, texts, actors, groups or institutions special or appear to partake of the sacred, and others profane. Such questions of knowledge and identity are central to social and intellectual change. In 'knowledge societies' experiencing exponential growth in the volume, complexity and sources of information and where growing demand beyond the academy for more knowledge to ameliorate the uncertainties of everyday life accompanies a loss of public trust in 'expert' knowledge (Muller 2000), issues of *who* knows *what* and *how* have become crucial far beyond the academy. At the same time, within higher education increasingly marketized funding regimes encourage the proliferation of publications, while credential inflation threatens to expand research student numbers. These developments make the tasks of determining what constitutes an original contribution to knowledge, who is a scientist or a sociologist, or what article is worth reading, recurring threads running through the everyday lives of academics. Questions of the basis of claims to be heard, recognized, published or resourced are thus far more than philosophical speculation or epistemological ground-clearing.

In this chapter I discuss how using Bernstein's analysis of curricular and knowledge structures can help shed light on the ways such questions of the specialization of actors and ideas are answered. I will also show how focusing on the role played by knower structures augments and develops these insights.

In Bernstein's work the latter represent a kind of shadow structure, implicit within the theory but not explicitly foregrounded, conceptualized and elaborated. Here I shall show what bringing knower structures into the light and making them an integral part of the analysis can offer. At the same time I shall illustrate and develop the concepts of legitimation code and epistemic device that are being used elsewhere to analyse institutional, disciplinary and pedagogic formations.[1] I am thus setting forth a way of thinking about intellectual and educational knowledge using some simple tools that researchers are finding useful to think with. I do so by briefly discussing two different substantive research projects I am using these tools to think about, which examine intellectual and educational fields. First, I address fields of knowledge production by discussing the famous 'two cultures' debate about relations between science and the humanities that erupted during the early 1960s. Second, I focus on fields of knowledge reproduction by discussing the early findings of exploratory research on the school curriculum that asks why comparatively few children choose to take qualifications in Music.

Knower structures in intellectual fields: the 'two cultures' debate

In 1959 C.P. Snow gave a lecture in which he claimed that the intellectual life of 'the whole of western society' was increasingly being split into 'two polar groups' that 'had almost ceased to communicate at all' with 'between the two a gulf of mutual incomprehension – sometimes ... hostility and dislike, but most of all lack of understanding' (Snow 1959: 3, 2, 4). These 'two cultures' were quickly associated in the ensuing debate with the humanities and science and the debate itself construed as a struggle over which of the two could lay claim to the title of 'culture' and so status in the academy. Though the idea that intellectuals were divided into rival cultures had been made before, it is difficult to overestimate the ferocity and intensity of the debate which raged following the publication of Snow's lecture – as Snow put it, 'a nerve had been touched' (1964: 54). The debate quickly became famous and remains widely discussed; indeed, current discussions of 'two cultures', relations between science and the humanities, and the position of social science, all remain deeply indebted to the grounds established by this original debate.

The answer to why such a well-established portrait of the disciplinary map aroused such passion can be found within the public pronouncements of contemporary participants in the debate.[2] Common across positions in the debate was a striking picture of contrasting fortunes. On the one hand, what Snow termed 'scientific culture' was portrayed as enjoying a meteoric rise in stature; as one commentator tartly expressed:

> You cannot open a newspaper, let alone the 'quality' journals, without the importance of science and technology being trumpeted at you from the headlines.

> (Morris 1959: 374)

By the late 1950s the term 'science' had about it something of the sacred: 'for non-scientists it is magic' (Allen 1959: 67). Fêted by and enjoying massive funding from industry and the state, revered by the media and worshipped by the public, scientists were said to be enjoying unprecedented prestige. In contrast, the humanities were portrayed as embattled, in decline and insecure. An influential collection of essays entitled *Crisis in the Humanities* (Plumb 1964), for example, included accounts of proclaimed crises within classics, history, philosophy, divinity, literary education, sociology, the fine arts, and economics, as well as the humanities in schools. They were said to be unwanted by better-quality students, considered irrelevant to a modern economy by industrialists, increasingly excluded from the corridors of power by politicians, no longer considered the repository of culture, and publicly ridiculed as offering little genuine knowledge. In short, while scientists were feeling strident and secure, humanist intellectuals were suffering from shattered self-confidence. The contemporary view of the disciplinary map, therefore, portrayed a fundamental shift in the balance of power between humanist and scientific cultures in their long-acknowledged struggle for status and resources. This raises two questions that I shall explore in turn: (1) What was the basis of their differences?; and (2) Why was this shift of power occurring? A common contemporary explanation of their differences held that scientists and humanist intellectuals 'speak different languages' (Editorial, *The Listener,* 3 September 1959b: 344). Using Bernstein's approach would suggest it was instead the *underlying structuring principles* of their languages that were different. I shall explore these principles in terms of knowledge structures and then knower structures, before illustrating how an analysis incorporating both can shed light on what was underlying this changing disciplinary map.

Knowledge structures

Analysing the form taken by knowledge in intellectual fields of production, Bernstein (1996, 1999) distinguishes first between horizontal discourse (everyday or 'commonsense' knowledge) and vertical discourse (scholarly or professional knowledge) and, second, within vertical discourse between horizontal and hierarchical knowledge structures. These different forms of knowledge structure can be used to describe the two cultures.[3] Beginning with the humanities, humanist culture was portrayed by participants in the debate as riven by competing claims for supremacy between strongly bounded disciplines. Commentators argued that classics had served as the basis of a 'common culture' or 'unifying force' (Lee 1955) and its decline was leaving a hole at the centre of the humanities; what had been a single, organic culture was fragmenting into a series of rival subcultures, with little dialogue across disciplinary boundaries and no means of adjudicating between competing claims to be the new unifying centre. Humanist culture thereby resembled what Bernstein defines as a *horizontal knowledge structure:*

a series of specialized languages, each with its own specialized modes of interrogation and specialized criteria ... with non-comparable principles of description based on different, often opposed, assumptions.

(Bernstein 1996: 172–3)

A horizontal knowledge structure comprises a series of segmented, strongly bounded languages which, developing Bernstein (1999: 162), I shall visually represent as:

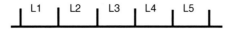

Where humanists were said to be riven by disagreement, and thought and acted differently, proponents of scientific culture claimed scientists comprised an organic community; as Snow put it, scientists shared 'common attitudes, common standards and patterns of behaviour, common approaches and assumptions' (1959: 9). Unlike the pluralized humanities, science was often referred to in the singular and portrayed as integrated and whole. Though science was proliferating specialisms at a rapid rate, scientists were said to know how to bring them together; they understood 'the essential principles' (Halsey 1962) and so were able to generate new knowledge without splitting into competing factions. Scientific culture thereby resembled what Bernstein describes as a *hierarchical knowledge structure:* 'an explicit, coherent, systematically principled and hierarchical organization of knowledge' which develops through the integration of knowledge at lower levels and across an expanding range of phenomena (1996: 172–3). This Bernstein represents as:

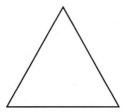

where the point of the pyramid represents the smallest number of axioms or theories and the base represents the maximal number of empirical phenomena explainable by these propositions.

Knower structures

Using Bernstein's concepts enables the form taken by the knowledge structures characterizing the two cultures to be described. If we now turn to look at each culture again but in terms of their knower structures, it shows a different picture (see Table 3.1). I described how the humanities were portrayed as having previously been a 'common culture' with the classics at its centre

Table 3.1 The 'two cultures' as knowledge structures and knower structures

	Humanist culture	Scientific culture
Knowledge structures		
Knower structures		

serving to integrate and bring the various disciplines into relation. However, it was not classics understood as knowledge, techniques, skills or procedures that formed the basis of this integration but rather the dispositions or 'gaze' that an education in classics was said to guarantee. The ideal humanist intellectual was a gentleman amateur who pursued (usually) his studies 'for the love of it', viewing them as secondary to a clerisy role of cultivating the cultured sensibility of the 'English gentleman' among students selected on the basis of fitting in with the character of the university (Maton 2004). Everything focused on the personal attributes, sensibility or character of the knower and an education in classics served as shorthand, indicating this requisite *habitus*. It was in effect a cultural veneer for a tacit social hierarchy by being associated with specific social and educational backgrounds (historically, upper-class, public school and Oxbridge). In other words, the humanities represented what I shall define as a *hierarchical knower structure:* a systematically principled and hierarchical organization of knowers based on an image of an ideal knower which develops through the integration of new knowers at lower levels and across an expanding range of different dispositions.[4] As shown in Table 3.1, this can be portrayed as a pyramid of knowers with, in the case of humanist culture, the ideal of the 'English gentleman' at its pinnacle. The recontextualizing principle of the humanities and its ruler (in both senses) was thus a *knower;* this idealized knower served as the basis for the selection of actors and ideas and their recontextualization into the field's hierarchy of knowers.

Where the humanist intellectual's 'ability is a personal matter, which on the whole he does not owe to his advanced training', scientific knowledge was widely portrayed as 'fairly independent of the personal merits of its possessor' (Gellner 1964: 75–6). Proponents of science claimed that *anyone* could enter the sacred. Snow compared scientific culture as a democratic and meritocratic endeavour to the class-bound patronage and social snobbery of humanist culture and claimed science was blind to colour, race, creed; it cut 'across other mental patterns, such as those of religion or politics or class' (1959: 9). In short, anyone could do science so long as they followed the correct scientific procedures. Scientists could, therefore, have very different social backgrounds and sensibilities because these did not matter. Science was thus portrayed as what I shall term a *horizontal knower structure:* a series of strongly bounded knowers, each with its own specialized modes of being and acting, with non-comparable habituses or embodied dispositions based on different social backgrounds or experiences. In science, according to its proponents, each type of knower could be strongly bounded from other knowers such that scientists could represent a series of segmented knowers (see Table 3.1), each 'gaze' strongly bounded from one another and capable of being based on very different, even opposed, assumptions.

Exploring these knower structures highlights something not immediately obvious from studying knowledge structures alone: it is not only hierarchical knowledge structures that have a hierarchy. As illustrated in Table 3.1, hierarchical *knower* structures also possess a systematic principle for arranging actors and discourses into a hierarchy. The difference between intellectual fields may thus be less whether they are hierarchical or not and more where their hierarchizing and recontextualizing principle lies: in the knowledge structure or in the knower structure (or in both). I should emphasize that 'knower structure' does not add a 'field of positions', as Bourdieu (1993) would put it, to the knowledge structure's 'field of stances'. The analysis remains focused on what Bernstein (1990) termed 'relations within' rather than 'relations to' knowledge (see Chapter 2, this volume). Analysing knower structures simply reveals another dimension to the knowledge formation. To explore this more concretely, I shall now examine how actors and discourses were related to each of these two structures in the 'two cultures' debate using the concept of legitimation codes.

Legitimation codes

The notion of legitimation codes is based on the simple idea that actors are not only positioned in both a structure of knowledge and a structure of knowers but also establish in their symbolic practices different forms of relations to these two structures. One can thereby analytically distinguish between an *epistemic relation* (ER) to the knowledge structure and a *social relation* (SR) to the knower structure.[5] Each of these relations can exhibit relatively stronger (+) or weaker (–) classification and framing. Varying their strengths for each relation independently generates four principal codes: $ER^{+/-}$, $SR^{+/-}$ (where 'ER^+', for example, condenses '^+C, ^+F of epistemic relation'). In other words, actors may emphasize the knowledge structure, the knower structure, neither or both as the basis of distinctiveness, authority and status; conversely, their identity, relations and consciousness are shaped in different ways by these two kinds of structures. These legitimation codes represent different 'settings' of the epistemic device, the means whereby intellectual and educational fields are maintained, reproduced, transformed and changed (Moore and Maton

2001). Whoever controls the epistemic device possesses the means to set the shape of the field in their favour, making what characterizes their own practices (in terms of legitimation codes) the basis of status and achievement in the field. This brief and somewhat formal definition of these concepts can be fleshed out by considering the different ways in which the two cultures established relations to their knowledge structures and knower structures.

Perhaps the most controversial claim Snow made in his lecture was that science and not the humanities was the *true* 'common culture': 'the scientific culture really is a culture ... Without thinking about it, they respond alike. That is what a culture means' (1959: 9, 10). The basis of this culture was scientists' 'sense of loyalty to an abstraction called "knowledge"' (Mackerness 1960: 15), commitment to 'truth' (Bronowski 1961) and allegiance to their discipline (Pakenham 1963), which specialized their identity and claims to insight. In other words, for science the epistemic relation to its knowledge structure was central to the field; this structure strongly classifies and frames actors and discourses within the field (ER⁺), while the social relation to its knower structure was less significant (SR⁻): what I have elsewhere defined as a *knowledge code* (see Table 3.2), which is predicated upon the rule 'What matters is what you know, not who you are'.

In the case of the humanities, knowledge itself mattered a lot less; possession of procedures and skills was relatively unimportant in defining identity and achievement, so the epistemic relation to its knowledge structure was weakly classified and framed (ER⁻). Instead, the basis of specialization was possessing the right kind of dispositions or character. In other words, the field strongly classifies and frames knowers (SR⁺); for the humanities, the social relation to its knower structure was the key to the field – a *knower code*, predicated upon the rule that 'What matters is not what you know but who you are'. Comparing the two cultures in Table 3.1 shows that it is that which is hierarchical (the pyramids) that strongly classifies and frames actors and discourses within the intellectual field (in bold type in Table 3.2): the epistemic relation to the knowledge structure for scientific culture and the social relation to the knower structure for humanist culture.

Having conceptualized the two cultures in terms of their knowledge structures and knower structures and brought these together as legitimation codes,

Table 3.2 Legitimation codes of specialization for the two cultures

	Humanist culture	*Scientific culture*
Epistemic relation (to knowledge structure)	$C^-\ F^-$	$^+C, {}^+F$
Social relations (to knower structure)	$^+C, {}^+F$	$C^-\ F^-$
Legitimation code	knower code	knowledge code
	(ER⁻, SR⁺)	(ER⁺, SR⁻)

Note: Classification (C) refers to relative strength of boundaries *between* categories or contexts; framing (F) refers to relative strength of control *within* these categories or contexts; ER/SR refers to epistemic relation and social relation; '+/–' indicates relatively stronger/relatively weaker.

we can now return to the two questions raised earlier: the basis of difference between the two cultures and reasons for the shift of power between them. First, the debate can be redescribed as a struggle for control of the epistemic device between fields characterized by contrasting rulers or measures of achievement (legitimation codes). These different codes characterize the kind of resources or capital actors bring to the struggle: a struggle here between 'who you are' (knower code) and 'what you know' (knowledge code) as measures of status. It is little wonder that between the two was said to lay 'a gulf of mutual incomprehension'. Moreover, the rise of science and the proclaimed crisis in humanities are intimately interrelated: rising status for science threatened to change the basis of the distribution of resources and status within the field and relegate humanists to second-class citizens. If scientists controlled the epistemic device, then the field would tilt in their favour by making a knowledge code the basis of achievement.

Second, the difference in codes also suggests reasons for why this shift in power seemed imminent. One reason lies in the different relationships the codes establish between their knowledge formations and horizontal discourse (or everyday knowledge). As discussed, science was portrayed as specialized by its language rather than its speakers: who was speaking was said to be less important than what they were talking about and how. The mathematization of science from the seventeenth century onwards had made this language progressively different to commonsense understanding, making *discursive distance* from the contents and form of horizontal discourse the basis of the specialization of science. The scientist B.C. Brookes, for example, claimed 'it will never be possible' to translate between the two and that 'the learning of science is the learning of a *first*, not a foreign, language' that needed 'lengthy and ruthless indoctrination' (1959a: 502–21, 1959b: 783–4). Measured in terms of its knowledge code, science was thereby becoming ever more specialized in relation to horizontal discourse.

In contrast, the knower code basis of identity and status in the humanities made *dispositional distance* the basis of status; i.e. the distinction between the dispositions of humanist knowers and those of the laity, rather than the possession of specialized knowledge and skills. In these terms the position of humanists was being undermined on two fronts. First, expansion was bringing more varied knowers into higher education, presenting challenges to its hierarchy of knowers; maintaining the code depended on successful accommodation of different dispositions. Second, when judged by the discursive distance of science's knowledge code, the humanities were becoming less special. The extension of literacy under educational expansion was giving birth to 'the articulate society' where everyone felt entitled to speak and in which the 'clerk is a nobody not merely because he is not a scientist, but also because in the developed societies *everyone* is now a clerk' (Gellner 1964: 78). The humanities did not involve learning specialized procedures or skills – there 'is no enormous discontinuity, a yawning gap, bridgeable only by prolonged training'; instead one could pick up a discipline 'simply by soaking in the ambience' (Gellner 1964: 70) – and so were vulnerable to being viewed as little more than a convoluted or jargon-ridden form of everyday understanding. As the historian Asa Briggs had complained:

> Everyone feels entitled to judge, even to condemn, and to say, for example, with Henry Ford that 'history is bunk'. This is a charge which few men-in-the-street would care to make against physics or chemistry.
>
> (Briggs 1956: 55)

In summary, the two cultures exhibited different legitimation codes, the debate represented a struggle for ownership of the epistemic device, and the state of play in this struggle was being affected by the different relationships each code established with lay knowledge and knowers. In his paper on knowledge structures, Bernstein (1999: 166) states that a field and its discourse are interdependent and interrelated and must be analysed together; the analysis presented here illustrates how they relate together in specializing identity and achievement within intellectual fields. That is, thinking in terms of how both knowledge and knower structures specialize actors, and how discourses can shed light on the different things they define as marking what is sacred and what is profane, the way they establish different relations between their sacred and profane, and the possible effects this may have for intellectual fields. I shall now use this simple idea to look at a different context: the school curriculum.

Knower structures in educational fields: Music in the school curriculum

Thus far I have focused on fields of knowledge production; in terms of educational fields of reproduction the notion of knower structures can be illustrated by returning to Bernstein's paper on classification and framing (1971) where he describes *inter alia* how educational knowledge codes shape educational identities. Bernstein identifies two codes as being predominant in educational systems: a collection code of relatively stronger boundaries between subject areas and control in pedagogy; and an integrated code of relatively weaker boundaries and control. Exploring the ways in which these shape identity and consciousness, Bernstein describes how collection codes emphasize educational knowledge, producing a 'clear-cut and bounded' or 'pure' educational identity based on one's academic subject ($^+$C,$^+$F), while in integrated codes the role of disciplinary knowledge in shaping one's educational identity is less clear-cut, more complex and must be constantly negotiated ($^-$C, $^-$F). From the perspective being advanced in this paper, one can describe this analysis as coding the way *educational knowledge structures* (such as a curriculum) specialize actors and discourses (ER$^{+/-}$). Just as for intellectual fields, we can additionally focus on the role of the *educational knower structure* and code its influence on specialization (SR$^{+/-}$). As I shall emphasize, it depends on the empirical context under investigation but it is likely that in contexts characterized by a collection code curriculum the significance of a knower's dispositions is diminished (⁻C, ⁻F), while in integrated codes there is more space for knower dispositions to play a greater role in the negotiation of identity and consciousness (⁺C, ⁺F), whether these dispositions are seen as 'natural', inculcated or resulting from one's social position (depending on the model of the knower).[6] In other words, examining the knower structures of collection code and integrated code curricula reveals unexpected strengths of classification and framing. If we consider Bernstein's original formulation as coding the epistemic relation and these unexpected readings as coding the social relation, then it is clear they represent a knowledge code (ER⁺, SR⁻) and a knower code (ER⁻, SR⁺) respectively.

In short, I am suggesting that there are two dimensions of educational contexts (knowledge structures and knower structures), that relations to both can be coded (using classification and framing), and that bringing these two modalities together gives the legitimation code. I stated above that this code depends on the actual example under investigation because the modalities characterizing the epistemic relation to the knowledge structure and social relation to the knower structure may vary independently of each other. The inverse relationship between knowledge structures and knower structures in the example of the two cultures (see Table 3.1) is not always necessarily the case; one can, for example, envisage a collection code knowledge structure which also exhibits strong boundaries around and control over knower dispositions (i.e. one characterized by a hierarchical knowledge structure *and* a hierarchical knower structure). Varying the relative strengths of classification and framing for the epistemic and social relations generates four principal legitimation codes (see Figure 3.1). This generates further possibilities than those already encountered. Analysing the knower structure and integrating this with an analysis of knowledge structure within the concept of legitimation code thereby expands the range of possible phenomena brought within the theory. I have already discussed:

- *knowledge code* (ER⁺, SR⁻), which emphasizes possession of specialized knowledge, skills or techniques; and
- *knower code* (ER⁻, SR⁺), which foregrounds dispositions, whether 'natural', cultivated or related to social background.

In addition, one can also identify:

- *relativist code* (ER⁻, SR⁻), where one's identity and consciousness is ostensibly determined by neither knowledge nor dispositions, a kind of relativist 'anything goes'; and
- *élite code* (ER⁺, SR⁺), where legitimate insight and membership is based not only on possessing specialist knowledge but also having the right kinds of dispositions.

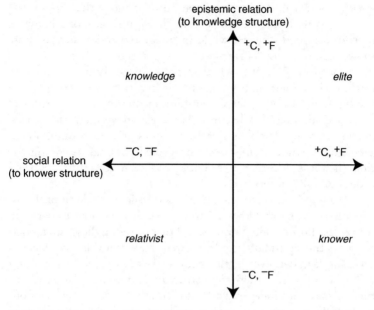

Figure 3.1 Legitimation codes of specialization

This conceptual framework thereby explores not only the strength of boundaries and locus of control but also what those classification and framing strengths are of. Put crudely, it asks what the entry requirements are to being considered legitimate, offering a legitimate performance or showing legitimate competence: is it knowledge, dispositions, neither or both? I have already discussed two of these codes. To explore the value of this generative theorization I shall now focus on the élite code by briefly discussing empirical research using these concepts to look at the problematic position of Music in the curriculum.

Music GCSE: an élite code?

There is something rotten in the state of Music in English secondary schools. Concern over its current status led to the launch in July 2004 of a 'Music Manifesto' by the British government that aims to champion the status of the subject and encourage more young people to remain involved in music making. In school the problem is that though Music is very popular among pupils up to the end of Year 9 (age 14) (Lamont *et al.* 2003) there is exceedingly low uptake for GCSE qualifications: approximately 7 per cent of children choose to take GCSE Music, compared to 38 per cent for History, 38 per cent for Art and Design, and 15 per cent for Drama.[7] The question this raises is why Music GCSE is so comparatively unpopular. So far little research has directly and systematically addressed this issue. Most studies of Music focus on the learning and playing of musical instruments in formal and informal settings outside school; Music in the school curriculum is typically described as simply being 'out of touch' or viewed as irrelevant by most children (e.g. Green 2001, Sloboda 2001). Research that focuses on school Music, including the limited number of studies on the GCSE problem itself, describe it as problematic but offer speculation or ad hoc, piecemeal and largely descriptive accounts of best practice (e.g. Bray 2000, Harland *et al.* 2000). This lack of explanation represents the starting point for a collaborative, interdisciplinary research project using the conceptual framework presented here. I shall report very briefly on the early stages of this research, focusing on two pilot studies: (i) an analysis of attainment targets and programmes of study set out in curriculum documents and syllabi for Music; and (ii) a survey of pupils' perceptions of a range of academic subjects including Music.[8]

Curriculum documents

The first study analyses the content and language of levels of achievement expected of pupils at different Key Stages, as expressed in National Curriculum attainment targets and programmes of study, and in the GCSE syllabi of major examination boards. These have been analysed in terms of whether they focus on and emphasize: skills, techniques and knowledge; knower dispositions (such as aptitude, attitude, personal expression); neither; or both. Preliminary analysis suggests that the legitimation code changes for different Key Stages through the curriculum. In Key Stages 1–2 (ages 5–11) there is an emphasis in the documents on the pupil's personal expression and inner attributes above all else. For example, at the end of Key Stage 2 (age 11) pupils are expected to be able to 'develop their own compositions ... with increasing personal involvement, independence and creativity' (DfES/QCA 1999: 18) – a knower code. In Key Stage 3 (ages 11–14), the emphasis shifts as issues of aptitude, attitude and personal engagement are replaced by a focus on the demonstration of skills and possession of knowledge. The attainment target here emphasizes, for example, that pupils should show an 'increasing ability to discriminate, think critically and make connections between different areas of knowledge' (DfES/QCA 1999: 20) – a knowledge code. Crucially for our focus here, a second change of code occurs at GCSE level (Key Stage 4). Examination syllabi for GCSE require both personal expression *and* technical skills and knowledge. For example, for the syllabus of the examination board Edexcel, pupils are required to include a solo musical performance which is assessed for being both 'accurate and fluent' and 'an expressive performance that is generally stylish', with equal emphasis on technical accuracy and personal interpretation – an élite code. These preliminary results suggest a possible reason for low uptake worthy of investigation to be this move from knowledge code at Key Stage 3 to élite code at GCSE, one which is not merely a shift of code (as also occurs between Key Stages 2 and 3) but one that becomes doubly demanding: it is not enough one be knowledgeable, one must also possess the requisite dispositions.

Pupils' perceptions

The second part of this pilot study is a survey of children's definitions of the basis of success in different academic subjects. The survey was constructed to explore pupils' attitudes towards a range of school subjects, using the four codes as potential responses. Pupils were asked about Music alongside the core curriculum subjects of English, Mathematics and Science and the comparison subject of History, to compare their responses across a range of different school subjects. The questionnaire was administered to 912 pupils aged 8–14 from school years 4, 6, 7 and 9 at four comprehensive schools (all of average size and average achievement rating) in the north-east and south-east of England between March and May 2004. For each subject children were asked to: (i) rate the significance of being good at the subject; (ii) rate their own ability compared to their peers; and (iii) describe the basis of success at the subject. I shall focus on the last of these here. For all five subjects, children were asked 'What do you think makes someone good at [the subject]?'; four possible responses were provided, of which one only could be chosen:

[A]   Anyone can do it, nothing special is needed
[B]   You need to learn special skills or knowledge
[C]   You need to have 'natural ability' or a 'feel' for it
[D]   Only people with 'natural ability' can learn the special skills needed

It was designed for the responses to indicate a relativist code, knowledge code, knower code and élite code, respectively.

I shall briefly highlight two results from a preliminary descriptive analysis of the resulting data. First, taking the sample as a whole, the reasons for success in Science and the humanities were viewed differently by pupils: in Maths and Science (and Music) the modal response was that success required knowledge or skill, while the modal responses for English and History were that 'anyone can do it'. (Further work is required to explore this characterization.)[9] Second, among pupils who had already chosen their GCSE subjects in Year 9 (age 14), Music stood out from the other subjects in terms of the élite code response. Success in Music was far more likely to be viewed as attainable only by those with both natural ability and special skills than was the case for any other subject: 19 per cent chose this option for Music compared to a maximum of 3.6 per cent for the other four subjects (see Figure 3.2). This figure almost doubled to 35 per cent among those pupils who had chosen to study Music at GCSE. The difference is quite striking: GCSE Music was far more often characterized as exhibiting an élite code by pupils, especially those who had chosen to take the qualification, than other subject areas.

I have reported here only part of the early results of this study, and further research is required both to deepen this pilot work and to broaden its focus. For example, we have reservations about the wording of the questionnaire and research is required, particularly focus group work, to better capture possible

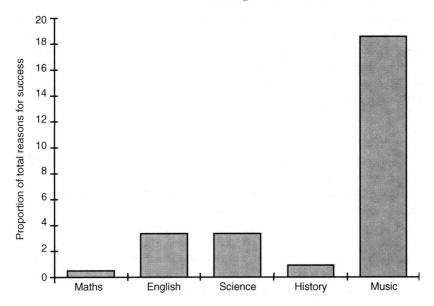

Figure 3.2 Proportion of Year 9 responses choosing 'élite code' as basis for success

options. Further analysis of the results may also reveal changes in the coding of Music in pupils' perceptions for different Key Stages that can be compared to those found in the National Curriculum documents. Both studies also form part of a bigger picture. For example, one hypothesis from the study of curriculum documents is that the élite code of GCSE Music may reflect a dominant view of professional music among actors in higher levels of education, such as universities and conservatoires; distinguishing between professional, élite performers combines exacting standards of both technical proficiency and sensibility and this may shape the nature of qualifications in Music at lower levels of the educational system. The genesis of the élite code within the official and pedagogic recontextualizing fields generating the National Curriculum and how the code is refracted within teaching and learning in schools and classrooms are thus areas for future research. However, the point for this paper is less the specificities of the substantive focus here and more the way it suggests that analysing both knowledge structures and knower structures together in terms of legitimation codes offers fruitful ways forward for empirical research. It reveals not only contexts exhibiting stronger or weaker classification and framing but also those with both; such contexts may appear contradictory or confusing if one considers educational knowledge structures on their own. Elite schools, for example, may operate with selection criteria based not only on qualifications but also issues of character and dispositions, or with what appear to be both performance and competence models of pedagogy. Integrating knower structures into the analysis may show such contexts exhibit an élite legitimation code. By being firmly anchored on the concepts of classification and framing, the strong external language of description of legitimation code theory also enables analysis of the underlying principles structuring curriculum guidelines, teaching practice, pupils' perceptions, school structures and so forth in a manner enabling systematic comparisons within and between these contexts, something lacking from existing research on Music in the curriculum.

Conclusion

In this paper I have highlighted a second dimension to the analysis of intellectual and educational fields. Bernstein conceptualizes knowledge structures in fields of intellectual production and educational knowledge structures in fields of educational reproduction. I have suggested we can also analyse these fields in terms of the knower structures encoded into their discourses and practices. For every knowledge structure there is also a knower structure. This dimension lay tacitly present as a potential of the theory but is here brought into the open. This by itself can reveal interesting issues; for example, it leads us to recast the question of hierarchies in intellectual fields from 'whether' to 'where' – horizontal knowledge structures may be characterized by hierarchical knower structures. It also offers further insights into the underlying principles of knowledge formations. In the example of the 'two cultures' debate, analysing both its knowledge structure and knower structure shows how humanist culture was, according to its protagonists, being threatened by both new knowers and by the ascendant knowledge code of science. Integrating the analysis of knower structures with that of knowledge structures within the concept of legitimation code not only enables their different insights to be brought together but also enables us to generatively conceptualize new possibilities, such as relativist and élite codes. This conceptualization expands the range of phenomena encompassed within the theory not by displacing or adding to the insights of educational knowledge codes and knowledge structures but by *integrating* them (see Moore and Muller 2002). That the ideas can be extended to analyse fields of recontextualization and reproduction was illustrated by briefly discussing an ongoing research project into Music in the school curriculum. Preliminary results from this study suggest that the very low uptake of Music at GCSE level may be related to its élite code of legitimation. In summary, both the examples illustrate that the ways in which actors and discourses are specialized help shape the development, position and standing of knowledge formations and the opportunities available and constraints presented to actors within these fields – as Bernstein argues, such 'relations within' have their own structuring significance, with real effects for the position and status of subjects in the curriculum, career opportunities for teachers and academics, and numerous other pressing, everyday realities. Looking at how actors and discourses are specialized by both knowledge structures and knower structures thereby not only offers interesting possibilities for research but also highlights issues of crucial significance for understanding and changing those intellectual fields and educational contexts which form our material and intellectual conditions of existence.

Notes

1 See Maton (2000, 2004) for analyses in terms of legitimation codes of changes in the disciplinary and institutional maps of higher education; Moore and Maton (2001) on the epistemic device; and Doherty (2004), Lamont (2004) and Wheelahan (2005) for examples of educational studies using legitimation codes.

2 The following draws on a more extensive study of the 'two cultures' debate which forms part of a wider analysis of the conditions of the emergence of British cultural studies in post-war higher education (Maton 2005). My coverage will be necessarily brief here as the principal focus is elucidating the notion of 'knower structures'; I shall analyse the debate more fully in a future publication.

3 The following is how science and the humanities were *portrayed* by numerous contemporary contributors to the 'two cultures' debate – a self-portrait of the disciplinary map by its participants – rather than an anthropological description of their enacted practices.

4 Integration of new knowers may be through resocialization (such as was attempted by the creation of new campus universities as resocializing institutions in 1960s English higher education; Maton 2004) or through a mixture of indoctrination and coercion (such as that underlying the Great Chain of Being of monarchical and papal hierarchies; Maton 2002). Educational expansion has typically accommodated new knowers through a combination of resocialization as the condition of entry into higher-status institutional and disciplinary positions or relegation into lower levels of these status hierarchies (cf. Hickox and Moore 1995).

5 I am broadening the original definitions of the concepts (Maton 2000) which reflected their basis in highlighting a specific issue: the significance of epistemological considerations in knowledge production. Moore and Maton (2001) argued and Maton (2004) showed that the epistemic device is also active in fields of recontextualization and reproduction. In other words, all discursive practices can be analysed in terms of a distinction between their epistemic and social relations.

6 Examples of these three include the focus in music educational research on notions of 'genius' and 'natural ability', emphasis in literary and art criticism on the cultivated sensibility of the reader or viewer through immersion in great works of culture, and standpoint epistemologies which base claims to privileged insight on membership of a specific social group. The definition of the form taken by 'dispositions' depends on the model of the knower; this analysis, however, reveals that despite surface differences, avowedly antagonistic positions, such as Leavisite and feminist literary criticism, share underlying structuring principles: a knower code.

7 GCSE is a public qualification taken through a combination of coursework and examination between age 14 and age 16. It is the first stage in the school system in England and Wales at which subjects can be chosen.

8 This research is being jointly conducted with Alexandra Lamont, a music psychologist at Keele University (see Lamont 2004 and QCA 2004). We shall report the results of this ongoing research more fully in future publications; my focus here is primarily on illustrating the conceptual development outlined in the current paper.

9 The results for English and History may reflect our wording of the options, particularly this first attempt to capture a dispositional emphasis. (Or it may be that humanist intellectuals in the 'two cultures' debate were correct and the humanities are indeed seen as nothing special.)

4 Climbing the ladder of knowledge
Plato and Bernstein

Wayne Hugo

> Wherever there is pedagogy there is hierarchy ... the language of description should attempt to sharpen its possibility of appearance.
>
> (Bernstein, 2001a, p. 375)

Let us begin in a place where student and teacher meet, a place that holds in a disciplined middle-ground bacchanalian excess and Apollonian principle – a Symposium where friends and lovers gather to deliver edifying speeches, eat good food, drink some wine and have a good time. It is in this setting that Plato contrives to provide an account of hierarchy within pedagogy through the speech of Socrates and from this primal scene where we will be able to build up a picture of how the work of Bernstein relates. Friend after friend stands to deliver a speech on love until we get to the ugly magnificence of Socrates. He points to the medium of love as that which enables a travelling up the ladder of beauty from its most concrete and physical manifestation to its purest and most abstract form. Love is precisely the power to straddle the various levels of ascent in an integrating spiral. Socrates points to Eros as a desire that has a notion of height and a smack of depth but strives in that liminal space between full knowing and ignorance. It occupies middle ground, a ground that has been tasted but not reached. It is the great facilitator between the sacred and the profane. In this intermediate world Eros is *both* and *neither.* It is a great spirit, a *daemon*, able to allow communication in the opening between the heights and the depths that otherwise would not touch each other (*Symp.* 202d – 204b). It is this force that Socrates uses to climb from the individual, concrete and temporal to the universal, abstract and timeless. For Plato, structured guidance up and down this ladder of beauty is what pedagogy is in its essence.

Socrates' account of how to educate towards this repeats what he heard at the feet of his own teacher, the high priestess Diotima. It begins with the love of a single body and quickly expands outwards to all bodies before suffering exhaustion and boredom in excess. The more subtle and interior qualities of mind then become increasingly attractive and this expands outwards to a fascination with the socio/cultural institutions and frameworks that encourage and produce good minds as well as the knowledge fashioned from this unity.

Now he has beauty before his eyes in abundance, no longer a single instance of it; now the slavish love of isolated cases of youthful beauty or human beauty of any kind is a thing of the past, as is his love of some single activity. No longer a paltry and small-minded slave, he faces instead the vast sea of beauty, and in gazing upon it his boundless love of knowledge becomes the medium in which he gives birth to plenty of beautiful, expansive reasoning and thinking.

(*Symp.* 210a–d)

A hierarchy emerges that includes a previous stage and then transcends it, a hierarchy that expands to gracefully include more and more within its ambit, slowly imparting beauty to everything that crosses its inclusive spiral upwards.[1] The ladder increases in both depth and breadth as it expands upwards and inwards. The individual beauty of a single lover is not forgotten, only properly placed in a mind and cultural milieu that is also beautiful. To focus in on individual beauty in a mortal world is to enter suffering, not only because the magnificence of the rest of existence pales, but because that particular manifestation of beauty is destined to wither. Diotima points away from this immersion in particularity towards a structured hierarchy that works from physical individuality to abstract knowledge. It is the taking of a more interior and intensional view. Hold onto the individual expression of beauty, but see its charm in relation to the radiance that flows all around it and scaffold a path from the one to the other – such is the teaching of Diotima.

A further consequence of the ladder is that the *autonomy* of the lover increases with ascent while degrees of *commitment* expand. As higher levels are reached, the lover is able to work in ways that increasingly release from previous bonds. Seeing that many are beautiful releases the lover from exclusive dependence on one body. Seeing that minds, institutions and principles are beautiful releases the lover from dependence on bodies. Each release brings with it an expanding area of commitment, until, with the final vision of the Beautiful, the lover is freed from all particular bonds yet committed to all, as we will see again with the cave metaphor. For now, let us return to the heights of beauty.

What he'll see is, in the first place, eternal; it doesn't come to be or cease to be, and it doesn't increase or diminish. In the second place, it isn't attractive in one respect and repulsive in another, or attractive at one time but not at another ... depending on how people find it. Then again, he won't perceive beauty as a face or hands or any other physical feature, or as a piece of reasoning or knowledge, and he won't perceive it as being elsewhere either – in something like a creature or the earth or the heavens. No, he'll perceive it in itself and by itself, constant and eternal, and he'll see that every other beautiful object somehow partakes of it, but in such a way that their coming to be and ceasing to be don't increase or diminish it at all, and it remains entirely unaffected.

(*Symp.* 210e–211b)

The art of pedagogy is to take the student on a path that expands the love of beauty until it touches pure form. It is a hierarchical path that reveals beauty in its most abstract clarity at its highest point and this imparts meaning to everything else below it.

This is the shimmering vision of Diotima that the older Socrates remembered hearing when sitting at her feet as a young man. She revealed to him the nature of pedagogy – the art of understanding the necessary stages to go through on a path that facilitates seeing the Still Main of Beauty. It is a course that Socrates in his younger years had not fully worked through. As her pupil then, he was still caught up in the earlier stages, as Diotima had wisely pointed out to him (*Symp.* 211d). The young Socrates still got overly excited by the sight of an attractive boy, was immersed in the particular and the sexual, the concrete and the physical, and had not yet glimpsed beauty itself, immaculate and pure. It is with these qualifications in mind that we meet Alcibiades, the most beautiful, controversial and desirable of Socrates' students, and it is in this pedagogic relationship that we see the art of pedagogy working with the nature of hierarchy.

Alcibiades arrives at the Symposium already wasted and pandemonium erupts. He is encouraged to also give a speech on love but insists that the only person he will deliver a eulogy on is Socrates. He is so drunk that what comes out is the most honest, affecting, searing and heartfelt description of what Socrates meant to him as a teacher and who Socrates is as a person. Yet it is also a test case for everything Socrates has said about the nature of pedagogy and love. At the feet of Diotima he craved the beauty of young boys, and now here, in full flesh and sexual splendour is the most gorgeous of Athenian men. What effect has the teaching of Diotima had on her student Socrates; will he be able to transcend the Dionysian beauty of Alcibiades? This is the dramatic impetus that drives the second half of the *Symposium.*

To understand the nature of Socrates, Alcibiades maintains, one must open him up and look inside and there you will find an image of the gods. He is able to reveal this divinity through mere words, words that are so powerful that even when repeated in differing contexts they still have the power to spellbind listeners (*Symp.* 215d). Alcibiades, when hearing the words of Socrates, found himself wrapped in ecstasy while at the same time feeling deep within the inadequacy of how he was conducting his life. Yet Alcibiades was not a compliant victim to the context-liberating words of Socrates; he was a robust and stubborn student, refusing to give up a life of ambition, fame and indulgence for eternal beauty. He might have liked the idea of pure form and felt its force, but he preferred to wander around in the quicker pleasures of sex and power with the refrain 'not yet, not yet' easing his way. Such a student would be a worthwhile type for a wise man to educate in exchange for bodily favours. Alcibiades suffered under no illusions and was happy to effect just such a deal with Socrates – body for mind. To this end he undertook the seduction of Socrates, a task that should not have been too difficult, given Socrates' proclivity for handsome young boys and the good looks of

Alcibiades. He contrived to get Socrates alone in his house and gymnasium so that a space could be created for the bold declarations of lovers. Yet Socrates' actions in private were no different from those in public. A determined seducer, Alcibiades finally decided on a direct assault, invited him to dinner and got him to stay the night (*Symp.* 217c–e). Socrates greeted his seducer's advances with the following epigram: '[I]t's only when your eyesight goes into decline that your mental vision begins to see clearly...' (*Symp.* 219a).

It is obvious that Socrates had learnt well from Diotima – the physical beauty of Alcibiades could not stand ground with pure beauty. As the circle of beauty widens from the individual to the ocean of beauty that is existence, true beauty is seen within, in a glimpse that does not look to any outward manifestation, but in a moment of total concentration catches something abstracted from all physicality, shining within one's own mind in an unchanging way. Alcibiades still had his mind fixed on externals and had not turned his mind around into itself, and thus had not begun to walk the inward and abstract path upwards. By brutally demonstrating to his student the paleness of the exterior beauty he held so dear, Socrates attempted to break the hold that physicality had on Alcibiades. Socrates wanted to turn Alcibiades around, stop him pouring his energy into the seething world of time and change, and channel that energy hierarchically upwards into the still point that offers a glimpse of immortality and widens beauty outwards from an individual point towards all of existence.

If the *Symposium* offers us a first take on the hierarchical complexity of the pedagogical task facing the teacher using the modality of love, it is the *Republic* that develops a similar but different pedagogic hierarchy using the modality of intellect. Just as at the heart of the *Symposium* lies the diamond of Diotima's wisdom, so does the *Republic* open out to reveal at its centre an image of pedagogic hierarchy in the cave metaphor (*Rep.* 514a–517a). Two different vertical paths, one for the heart, the other for the mind.

For the learner to begin a hierarchical journey towards increasing abstraction we need to know the initial conditions. Plato describes this as being tied down by chains and forced to look in one direction only, towards the dark end of a cave where shadows play on the wall, cast from a fire behind. All the captives have ever experienced is the dance of shadows, so naturally it is their reality. There is no questioning of what is going on behind them to cause such a display, for it has never been seen. We are in this state in our everyday consciousness; it is our normal taken-for-granted existence at its most elementary level that Plato is capturing. We are bound tight and then driven by a single context and the manifestations it displays. We chase after its representations, pouring ourselves into them, investing what we are in it, naming it, interpreting it, valuing it, twisting it and criticizing it to suit our desires.

The key point is that there is no recognition of being a prisoner in this state. It is experienced as freedom and, indeed, the captives are free to make what they will of the display in front of them, free to shift the discourses horizontally depending on what their current state demands. It is a freedom held in chains by the inability to work on another level apart from the located one in front of them. It is a freedom that allows for any and all attempts so long as they segment and saturate themselves against the same flat wall.[2] This allows for a sense of *complexification* but not of *complexity* and order. Complexity needs one level ordering or emerging from another; complexification is all about various activities happening on the same level without an ordering device. Put paradoxically, complexity involves simplification. The prisoner suddenly recognizes that all the various shadows have higher ordering devices that simplify the various shadows into stabilizing categories that are hierarchically organized.

Only with the ability to work on another level that places and organizes the first does a pedagogic relationship appear. The only way to understand the nature of shadow is to understand the form that causes it; otherwise all one is doing is playing with more shadow. As Muller reminds us in Chapter 1 of this book, it is the first step in standing on the shoulders of giants. What the learner must do is turn around and look into what is causing the display. It is a wheeling around of the whole person from being focused on the instability and momentariness of existence towards a more stable force that lies behind the production. As the learner turns from the outside world of display to the inner and more abstract world producing it, a journey out of the cave begins that echoes the *Symposium*'s ladder of beauty and its shift from the physical to the abstract.

The first thing seen by a prisoner who is set free from dependence on horizontal shadows is a higher ordering device that regulates its lower field. What regulates this higher field is still not clear; this will only become comprehensible as the learner moves vertically up the ladder and it is this logic that is repeated continuously in the cave metaphor. Clearly the 'more real' object is itself a copy of something 'more real' outside the cave but the cave dweller does not know this yet – he is still struggling to make out what this new world and its objects are. Even the firelight is dazzling and obscures his attempt to see the models responsible for the shadows. Yet slowly this new reality stabilizes, and with training and discipline the shadow lover is able to identify the new objects seen although he does not yet know that these new objects are things made in imitation of the world outside the cave. A Hierarchy of Being slowly emerges and it is a deeper and more complex world that the cave dweller now moves within.

The world beyond the cave is not a physical world that can be touched, tasted and smelt. It is an abstract, immaterial world, but for Plato it is the most real of worlds, a world that contains truth, beauty, goodness as its very Being, an eternal world beyond this world of becoming. The pressing pedagogical question that arises is how to introduce the learner to its vertical delights, of how to take the cave dweller to the mouth of the cave so he can emerge into the sea of beauty out there in the 'real' world of Being. It is a question of how to shift a student's interest from the visible towards the intelligible, from physical objects and their models to an increasing hierarchy of abstract forms. It is an education of hierarchical abstraction that Plato is *enacting* for us in words. This journey is a difficult task, for students still desire the satisfactions offered by the cave with its models and shadows, as we saw with Alcibiades. Besides this, looking into the higher reality that opens out at the cave mouth is a blinding activity, especially when it is only the physical world of becoming that a learner is used to contemplating. The student would still feel that this new world outside the cave is actually the imitation of the 'real' world of the cave. He has only a shaky grasp of its movements and forms, and this unfamiliarity makes this new world appear ghostly and vague in comparison to his own locale. Much practice would be needed before the student was capable of contemplating the forms in themselves; initially the cave will continually pull the student back with its attractions. Slowly, with diligence and discipline, abstract ideals and principles will begin to emerge as worthy of emulation and honour.

A hierarchical process takes place, with the student continually searching for a deeper reality that underlies the object contemplated, continually questioning assumptions and abstracting until the deepest reality is attained. An integral vision will begin to unfold that holds gradients of reality in perspective until the student is finally able to turn his eyes heavenwards and contemplate the generating source of light that illuminates everything – the Good – that which sits at the heart of existence in the purest, most abstract state. Once this utmost level of abstract contemplation has been reached the student will, for the first time, understand the full nature of existence in all of its complex depth and height and understand how it fits together. He will have come to an understanding of the Good, the Beautiful, and the True as well as the murkiness of the cave. The levels of existence will hold together in a graded ladder that includes and places all in a hierarchy that ranges from darkness to light, concrete to abstract, image to reality, becoming to Being.

Only once pedagogy has taken the student from the depths to the heights can the true nature of this world of becoming be seen. He would rather be a serf in this glorious sphere than king of the shadows. In this newly illuminated world he will see grades of abstraction, running from the purest of forms to its various dependent realizations contained within. Yet an obligation awaits all who have ascended to the heights: it is the call to return to their fellows still chained below and assist them on the journey upwards. It is the call to teach, a call to return from the monad to plenitude, from principle to application, from contemplation to praxis. It is the call to *recontextualize*. First, the teacher mostly has no desire to return to the cave, preferring a world that is close to the production of things rather than having to enter the world of reproduction once again. Second, his fellows have no desire to leave their located context. It will sound like a madman's talk to them. Third, as the teacher enters the cave of becoming again, he will be blinded anew, unable to see even the shadows so easily worked with before. He will seem idiotic to the shadow lovers, even more stupid than before he left their company, or be seduced by the shadows again, recalled by the attractions of the flesh. The cave is a beautiful place – it is only in a widening and deepening reality that it becomes shallow, its diversity segmented and exhausted on the cave wall.

The task of education is to devise the simplest and most effective manner of turning the mind away from its fascination with the world of becoming and make it capable of bearing the sight of real Abstraction. Education becomes the art of correct alignment, of proper orientation, of turning the mind around (*Rep.* 518d–e). It enables the darkling to increase depth by one, to gain control of desire and wander around in a useful way throughout the world of becoming. The question remains as to what kind of education would enable a leaving of the cave and an entering of the Light, of how to close the route of everyday common sense and open up the road to the Invisible.

Plato's famous recommendation is an education in abstraction, a shifting of focus from the visible to the intelligible, from becoming to Being. It awakens reason and provides tools for its strengthening until eventually the soul can make a leap towards a level of reality beyond Mathematics – Goodness. In working with numbers it deals with a phenomenon not encountered in the physical world, for there is nothing in the world that has every single unit exactly equal without any remainder (*Rep.* 526a). It thus forces the mind to rely on intellectual rather than physical processes. The lifting of the learner into the heights entails a separation from the physical world so that a contemplation of essence can occur.

Once this is achieved, a sea of knowledge opens out to the learner. If he manages to work in a totally abstracted world, everything unwraps itself. An affinity between all subjects is revealed, uncluttering the student's mind and enabling him to see the relation of everything to all. The vertical ascent leads to an integral vision developing that is able to take in local and generic levels of reality as well as having a tool to work across these levels. Yet all of this is only a prelude for the final great leap of learning; it is all only preparation for the best part of the mind to reach out for the best part of reality (*Rep.* 532c). This is the great discipline of Dialectic whereby 'without relying on anything perceptible, a person perseveres in using rational argument to approach the true reality of things until he has grasped with his Intellect the reality of goodness itself' (*Rep.* 532a–b). It is a process of actively questioning assumptions until a point is reached beyond abstraction. Even Mathematics, the technique that turns the mind from the physical to the abstract, has to work with definitions and assumptions that it does not question. The nature of a point, of a number, or of a line is defined, but how they came about is left unanswered.

> There is no chance of their having a conscious glimpse of reality as long as they refuse to disturb the things they take for granted and remain incapable of explaining them. For if your starting-point is unknown, and your end-point and intermediate stages are woven together out of unknown material, there may be coherence, but knowledge is completely out of the question.
>
> (*Rep.* 533c)

Mathematics can only dream about true reality; it is Dialectic that enables the final lifting upwards into the Good. In a radical doubting of all assumptions, in a searching for the context behind the context, in a quest to find the mother of all abstractions, a sudden flash of insight comes with pure mental clarity. A limit point of the thinkable is reached, and as the mind attempts to work at this end-point it is abruptly pitched into a world beyond assumptions, a first world, a world that makes assumptions possible. The ladder is thrown. It is a peculiar process; on the one hand thought expands outwards, including more and more within its grasp. At the same time it radically simplifies and abstracts as more and more contexts are held within generating principles. Its end result is more than a founding assumption; it is what makes founding an assumption possible and enables an analysis of the founding principles of knowledge structures.

It is an arduous curriculum that entails a good basic education and a thorough grounding in the mathematical sciences, beginning the shift from the tangible to the conceptual. Dialectic is then actively practised to eliminate all assumptions and direct the student to the First Principle that informs all. Only then is a student ready to begin the descent back into the cave as a teacher of others and there he must work until he is able to teach in the cave in an adroit and illuminating way. At this stage the teacher is equally comfortable in the world of becoming and Being, skilled in polymorphically working on the interface between the two, unblinded by the continual shifts of perspective needed. Now the ascetic path upwards and the creative pouring downwards hold equally for the adept. Only then can they be guided to the climax of their lives.

> You must make them open up the beam of their minds and look at the all-embracing source of light, which is goodness itself. Once they have seen it, they must use it as a reference-point and spend the rest of their lives ordering the community, its members, and themselves.
>
> (*Rep.* 540a–b)

How does the Bernsteinian corpus square up to this archetypal vision of hierarchy and pedagogy? Here I can afford to be fairly brief as extended discussions of Bernstein's work on hierarchy can be found in the contributions of Moore and Muller in this volume. The easiest place to begin is with Bernstein's description of the sacred and the profane and the space that opens between them. Within any society there is a distinction between sacred, esoteric, unthinkable otherness of knowledge and profane, mundane, thinkable knowledge of the other (Bernstein, 1996, p. 43). It is a splitting up of the world into immaterial transcendence and everyday mundane materiality. What interests Bernstein is the force that relates these two to each other, a force that Plato described as Eros in his ladder of beauty. This force must break through meanings that are directly tied to a material base, that are wholly consumed by and embedded within context without hope of uniting with anything but themselves, much like the state Plato described his prisoners being in within the cave (ibid. p. 44). For Bernstein it is the pedagogic device that plays the specific role of breaking this grip of materiality and uniting context-bound meaning with other contexts and abstracting concepts. To enable this release there must be a prising open of the context in such a way that the direct relationship becomes indirect by introducing a higher level of abstraction that depends on the context but works differently to it, shifting meaning by degrees from the material and concrete to the immaterial and transcendent. This is what pedagogic *enhancement* is – experiencing boundaries in a way that breaks their chains through the *discipline* of hierarchy, for it is through hierarchy that one is able to step onto the other side of the boundary, able to walk up and down the ladder into new worlds of possibility and probability (ibid. p. 6). As this gap opens it creates the space for change, for it has released possibility from necessity and this is where we see the first crucial difference between Plato and Bernstein. Both understood the nature of this gap between the sacred and the profane but Plato wished to regulate this gap with specific political, economic, social, educational and personal practices that ensured a specific distribution of power. Hence his tying of the personal model of the shift from the shadows to the light with the *Republic* and its philosopher kings. Bernstein, on the other hand, wished to think through the way *power and control relations distribute the sacred and the profane* (ibid. pp. 18, 45). It provided Bernstein with a certain kind of critical edge that is different from Plato. He is able to describe not only the nature of the divide between the sacred and the profane and how to bridge the two, but also the variations/possibilities opened up in this gap and the power and control relations that attempt to regulate its functioning. Plato's ladder attempted to set up a pure Euclidean space in which philosopher kings ruled within a mythology of gold; Bernstein's ladder recognized a topology twisted in space and time by the gravity of power and the reproduction of inequality.[3]

This does not mean that there was no movement in the Platonic hierarchy or a questioning of its functioning; we only have to turn to his *Parmenides* for an internal critique. We did see two essential movements in the cave metaphor and the ladder of beauty: a movement upwards from the profane to the sacred and then a movement downwards from the light back into the shadows. The task of the sun gazer is to return into the cave and recontextualize what he has experienced for those still bound in a specific, limiting context. It is a descent down the hierarchy and this is also how Bernstein describes the pedagogic device, beginning with how it *distributes* the sacred forms of knowledge, then how it *recontextualizes* it downwards into the shadows as thinkable knowledge, and finally how within the profane this recontextualization is received and *evaluated,* of how it impinges on the consciousness of the prisoner. It is the hierarchical shift downwards from creation to transmission to acquisition, from inspired production to reflective simplification to reproductive acquirement. It is a movement from abstract design to repetitive copy.[4] The prophet seer on the top of the mount is recon*text*ualized by the priest who makes what he saw understandable to the laity in the foothills still worshipping concrete images. One founding type produces type/token trees below it that increasingly make explicit and specific what was contained in its abstract glory. But it is also the story of return from the many to the one, of what the reproductive acquirers make of this downward flow of light into the cave and here again the similarities between Bernstein and Plato become apparent. Bernstein continually points to how this device is not deterministic in both its flow downwards and clambering upwards, in both efflux and return. There is always space for this device to work differently, for in making the sacred accessible to those who it wishes to acquire it, paths are created that others can follow and exploit. The sacred vow unlocks to profane articulation (Bernstein, 1996, p. 52). But it also finds in its successful charting of a path between the sacred and the profane that others begin to challenge for its ownership, redefinition and use (1996, pp. 64–81). In Bernstein's explicit pointing to how power and control relationships can be understood in terms of classification and framing relationships he encompassed not only a similar height and depth of vision to Plato but enabled a clearer placing of its majesty within the power and control relationships it was always already a part of.

Yet this placing of hierarchy within the fields of power and control should not make us ignore the nature of hierarchy in its own right and its intimate relationship to pedagogy. There is a deep educational logic to hierarchy that works its specific claim and the easy mistake is to critique hierarchy wherever it is found as if hierarchy itself is responsible for inequality and not a device that can both address and cause inequality in education, depending on its use. With both Plato and Bernstein we saw a use of hierarchy to liberate, not enchain, and it is incumbent on us to point explicitly to how this is the case.

The first point already made is that any 'pedagogy' that works without any hierarchy results in complexification, not complexity. Each unit works on its own and is exhausted within itself as its own type. It does not relate to any other unit for to do so would assume some higher abstraction that related the two to each other. It is a wasteland pedagogy of immense variation and multiplicity without an ordering or emergent device to hold the diversity together. It is a horizontal plane where each feature holds separate and pure, a deflationist account where each unit holds in its own right and has nothing to do with the truth of the other. There is an illusion of growth in the diversity but these form a horizontal chain that binds the learner to whatever the specific context is, without providing the tools to move beyond. Those who already have such an ordering tool can begin to build from the elements and climb the ladder; those who don't can only rearrange the types into different patterns on the same cave wall.[5]

As soon as there is another level then hierarchy appears and the pedagogic relationship takes on one of three possibilities. First, it can explore how a new level *emerges* from the elements below, how the many become one and are increased by one, how types become tokens for a new type. This is a pedagogy that works with hierarchy from the bottom up. Second, it can reveal how the higher level (type) *constrains* or provides boundary conditions on the elements (tokens) below, how the one makes of the many below it a specific order necessary for itself to appear. Either pedagogy works from the fundamental to the significant or from the significant to the fundamental. The third pedagogic option is to work *horizontally* within this hierarchy, building up fundamental components so that possibilities can be created for significance or creative play. This allows for the possibility of pedagogy working with three levels: an upper level that constrains the middle level with its boundary conditions and a lower level that enables the middle level to emerge from its components. At this level of working with a pedagogic hierarchy a unit would hold within itself both its own conditions of *possibility* from below and its higher levels of *probability*. It would not only have been built up from elements below but also have been formed by constraints above it that are pulling it towards itself as an attractor.

These are the simplest components of a model of hierarchy and pedagogy placed together and both Plato and Bernstein work its logic for the enhancement of educability. Both also work with two types of hierarchy, one that goes from smallest to biggest and another that goes from concrete to abstract. Within hierarchy theory[6] there are two basic kinds of hierarchy: extensional and intensional. The first works with increasing levels of scale (from classroom to school to district to province to country), the second with increasing levels of complexity (from the concrete to the abstract) where there are greater levels of generalization, structuration and organization as one moves up the hierarchy. Plato works with both types in his two guiding images of pedagogic hierarchy. There is a shift from one body to many bodies (scalar/extensional) and then from bodies to mind (intensional/conceptual). Then there is the extension of minds working together in cultural institutions, before the intensification of knowledge produced into *formal* principles that finally lead to the great attractor of all – the Good. But the highest point of an intensional hierarchy is not the largest, indeed in Plato's case the Form has no extension at all for it is immaterial. It might have great extensional *implication* in that it contains within itself these fundamental constituents as its earlier levels, but its higher levels go beyond these more concrete units by having included what is necessary from them and then having introduced new and more abstract levels on its foundation.

We see a similar logic operating in Bernstein's pedagogic device. It is an intensional hierarchy in that its highest point is what is most sacred and abstract and then it recontextualizes downwards and outwards into increasingly more concrete and specific formulations that reach right down into the trenches of the classroom. But it can also appear as an extensional hierarchy with the national department providing the highest/largest level of organization that increasingly breaks itself down into smaller units until we again reach the classroom. Both kinds of hierarchy are needed to think through the device's implications for pedagogy. The danger is getting the two mixed up and maintaining that the biggest has to be the most abstract, or the abstract has to be the largest. Anyone who has worked with national departments will recognize the absurdity and danger of this link being absolute. Bernstein's strength was that he was not only able to think through the implications of both hierarchies separately and together within the educational field but was also able to provide a language of how these all held together. This enabled an analysis that can function on different levels, but with those levels still able to work with each other. His language enables a translation device that works across both macro/micro and intensional/extensional hierarchies as well as their cross-fertilizations.

As Bernstein reached the end of his highly productive life he pointed to precisely that sacred end point of Plato's ladder, the terrain beyond Dialectic where assumptions and principles of knowledge are generated. He wished to find out from this place of great height and abstraction not who its first mover was but how there are 'changes in knowledge forms and displacement of and replacement by new forms, creating a new field of knowledge positions, sponsors, designers and transmitters' (2001b, p. 368). It is from this great height that Bernstein peered down with intelligent love into the classroom in the hope of making the climb upwards recognizable and realizable. We have already seen Plato describe what should happen to someone privileged enough to reach this point. After contemplating the nature of the Good they should

> use it as a reference-point and spend the rest of their lives ordering the community, its members, and themselves.
>
> (*Rep.* 540a–b)

What Bernstein used as his reference point was not the nature of the Good itself, but how the Good has been structured within poverty and plenty. The pedagogic love that is born from this union is the need to structure a path towards *justice* that works with broken ladders. However, it is not only broken ladders that Bernstein worked with but the grammars of different ladders (Bernstein, 1999) and the various recontextualizing effects this has as the pedagogic device shatters downwards. Perhaps now we can see why Plato not only wrote of a ladder of beauty that worked with the verticality of love but also of a cave of shadows that worked with the differing verticality of intellect. Yet Plato did not only provide us with differing paths through that complex middle ground of the profanely sacred, he *performed* the journey for us through his writing. His writing is precisely the principles of hierarchical pedagogy enacted before us in such a way that it still takes us on the journey in all its warm, phenomenological richness and complexity. It is this performance that makes of us all bloody footnotes.

Notes

1 Hierarchy comes from two Greek words: *hieros* meaning sacred; *archein* meaning rules/order.
2 See Bernstein, 1996, pp.170–171 for a comparative account in terms of horizontal and vertical discourses, well elaborated on by Moore and Muller (2002) and their respective contributions to this volume.
3 This is a broad generalization, as so much of this paper is. Plato does think through the implications of power and justice being intimately connected through the articulations of Thrasymachus (*Rep.* 338c), a position he gives full attention to in his *Gorgias*.
4 We see a similar logic in Bernstein's distinction between internal and external languages of description, where the first works in the light and the second asks how these concepts can be made more material for the cave. Morais and Neves (2001), Ensor and Hoadley (2004) provide useful guidance in how to work from the light into the shadows.
5 See Holland (1981) for experimental confirmation of this vision in terms of elaborated and restricted codes, where middle-class learners are free to move through conceptual and contextual hierarchies and working-class learners are condemned to repeat the same everyday patterns again and again.
6 Koestler (1967); Ahl and Allen (1996); Wilber (1995). Set theory and computer programming, especially object-oriented programming with its concepts of inheritance, polymorphic resonance, yo-yo effects, etc. provide rich resources to elaborate on this field. In education the classics can be found in Bloom (1964) and Gagné (1985) although its presence is seen throughout the instructional design field.

Part II

Knowledge, identity and voice

5   Power, pedagogic voices and pupil talk

The implications for pupil consultation as transformative practice

Madeleine Arnot and Diane Reay

> ... normalising processes produce norms and their agencies, which are rarely free of the contradictions, cleavages, and dilemmas they are set up to control. Socialisation into norms from this point of view, is then always socialisation both into another's voice and into one's own 'yet to be voiced'.
>
> (Bernstein 1990: 159)

This chapter focuses on the nature of pupil voice which expresses socialization into what Bernstein called 'another's voice'. Our interest in this aspect of Bernstein's sociology of pedagogy results from our recent research on what pupils have to say about the social conditions of learning. In the context of the growing interest in pupil consultation as a means of ensuring more effective knowledge acquisition, we believe much can be learned from a consideration of what constitutes pupil voice and what significance it could have in mediating such knowledge acquisition. The concept of pupil voice, whilst associated with democratic agendas of social inclusion and participation, is nevertheless deeply problematic, since from a Bernsteinian perspective it is itself produced by the very power relations which it is meant to help transform. In this chapter, we consider the nature of Bernstein's claim and reflect on the issues which face those committed to pupil consultation in schools. Our purpose is to relocate pupil voice in the context of the pedagogic encounter and to understand its complexity, diversity and significance. In this paper we argue that Bernstein's conceptualization of 'voice' and the range of research associated with it which we wish to call a *sociology of pedagogic voices* is substantially different from 'voice sociology in education' that is associated with standpoint epistemologies and concepts of empowerment.

Our research project conducted in 2003–4 employed a range of qualitative methods that purposively elicited the voices of pupils from different social classes, different ethnic groups and both genders. We established focus groups with one class of Year 9 (13–14-year-old) students in two English secondary schools and with one class of pupils of Year 6 (10–11-year-old) pupils in two feeder primary schools. We also observed lower-achieving pupils in Maths and English classes and interviewed the smaller sample individually. Our contribution to a research programme on pupil consultation focused on what different groups of pupils could tell teachers about the rules which govern the pedagogic encounter and their access and participation in learning. In effect, we encouraged pupils to 'voice' their understanding of the social conditions of learning – the interface in Bernsteinian terms between the regulative and instructional discourses of schooling.

The design of our instruments operationalized Bernstein's (2000) concepts of democratic pedagogic rights. We identified key questions around the notion of learner identity (enhancement), pupils' perception of the processes of social inclusion in relation to learning and their experiences of participation (Reay and Arnot 2004; Arnot *et al.* 2004). Having collected the data, we found ourselves reflecting critically on both the voices we collected and what they represented within processes of pupil consultation. What exactly are we tapping when we ask pupils for their views about schooling? In this paper we stand back from the findings of this research to reconsider the nature of pupil voice and in particular its relationship to pedagogic and social identities.

There has recently been much debate concerning voice research in sociological studies of education (cf. Moore and Muller 1999; Young 2000). However a distinction has to be made between voice sociology in education and *a sociology of pedagogic voices.* Voice sociology refers to standpoint epistemologies and the concept of empowerment through the making visible and audible the voices of oppressed groups. Such sociology has been criticized by Moore and Muller and by Young for its relativism and its weak epistemology. In this chapter we wish to distinguish Bernstein's concept of 'voice' from such voice sociology and show how the concept of 'voice' (usually expressed in inverted commas) as an analytical category is particular to his theory of transmission and the relay of power relations through pedagogy. Power, as we shall see, works through pedagogy shaping the forms of voice realizations. Yet Bernstein's particular concept of 'voice', although central, has not been addressed in any depth. Below we address the following questions:

- What concept of voice is embedded in Bernstein's sociology of pedagogy?
- What are the implications of Bernstein's concept of voice for the use of perspectival pupil data?
- Under what conditions could the elicitation of collective or individual pupil voices provide insights in the processes of teaching and learning?
- Can the concept of pupil voice have transformative consequences if used in consultation processes?

We begin by identifying the development of Bernstein's concept of 'voice' before distinguishing between a number of 'voice' terrains. The first section focuses on how Bernstein's theorization of 'voice' moves us from the sociolinguistic into the framework of pedagogy, power and identity. The second section draws on the classroom research of Bernsteinian scholars and our own work to explore the relationship between 'voice' and pedagogic practice. The final section engages directly with the issue of pupil consultation and Bernstein's underdeveloped but nevertheless interesting notion of the 'yet to be voiced' as the conditions for social transformation.

Power, 'voice' and the pedagogic device

Although at times critical of quasi-ethnographic voice research within sociology of education, the concept of 'voice' was central to Bernstein's sociology of pedagogy. In 1990, he acknowledged that D. Silverman and B. Torode's 'impressive' book *The Material Word* (1980) had drawn his attention to the possibilities of the concept of 'voice', although he admitted to putting the concept to different use (Bernstein 1990: 62). Silverman and Torode employed the concept of 'voice' to analyse pupil talk in relation to restricted and elaborated codes. By 1981, however, Bernstein had started to employ the concept of 'voice' as pivotal in his understanding of the nature of the subject. 'Voice' for Bernstein, became:

> a semiotic category that introduces a symbolic dimension to the concept of subject. ... Through the development of the notion of voice, Bernstein questions the supposed unity of the subject with an independent and individual consciousness. For Bernstein, the conditions for experience are not experience itself but the limits that locate or position individual experiences in fields of meanings and practices. This theoretical formulation requires description of the ways power is inscribed in the subject and realized through voice ...
>
> (Diaz 2001: 85–86)

In his educational theory, the 'moral, cognitive and communicative principle of which voice is a central element, links the school to a "complex social structure" and even more importantly, distributes social privilege' (Tyler 1988: 151, quoted in Davies 1995: 144). Bernstein had observed that, within sociological studies of education, pedagogic discourse has often been understood only as 'a medium for other voices: class, gender, race' (Bernstein 1990: 165):

> The discourses of education are analyzed for their power to reproduce dominant/dominated relations external to the discourse but which penetrate the social relations, media of transmission, and evaluation of pedagogic discourse ... what is absent from pedagogic discourse is its own voice.
>
> (Ibid.)

However, if pedagogic discourse represented only a relay for patterns of discourse external to itself, arguably its form has no consequences for what is relayed. If this is the case, are pedagogies 'somehow bland, neutral as air?' (ibid. 169). As Bernstein pointed out, theories of cultural reproduction had essentially become theories of communication 'without a theory of communication'. The 'voice' of pedagogic discourse is a 'voice' that is never heard, only its realizations – that is, its messages, the voices of class, gender, race, region, nation and religion. An important task therefore was to construct a theory of pedagogic communication which focused on the 'inner structure of the pedagogic' (ibid. 171) – the 'intrinsic features constituting and distinguishing the specialized form of communication realized by the pedagogic discourse of education' (ibid. 190). It is here that 'voice' acquires its social meaning. He argues:

> The 'voice' is constituted by the pedagogic device. A more appropriate metaphor may be that the pedagogic discourse device is a grammar for producing specialized messages, realizations, a grammar which regulates what it processes: a grammar which orders and positions and yet contains the potential of its own transformation. Any sociology of education should have a theory of the pedagogic device. Indeed, such a theory could well provide its necessary foundation and provide the fundamental object of the discipline.
>
> (Bernstein 1990: 190)

The distinction between 'voice' and message – a distinction which Bernstein once described as rather perverse, but which became central to his theory (ibid. 22) allowed him to distinguish between modes of recognition and realization. Whilst 'voice' represented the mode of recognition, it had the power to constrain the message; message represented the realization, with the potential to transform 'voice':

> The voice of a social category (academic discourse, gender subject, occupational subject) is constructed by the degree of specialization of the discursive rules regulating and legitimizing the form of communication. In this sense, voice is a little similar to register. However, accredited knowledge of these discursive rules is one thing and their realization in a local context quite another. Thus knowledge of the rules does not necessarily permit knowledge of their contextual use. The contextual use is, from this point of view, the *message*. Voice sets limits to message but ... message becomes the means of change of voice. We can see that the distinctiveness of voice is a consequence of the relations between categories, where message is the consequence of the interactional practice *within* a context.
>
> (Bernstein 1990: 23)

Key to the concept of 'voice' is its relationship to power manifested in boundary and boundary insulation. Subjects are positioned through power relations and the social or academic classifications they sustain. The insulation between categories, the boundaries between categories, can vary in relation to each other, their identity, space and 'voice'. Boundary insulation therefore becomes the key to the specificity of voices and power relations which sustain such boundaries, and therefore establish the 'voice' of a category (subject, discourse). Here Bernstein, as so often is the case, uses gender as an example of this relationship between power and 'voice'.

> We can give examples of the relations between power, classification and 'voice' by examining the division of labour according to gender. When this division of labour generates strong classification, then there is strong insulation between each category and each category has its own specialized 'voice', and necessarily 'voice' will be specialized to gender. Further, any attempt to weaken the classification – that is, to reduce the insulation so as to change 'voice' (discourse) will provoke the power relationship to re-establish the relations between gender categories by restoring the insulation.
>
> (Bernstein 1990: 24)

Key to this analysis is not that voice change can change power relations, but that shifts in power relations can change 'voices'. As Bernstein comments:

> In Bourdieu's terms, 'symbolic voice' is accomplished not by communication but by *delocations that regulate differences between voices.* Inasmuch as the insulation of strong classification of gender categories produces an arbitrary (contingent) specialization of gender 'voices', it has created imaginary subjects whose voices are experienced as real, as validating and constituting of the specialized category (Althusser 1971). Here the insulation attempts to suppress the arbitrariness of the principle of classification by suppressing the contradictions and dilemmas that inhere in the very principle of classification.
>
> (Bernstein 1990: 25)

At this point, Bernstein appears to employ the notion of voice in relation to social identities, constructed through the hierarchically produced specializations within the division of labour. However, the development of his understanding of the relationship between recognition and realization focuses on the formation of *pedagogic* identities rather than social identities. Classrooms, for Bernstein, are communicative contexts in which the interactional principle dominates. This is a principle which regulates 'the selection, organization, sequencing, criteria and pacing of communication (oral/written/visual) together with the position, posture and dress of communicants' (ibid. 34). It offers recognition and realization rules which need to be acquired by communicants in order to achieve 'competence' (ibid. 35).

In this context, the relationship of 'voice' to text is highly complex, based as it is on the interactional rather than structural conditions for the production of pedagogic realizations. Interactional practices in education in the classroom shape the realizations of meanings which take the form of 'messages'. These messages are dependent on 'voice' since 'voice' limits 'the range of legitimate potential of the message' (Bernstein 1990: 33).

However, this distinction between voice and message (between recognition and realization) is hard to sustain empirically. Bernstein recognized that it is not possible to separate out voice from message since 'voice' is always announced or realized in message. Researchers therefore may find that they are unable to identify uniquely expressed or authentic social voices or pedagogic realizations that are not influenced by social categorizations. Nor is it possible to separate out different 'voices': the classificatory principle works through every pedagogic relation and interaction. As Bernstein points out:

> All the 'voices' are invisibly present in any one 'voice'. Socialization into one 'voiced message' involves socialization into all (i.e. into the principle of the classification).
>
> (Bernstein 1990: 33)

The tensions in the social order merge in the contradictions and dilemmas which are latent in 'voice'. As Diaz observed, Bernstein's notion of 'voice' is one which 'belongs to the field of subjectivity' with its 'fracture between conscious practice and its regulative principle':

> It emerges from social positions and boundary acquisitions within culture but also from the ruptures, discontinuities, and gaps inherent in such positioning, oppositioning, and transgressing.
>
> (Diaz 2001: 85–6)

The task for researchers in garnering and interpreting pupil talk becomes complex at this point. Not only are there empirical difficulties in relation to the separation of 'voice' and message, but also pupil talk could simultaneously offer different 'voices' and all 'voices'. Pupils, when consulted by researchers or teachers, express complex messages about the form of their socialization.

Of importance, too, is the relationship between the formation of a specifically pedagogic identity through official knowledge and 'voice'/message relations in pedagogic encounters:

> In the code theory, 'identity' and its realizations are constructed by variations in classification and framing relations. From this perspective classificatory relations establish 'voice'. *'Voice' is regarded somewhat like a cultural larynx which sets the limits on what can be legitimately put together (communicated).* Framing relations regulate the acquisition of this 'voice'

and create the 'message' (what is made manifest, what can be realized). The dynamics of the framing relations initiated by the acquirer can initiate change in the expected message and so in the governing 'voice'. Thus identity in the code theory is the outcome of the 'voice-message' relations. With respect to the definition of pedagogic identity – the embedding of a career in the principles of social order – acquisition would be regulated by the classification and framing relations $\pm C^{ie}$ and $\pm F^{ie}$ of the pedagogic practice.

(Bernstein 1999: 260, our emphasis)

Bernstein appears to be making an important distinction between the location of social identities and pedagogic identities. The social location of the former tends to:

vary with age, gender, social class, occupational field, economic or symbolic control ... these identities are not necessarily stable positions and shifts can be expected depending upon the possibility of maintaining the discursive or in some cases on the economic base of the identity.

(Bernstein 2000: 79)

This suggests that sociologists of education need to consider the relationship between the social identity shaped within the external fields, and those generated within the classificatory relations of schooling. Research on youth blurs this distinction with the implication that social identities are sustained independently of pedagogic identities.

It is interesting to note that in 2000, Bernstein returned again to talking about how classificatory principles form consciousness in the process of acquisition. His interest now was on the nature of the talk and the kinds of spaces constructed in which communication takes place. He returns to analyse 'the different forms of legitimate communication realized in any pedagogic practice', considering this time whether the concept of framing can address any pedagogic relation (Bernstein 2000: 12).

Framing refers to the controls on communications in local interactional pedagogic relations: between parents/children, teacher–pupil, social worker/client etc. If the principle of classification provides us with our voice and the means of its recognition, then the principle of framing is the means of acquiring the legitimate message. Thus classification establishes voice, and framing establishes the message; they can vary independently.

(Bernstein 2000: 12)

The complexity of his argument is the recognition that: '(t)here is more than one message for carrying any one voice. Different modalities of communication can establish the same voice. Different modalities of framing can relay the same voice (identity)' (Bernstein 2000: 12). Looking back to the 1981 paper 'Codes, Modalities and the Process of Cultural Reproduction: a model', Bernstein (2000) reminds the reader that there are a range of messages, different possibilities of specific codings of identity and different modalities of acquired identity (2000: 204). As Diaz (2001) argues, at the heart of Bernsteinian theory is the articulation of the voice–message relationship as the means by which the subject is constituted:

> Power is a means of constitution of voice in the multidimensional set of social relations or social games that both integrate and fragment. These social relationships take place in contexts where the interests of 'individuals' give rise to conscious actions and interactions, full of strategies. This is a crucial problem for the understanding of subject positions because voice becomes dispersed throughout the range of social practices and messages. In other words, practices and messages have to do with concrete events dispersed in space and time, however inscribed in the voice ... Thus, subject becomes a symbolic space for the realization of power positions that fragment voice into voices internal to the individual. In opposition to individual unity and freedom, Bernstein thinks of a subject as limited by what power establishes in actual voices. Voice is, in this sense, difference, is identity. Power is translated into voice, voice is translated into difference, and difference creates identity. But the translation is not mechanical; it is realized through the fracturing, dispersing and fragmenting of voice. The voice is, then, the living condition of power within the limits structured in and experienced by the subject ... From this view, we can understand Bernstein's thinking on the structuring power of the voice, that is, that instead of being the natural centre or locus of identity, voice is a function of identity. This means that voice, as power and discourse, is a field of multiple formations and transformations.
>
> (Diaz 2001: 86–7)

This brief summary of some of the key elements of Bernstein's concept of voice encourages researchers to take far more care in how they collect and read pupil or youth voice. Over twenty years, Bernstein's conceptualization of voice and its use in educational research developed. Distancing himself from 'extrinsic' features of education (such as class, race and gender voices), through the notion of voice he explored the formation of subjectivity at the interface between the communicative contexts of schooling and the locational, social positioning of the division of labour. His conceptualization of voice, although structurally determined by power relations, nevertheless was only expressed through its interactionally produced realizations. In this reshaping (or recontextualization), tense and contradictory interactions occurred between social voices and pedagogic voices, between dominant and dominated, and between voice and sub-voice.

Pedagogic voices and encounters

Bernstein saw the potential of what he called 'reading up' from voice-message through the structuring of the pedagogic encounter to the power relations which provide the conditions for those articulations and specialized voices. Although he recognized that he had never offered 'the possibility of a delicate description of the full repertoire of arabesques of interaction within any classroom, staffroom or family' (Bernstein 1990: 7), nevertheless his concepts of voice, message, recognition and realization were part of the principles of description which were capable of accounting for features relevant to a theory of classroom interaction and organizational contexts for the transmission of knowledge:

> it is crucial for students to know and feel that they, the experiences which have shaped them, and their modes of showing are recognized, respected and valued. But this does not mean that this exhausts the pedagogic encounter. For, to see the pedagogic encounter only in terms of a range of potential voices and their relation to each other is to avoid the issue of pedagogy itself i.e. the appropriate classification and framing modality. When this is considered, institutional, structural and interactional features are integrated in the analysis. The necessary resources (material and symbolic) can be assessed to become the site for challenge of what is and demands for what should be.
>
> (Bernstein 2000: 174)

Bernsteinian theory has encouraged a number of sociological studies of pedagogic practice. What distinguishes these projects from mainstream classroom research is their highly structured and focused attempts to get behind 'the choreography of interaction' – the educational performance (Bernstein 1990: 7). Bernsteinian scholars have attempted to demonstrate the consequences of different pedagogic devices and practices and the interconnections between social and pedagogic identities, although this distinction is not usually highlighted. It has involved reading pedagogy rather than reading pupil 'voice'. As Davies (1995: 7) pointed out, the particular form of qualitative research used by Bernsteinians to elicit pupils' view of classroom learning did not focus on pupil voice per se.

Using Bernstein's scaffolding, Bernsteinian scholars have drawn upon the voices of pupils as part of their research design.[1] Different types of qualitative data explore the consequences of different pedagogic practices for groups of children. Although not cumulative, these projects throw light on the creation of specialized voices and positions and the consequences for children of specialized dispositions and identities in the context of a broad range of subjects (e.g. English, Art, Science, Maths and ICT). They tend to be quasi-experimental comparative studies, differentiating and contrasting different institutional/structural pedagogic practices/devices. Open-ended questions, specially designed tasks and activities have been used to assess pupils' ability to identify whether they recognize the rules of the pedagogy and are able to generate appropriate texts. The intention is to use pupil voice to understand pedagogic practices and their implications for access to the rules of acquisition of different socially constructed groups.

On the basis of our reading of such research and our own data, which focused more specifically and purposively on eliciting pupils' voices/message, we became aware of a range of different types of pupil talk elicited by Bernsteinian researchers, tapping different aspects of the 'voice'/message relationship and its impact on identity. Below we offer a (somewhat crude) categorization of different elements in the realization of voice.

- *Classroom talk* and the styles of communication and language codes used between teacher and taught.
- *Subject talk* – making explicit the recognition and realization rules of particular subjects and specialized communicative competence.
- *Identity talk* – social bonding, humour, casual framing, friendship talk and what Bernstein called 'sub-voice'.
- *Code talk* – a focused representation of educational codes and their impacts (e.g. framing rules and pedagogic rights).

We illustrate this distinction between different types of pupil talk by giving examples from research.

Classroom talk

The particular formation of classroom talk is exemplified by the work of Silverman and Torode (1980) and of Edwards and Westgate (1987), who consider the linguistic registers used and expected in lessons and the sorts of pupil talk encouraged by teachers. Edwards and Westgate (1987), on the basis of their research, argued that school did not just teach in elaborated codes since teachers also employed restricted codes, and working-class pupils were able to cross registers. A detailed debate ensued between Edwards (1987, 1994) and Bernstein (1996: Chapter 8) about the 'underlying semantic of communication' and the nature of elaborated codes. Bernstein argued for the central importance of the use of different language codes within educational codes. Communicative competence is dependent upon satisfactory performance of the realization of language codes within the particular oral and written pedagogic traditions found in schools.

Subject talk

In 1992 Morais, Fontinhas and Neves, using three experimentally controlled pedagogic practices (differentiated by classification and framing configurations), linked the social positioning of Portuguese pupils with their access to the recognition and realization rules employed in problem-solving activities in Science. Data from structured pupil interviews supplemented data from tests and questionnaires, and helped uncover the fact that social class was highly correlated with recognition and less so with realization. Children of 'lower social levels' in the sample had greater difficulty in recognizing the difference between cognitively low-level competencies requiring less abstraction and cognitively high-level competencies requiring the use of knowledge in new situations. They also had difficulties producing, orally, the correct texts for the latter context except when the realization task was limited to a selection of alternatives. Social class and 'race', with gender as a mediating variable, were important discriminatory factors in terms of learning competencies.

Pupil interviews were also important in Morais and Antunes' (1994) analysis of data from the same experimental project which analysed the 'differential text production by students from different backgrounds'. Here they compared pupil responses to the three pedagogic practices which required different socio-affective dispositions and competences. Eighty children aged between ten and twelve were asked questions about, for example, what was important for them in the Science classroom, what were the objectives, which was the most important, what was meant by co-operation and class participation. The project suggested differential knowledge of the recognition rules and realization rules depending largely on the socialization practices within families and family–school relationships.

Identity talk

The type of talk generated by youth is often understood as representative of social identities, irrespective of the impact of pedagogy upon their subjectivity. Social identities then become the only 'voice' that can be realized. Youth studies which are heavily reliant on ethnographic qualititative data explore in effect what we call 'identity talk' – the type of voice research criticized by Moore and Muller (1999) for its romanticization of such talk as a form of political resistance. However, Moore and Muller's main criticism concerns the epistemological basis of such research. From a Bernsteinian perspective, it is not so much that researchers have concentrated on voice, but that they have failed to locate such voices as the 'messages' – the products of the interface between various communicative contexts. Pupil languages are to some extent the result of an arbitrary marriage between the culture of the child's socialization with the family and community and the pedagogic culture of the school. What contemporary ethnographic studies using pupil voice mainly fail to do is to locate those forms of identity talk within pedagogic practice – thus they fail to explore in greater depth the relation between such identity talk based on social categorizations and hierarchies, which creates insulation and difference, and the forms of pupil voice that are created within the relationship between transmitter and acquirer.

This connection can be explored through Bernstein's concept of voice and 'sub-voice'. Bernstein recognized that both the transmitter and the acquirer have different specialist voices, but they are also differentiated within by a range of sub-categories and voices:

> Within the category of transmitter, there are various sub-voices: age, gender, 'ability', ethnicity. In the process of acquiring the demarcation markers of categories (agents, discourse), the acquirer is constituted as a specialized category with variable sub-sets of voices depending on age, gender, 'ability', ethnicity.
>
> (Bernstein 1990: 26)

Thus the dominant voice within the school (power relations between teacher and taught) is shaped by the distribution of these various sub-voices. Power relations, however, also work through other sets of categorizations which might traverse and influence the hierarchical distribution of power within the pedagogic context.

> In the case of the school, the dominant 'voice' is given by the category of teacher/pupil, but the pupil may be subject to distributive rules which regulate the sub-voices (gender, race, ability etc). From another perspective, pupils (and for that matter teachers) may be positioned within the category relations of social class and this may well become the dominant positioning voice, with pupil as the sub-voice. Whilst we may be criss-crossed by diverse voices (discourses) from our point of view these are arranged not horizontally but hierarchically.
>
> (Bernstein 1990: 26)

Singh's (1993) research tackles this complex relationship in her seminal analysis of the social construction of technical competence in computer lessons in primary schools. She discovers through listening to pupil identity talk and subject talk and by observing pupils at work in the classroom how they position themselves within the technocratic discourse of ICT. The girls are found to 'deconstruct' the truth about their computer incompetence and passivity. Their struggle to redefine themselves as competent in terms of the pedagogic device of technocratic masculinity is represented by Singh as a 'constant struggle' between the inner and outer voice. In an important development that was recognized by Bernstein (2000), Singh describes how they have to reconcile their inner voices, their desires to be powerful, active and successful in the pedagogic skills required, with the outer voice determined by patriarchal controls which positions them as dutiful, subservient carriers of messages and passive rule-followers.

In another study which reveals the interface between dominant and dominated sub-voices, Daniels *et al.* (2004) used pupil interviews to understand the different communicative competences pupils achieved within two pedagogic settings – one which operated through a discourse of expertise and the other through a discourse of co-operation. Children were asked in friendship interviews what they thought about learning and were observed in a range of activities to see how they verbally and non-verbally engaged in, were positioned in and developed and displayed friendship in learning groups. They were also specifically asked whether boys and girls learn differently. Reading back from the 'voice' data, the research team was able to differentiate the experiences and communicative competencies of middle-class boys and girls and to discover that some were more able and more comfortable with particular pedagogic discourses and strategies. The qualitative data are quoted as revealing of the communicative competences and practices expected of children and the different male and female pupil positionings within different regulative discourses. In the case of performance/expertise focused pedagogies (+C+F), the association of specialized gendered discourses contributed to the marginalization of some groups such as lower-ability non-sporty boys and working-class girls:

> There was no pedagogic space in which their 'uniqueness' was allowed to shine. They worked in pairs closely with one another but rarely occupied central positions in the class. They continued to keep quiet, to help others and one another and were characterized as working hard but doing dull work. It is likely that performing a unique identity was not a desirable position for these working class girls.
>
> (Daniels *et al.* 2004: 129)

These studies illustrate in subtle and complex ways the working through of voice and message, of power relations which constrain what can be realized and of the different ways in which realizations are shaped by pedagogic practices. Embedded in these voice data are notions of subjectivity and identity.

Code talk

Our research project was essentially a study about educational codes, but from the pupils' perspective rather than through learning performances. We focused on what we now call 'code talk'. We wanted to ask pupils directly about the framing rules and the pedagogic rights that shape learning in classrooms – in that sense we explored through pupil perspectival data how the rules which govern framing operate in their different schools. Our research design took as its main feature the categorizations of pupils by gender and achievement, working with the academic positionings constructed by the school. These positionings often reinforced social class and ethnic differences. The data we generated not surprisingly articulated identity talk, but in ways that were deeply shaped by pedagogic practices.

Our analysis of 'code talk' suggests that it is not necessarily easy for pupils to speak the language of learning. In contexts where the principles which govern transmission are hidden (for example, invisible pedagogies), pupils struggle in our interviews to articulate the intrinsic criteria which govern their learning. In our study, we asked pupils to describe their identities as learners, their relations with teachers, the processes of inclusion in learning, and the degree of control they had over the selection, sequencing, pacing and evaluation of knowledge (Reay and Arnot 2004; Arnot and Reay 2004). Pupils are able to describe some of the classifications and positionings operating within their classrooms. In the example below, they articulate the extent to which the regulative discourse impinges on, and the reasons why it impinges on, the instructional discourse:

> Some of the boys just muck about then the rest of us have to wait while the teacher sorts them out. And like they slow everything down. Like the teacher has to go through it 100 times then they'll do it. But like they deliberately wait for the teacher to spell it out to them and it affects everybody's learning.
>
> (Lisa)

Pupils appear to be well aware of the presence of dominant and dominated voices in the classroom. However, they also record their own silencing in learning interactions, and in responding to teachers' demands. As Bernstein pointed out, 'contextually legitimate communication' (1996: 32) between teacher and taught is not possible without learning the recognition rules – as a result there are those who remain silent in the classroom.

> It may well be, at the more concrete level, that some children from the marginal classes are silent in school because of the unequal distribution of recognition rules ... Power is never more fundamental as far as communication is concerned than when it acts on the distribution of recognition rules.
>
> (Bernstein 2000:17)

The children of the so-called marginal classes may have the recognition rule (they can recognize power relations and their own position in them) but if they do not possess the realization rules, then they cannot speak the expected legitimate text or 'produce the legitimate communication' (ibid.). The consequence is that these children

> will not have acquired the legitimate pedagogic code, but they will have experienced their place in the classificatory system. For these children, the experience of the school is essentially an experience of the classificatory system and their place in it.
>
> (Ibid.)

This legitimate text may be 'no more than how one sits or how one moves' – even a slight movement: anything that attracts evaluation. However, it is not mechanically reproduced. There is, according to Bernstein, a 'dynamic relation between the text and interactional practice, with the possibility that the former can change the latter (ibid. 18). What is more likely, however, is the silencing of the classroom and subject talk of precisely those marginalized classes whom teachers find the most difficult to consult about their learning:

Matthew: The new teacher she doesn't respect the way we learn 'cos some of us learn at a slower pace than others and she has no respect for the slower ones.

Kenny: And she just treated us like a pile of shit, man.

Matthew: Because we don't speak right.

The sub-voice – for example, that of social class – may be the only voice that pupils can realize:

David: Some teachers are a bit snobby, sort of. And some teachers act as if the child is stupid. Because they've got a posh accent. Like they talk without 'innits' and 'mans', like they talk proper English. And they say – that isn't the way you talk like putting you down. Like I think telling you a different way is sort of good, but I think the way they do it isn't good because they correct you and making you look stupid.

Matthew: Those teachers look down on you.

David: Yeah, like they think you're dumb.

As pupils were aware, only some were able to speak the appropriate form of classroom talk in ways that communicated their priorities and concerns to teachers, and it was they who were therefore able to acquire learning support. Yet again recognition of the rules does not necessarily lead to appropriate forms of realization. As two working-class girls in our study commented:

Jenna: Yeah, our English teacher. He likes the three clever girls a lot because they are always answering questions. He never gives other people a chance to say ...

Sarah: If we put our hands up and we want to answer the question, the cleverest person, he will ask them, and we all know the right answer. And then he starts shouting at us saying that we are not answering.

Jenna: Like it's not as if we aren't trying but he always thinks we're gonna get it wrong.

Some pupils were more bilingual – they could work with the expectations and criteria of both strong and weak frames, moving between the language of learning and that of their homes. Some of the working-class pupils we spoke to, however, were well aware of the distance between the educational codes and languages of the home and the school. Working-class boys and girls especially talked in ways that suggested that they were not able to deliver the elaborated messages about 'I the learner' expected of independent learning and relatively weak framing, nor were they able to take control over their own learning through engaging with pacing rules, evaluation criteria or classroom order. For these pupils, more formal and less language-based options of pupil consultation were found to be a more positive option (see Arnot *et al.* 2004).

Below we consider in more depth the implications of such 'voices' for pupil consultation.

Pupil consultation and the 'yet to be voiced'

Our research caused us to reflect on how teachers overcome the strong boundaries and sometimes conflictual relations between themselves and those with whom they want to consult. How do pupils talk about such relations and with what purpose? Consulting pupils, eliciting and hearing their voices also makes assumptions about the value of such talk in transforming the hierarchical relations between teacher and taught and in reshaping pedagogic practices in line with students' expressed needs. As such, promises are made implicitly if not explicitly about the possibilities of transforming the power relations inherent in pedagogy. The articulation of these power relations by pupils suggests the possibility of a shift in the boundaries between teacher and taught.

However, from a Bernsteinian perspective, the process of pupil consultation is not substantially different from other pedagogic encounters. It too requires recognition and realization rules. Pupils are expected to communicate in a certain way about their learning with the teacher using appropriate language forms, topics, styles, expressing appropriate needs and at appropriate moments. They need to be fluent speakers of classroom and subject talk. And the identities they express should, arguably, be pedagogic identities as learners rather than their social identities. The displays or performances by pupils in these consultation moments are meant to reflect the instructional rather than the regulative, even though as Bernstein argues the instructional is always embedded within a dominant regulative discourse.

There are pupils, however, who have acquired the pedagogic voice that teachers expect and respond to the processes of consultation. Their voices are articulate, reflexive, focused and appear to be independently constructed. Their voice with its associated messages indicates that they have learnt both the recognition and realization rules not just of academic learning, but also the framing rules in which such learning is located. Thus middle-class girls were sufficiently confident within the existing spaces of the classroom not to need to value consultation. Such new spaces had little more to offer than that made available to them in the normal pedagogic practice.

There is a danger, therefore, that the process of pupil consultation is one which hides the social stratificational aspects of schooling. The mask of neutrality relocates responsibility for learning on the pupil rather than the transmission. Consultation, whilst appearing democratically grounded is a clearly bounded, pedagogic event with high expectations that pupils will actively realize their own potential to help themselves. Yet in reality, given the operation of power relations within the construction of voice and the constraints that it imposes on the messages that can be realized, the process of consultation with pupils represents potentially what Bernstein called a 'mythologizing discourse', masking such power relations. The pupil voices elicited through consultation are not independent or extrinsic features; they have been constituted by the pedagogic device and classificatory rules of the school.

However, as we have seen, Bernstein accepted the possibility that power relations could be challenged. The tension between voice and message lies in the fact that the latter could change the former. Weak framing of the sort implied by personalized/individualized learning arguably could lead to a change in classificatory relations. As we have seen, the possibility that the contradictions, cleavages and tensions latent in 'voice' mean that the practices themselves 'contain the possibility of change in the social division of labour and thus of their own change (Bernstein 1990: 33). Working-class boys like Matthew and David have learnt a recognition rule in so far as they recognize the power relations, even if they cannot find ways of shifting them. In our study a number spoke of their commitment to non-co-operation with teachers, the politics of confrontation and their preference for the support and back-up of their friends in the context of what they saw as teacher indifference, hostility or neglect. The opportunities for teachers to hear, through the voices of pupils, the embedded power relations and forms of control which organize pedagogy can be forceful. The code talk of marginalized learners, in particular, reveals the ways power is currently being exerted through pedagogic encounters. At a pedagogic level, there are therefore political possibilities in the opportunities which consultation provides, of teachers reflecting critically on the forms of specialized pedagogic and social identities and experiences the school creates. Pupil consultation might reveal to teachers the socially differentiated competencies and the ways in which children talk about different forms of recognition and realization. They might also consider the social/group effect of their pedagogic practices on children from different socializing contexts and different gendered/racialized positions.

Bernstein's conceptualization about the role of the 'yet to be voiced' in promoting change has interesting possibilities. Clearly it is the message for Bernstein that is critical – the realizations and sub-voices allow for the possibility of challenges to the power structures which condition voice. Dominated voices could challenge dominant voices by the different ways in which voice is realized. At the same time, there are also potentially the 'yet to be voiced' (1990: 30). The contradictions and dilemmas associated with a social order provide the 'source' of the 'yet to be voiced' (an alternative discourse). 'Yet to be voiced' could provide the 'basis for anomie', especially on the part of those dominating the distribution of power, but speak to change for the dominated. These 'yet to be voiced' voices could be suppressed, but as Bourne (2003) found, they could also be developed. The lessons of a black African Caribbean teacher of English provide the model classroom of what she describes as a 'radical visible pedagogy' in which learners are encouraged to come to an understanding of their own position in society by 'coming to an understanding of the relationship between social groups, and through this new appreciation the ability to change practice.' (Bernstein, 1990: 72, quoted in Bourne, p. 518). In a diverse constantly shifting range of teaching episodes, children learn 'to voice themselves' and to understand the workings of power in everyday English society'.

> Voicing oneself in this context does not mean leaving students to find some inner well of personal expression. The teacher offers students access to a new discursive network, through a vertical discourse of analysis and interpretation, part of a wider genre network of schooling.
>
> (Bourne 2003: 518)

This allows the 'yet to be voiced' to reveal itself – generating the possibility of a new 'pedagogic climate in the UK' (Bourne 2000, 2003).

There is a raft of ethical issues associated with voice and with pupil consultation. Bernstein would argue that such 'voice'-led initiatives could easily be used to imply transformation when none is delivered. The tragedy of democratically inspired pedagogies is likely to be their lack of consequence in being able to challenge classification structures. Frames are the source of change, as are messages, but the reality is, as Bernstein pointed out, that such emancipatory strategies generate equal and opposite reactions from those in power to reinstate and strengthen boundaries and forms of social insulation. Alternatively, such weakening of the framing may be used as a mythologizing discourse, which masks the continuing forms of social class stratification and transmission of class values. The illusion of a non-arbitrary order can be created by a 'listening school'.

Conclusion

In conclusion, as we have shown, we are now a long way away from the dangers and pitfalls described by Moore and Muller (1999) in relation to voice sociology. The possibilities for exploring the role of voice, message and text, or pedagogic encounters through qualitative studies of classrooms and the collection of pupils' pedagogic voices, are being developed whether in the normal practice of teaching or in the processes of pupil consultation. The forms of pupil talk have become the means by which the pedagogic device, and thus power relations, are relayed. At the same time, the opportunities for social challenge are represented by the ways in which power is realized. As Bernstein (2000) argued, 'it is by reading voice backwards (from speaker to hearer), that we may be able to recover the specialized pedagogic device, which through constructing the "imaginary subject" (Bernstein 1990) of voice, specializes and privileges the field position of the hearer'. We have found our exploration of 'voice' extremely helpful. It has revealed the potential as well as the complexity and 'slipperiness' of 'voice' as a concept. At the same time, it encourages us to develop a sociology of pedagogic voice, with all its different elements.

Despite his, at times, apparent dismissal of 'voice' research, Bernstein was playing with his own notion of 'voice' in his work. For Bernstein, the concept of 'voice' was in the end indicative of his own personal stance. He argued that 'to know whose voice is speaking is the beginning of one's voice' (Bernstein 1996: 12). In the interview with Solomon, he summed up his view about the role of voice in the shaping of his own theory in a very personal way:

> My preference here is to be as explicit as possible – then at least my voice can be deconstructed.
>
> (Bernstein and Solomon 1999: 275)

Notes

1   Recent examples are: Daniels 1988, 1989; Diaz 1984; Morais, Fontinhas and Neves 1992; Pedro 1981; Singh 1993; Ivinson 2002; Bourne 2000.

6   Disembedded middle-class pedagogic identities

Sally Power

British sociology of education over the last fifty years has largely concerned itself with the relationship between the education system and social disadvantage (Whitty 2001). Throughout this time, the middle class has had a shadowy and unsatisfactory presence. It hovers in the background – rarely the focus of the investigation, but rather the background against which the perspectives and experiences of the working class have been contrasted (Power 2000). However, exploring the relationship between education and the middle class will not only provide more sophisticated understanding of diverse educational careers, institutions and orientations, it will also help us to have a better grasp of the significance of struggles over education. As Bernstein points out: 'The middle class are specialists in the theory, practice and dissemination of symbolic control' (1977: 192). Therefore, while examination of the relationship between education and the middle class may be partly justified in terms of a social policy agenda (Whitty 2001), it also merits greater prominence on a sociological agenda.

The twentieth century witnessed the rise of the middle class, but this rise was also marked by struggles for ascendancy between distinct middle-class fractions. Many of the struggles were played out in the field of education – perhaps not surprisingly inasmuch as schooling provided the main vehicle for middle-class growth and consolidation. In the UK and the US, it is possible to identify divisions between the 'old' and the 'new' middle class which have contributed to oppositional allegiances to traditional and progressive forms of childrearing and schooling which in turn led to distinctive pedagogic identities. It is generally considered that the basis of this opposition derives from occupational location – with the 'old' middle class being located within the economic sphere and the 'new' middle class being located in the ascendant sphere of cultural production. However, as the twentieth century drew to a close, changes within the economic and symbolic fields have made the division less clear-cut.

My colleagues and I have explored elsewhere (Power and Whitty 2002; Power *et al.* 2003) the relationship between the 'new' and 'old' fractions of the middle class through analysing the biographies of a unique UK cohort of over 300 young men and women who were identified as being 'destined for success' in their early teens. These analyses revealed the logistical difficulties of finding any clear statistical patterns of allegiances in empirical research. The lack of clear division between our respondents from 'new' and 'old' middle-class backgrounds can be explained on a number of counts. First, the subdivisions *within* the new middle class are so significant that it is hard to gloss over them[1] and our sample size does not allow us to gain statistically significant correlations at subdivision level (it should also be noted that the picture is further complicated by the large number of 'cross-field' and 'cross-subdivision' families). Second, in the past two decades the middle class has undergone rapid change. There have been changes within the economic and symbolic fields which underpin the distinction between the old and new middle-class categories and which have made the distinction less clear-cut (Bernstein 2001). In particular, the extension of market principles into the public sector has brought the rationality of the economic field into the field of symbolic control.

This chapter explores whether Bernstein's later work on pedagogic identities (Bernstein 1996) provides a more appropriate framework for understanding the development of young adult middle-class identities than the model based on divisions between and within 'new' and 'old' fractions of the middle class. The first section outlines the premises and key elements of the framework. The second section describes my attempt to map the framework onto biographical data from our cohort of young adults through providing illustrative examples of 'matched' individuals. The original intention of this mapping was not to test out the framework, but to see whether re-classifying our cohort members in terms of the new categories of pedagogic identities could provide a more sophisticated and contemporary basis for understanding the differences between them. However, the difficulties of connecting the framework with the data raise a number of theoretical and methodological issues about the framework itself. These are explored in the concluding section of the chapter.

Framework

During the 1990s, Bernstein developed his theory of pedagogic codes to postulate the development of distinctive pedagogic identities that reflect the changing social conditions of modern (or postmodern) society. In line with other social theorists, he argues that the conventional 'ascribed' 'cultural markers' (age, gender, age relation) and 'achieved' locations (class and occupation) are no longer stable or strong enough to provide unambiguous identities. This new period of transitional capitalism, has, he claims, 'brought about a disturbance and disembedding of identities and so created the possibility of new identity constructions' (Bernstein 1996: 76). Bernstein identifies three 'fundamental' identity constructions: *decentred, retrospective* and *prospective,* which are built upon different resources. He represents his model diagrammatically[2] in Figure 6.1.

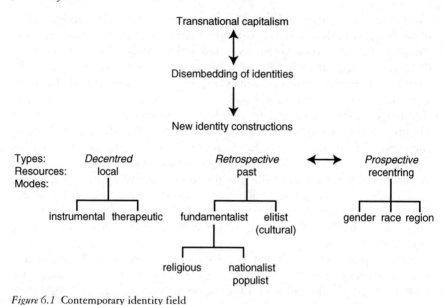

Figure 6.1 Contemporary identity field
Reproduced from Bernstein (1996: 77)

The characteristics of these identities can be summarized as follows:

Decentred identities

These identities are constructed by what Bernstein refers to as 'local' resources. They are decentred inasmuch as they are disembedded from and reject the old 'achieved' and 'ascribed' attributes that 'centred' previous identities. They tend to be highly individualistic rather than seeking new collectivities. There are, though, two variants which may align themselves to the economic and symbolic fields of production respectively.

Instrumental (market)

These identities are decentred in that they 'arise out of a *projection* on to consumables which relays to self and others the spatial and temporal attributes of the identity ... boundaries are permeable' (Bernstein 1996: 77). They are, argues Bernstein, anti-centralist in political orientation because of their close relation to the economic base. He specifically connects these identities with those in non-entrepreneurial positions, such as new technologies.

Therapeutic

These identities are also 'decentred', but rather than arising from projection, they are produced by *introjection*.

Here the concept of self is crucial and the sense of self is regarded as a personal project. It is an internally regulated construction ... It is a truly symbolic construction ... [that] takes the form of an open narrative which constructs internal linearity.

(Ibid.)

So that while both variants may be responses to decentring, they have oppositional bases. As Bernstein puts it in his typically elliptical way: 'If the market identity is dependent upon the segmentation of the shopping mall then the therapeutic is dependent upon internal making-sense procedures of the external segmentation' (ibid. 78).

Retrospective identities

Whereas decentred identities draw on contemporary and local resources, retrospective identities look to the past. There are, similarly, two variants that are oppositional in nature and this opposition may also relate to differences in the symbolic and economic fields of production.

Fundamentalist

These identities are 'unambiguous, stable, intellectually impervious, collective'. They produce 'strong insulation between conduct and modernizing or post-modernizing influences' (ibid. 78). Although some of these identities arise from religious fundamentalisms, others arise from nationalism and populism – 'drawing on mythological resources of origin, belonging, progression, destiny' (ibid. 78). These may well, argues Bernstein, be selected by those who have an entrepreneurial or 'threatened' base in the economic field.

Elitist

These retrospective identities draw on resources of high culture. Like fundamentalism, elitism is based upon strong classifications and internal hierarchies. However, as Bernstein notes, 'whereas fundamentalist identities have strong rules of membership, conversion is available; this is much less the case for elitist identities as they require a very long and arduous apprenticeship' (ibid. 78–9). Like therapeutic identities, elitist identities are likely 'to be distributed in agencies specializing in the field of symbolic control' (ibid. 79).

Prospective identities

These are future-orientated identities. However, unlike decentred identities, which similarly reject 'old' collectivities, prospective identities seek to build new narratives of collectivity. They involve a 'recentring' of identity on new bases for social solidarity – such as race, region or gender. Bernstein argues that, in their early stages of development, they may display some of the attributes of fundamentalist identities. These identities are likely, he claims, to be selected from those in the symbolic rather than the economic field.

Applying the framework

This section describes the attempt to map the framework onto biographical data from our cohort of young adults. These young people have participated in a series of research projects, funded by the Economic and Social Research Council (ESRC) that have followed them from the start of their secondary education into their early thirties.[3] When they were first researched in the early 1980s, they had just embarked on their secondary school careers. Although they were all identified as being 'academically able', they attended eighteen different schools that ranged from inner-city comprehensives to some of the most prestigious and selective schools in the private sector. Not surprisingly, given the close connection between social class and educational achievement, our pupils came from predominantly white (97 per cent) and middle-class families.[4]

The data used for this analysis are drawn largely from the 'Destined for Success?' project, which revisited the cohort when they were in their mid-twenties during the mid-1990s. At this point there were 347 participants (169 men and 178 women), the large majority of whom had completed higher education. All returned long and detailed questionnaires, and extended interviews were undertaken with just under half of the sample. The questionnaire and interview schedule invited respondents to offer their perceptions of their educational careers, their current position and priorities, and their aspirations for the future.

This analysis began by reading through all the interview transcripts with a view to categorizing as many individuals as possible into the distinctive pedagogic types developed by Bernstein. However, it soon became clear that categorizing a significant proportion of the cohort would be impossible. Although it was possible to locate some individuals within the framework, these were in the minority. Rather than re-classifying our respondents into different sub-groups, it has only been possible to provide illustrative examples of 'matched' individuals. In what follows, one respondent for each pedagogic type has been selected with the basis of the matching indicated through data from both interviews and questionnaires.[5]

Decentred identities: instrumental (market)

As already outlined, we are looking here for a respondent whose identity is decentred from the 'old' cultural markers and defined largely in terms of their relationship to consumables. Peter Abbott (who went to Bankside

College, an elite private school) displays some of these tendencies. Although his parents worked in the field of symbolic control (his father was a teacher at the school Peter himself attended and his mother worked as a researcher at the local university), Peter's degree in Product Design and Manufacture from Loughborough University brought him much closer to the economic sphere. Peter's approach to his higher education appears to be quite instrumental – valued in terms of its exchange value rather than any intrinsic interest.

> The thing is, to be honest, I probably got as much as I could have at university but I just saw it purely, really, ultimately as getting my degree and to get me to start doing the things I want to do. I didn't see it as another sixth form where you got a bit more freedom and you got all these other things to do and all these, I just wanted to get there, do my degree, enjoy it, but ultimately get my degree and get out.

When interviewed three years after completing his degree, Peter was undertaking casual work as a van driver for Securicor. This is, though, only part of his grand plan:

P: When I say I'll be retired in ten years' time, I've still, I've got my plan ... and basically the position I'm going to be in, maybe ten years is slightly out by a couple of years, I'm aiming for about mid-35 to be, when I say retire I'm not sitting there and watching the paint dry, I've got plans and things I want to do which don't involve being tied to an organization.

I: Plans to do with personal ambitions or work-related ambitions?

P: No they're totally personal. They're projects which have either come to light or I've thought up myself which I feel have sufficient financial reward in them and providing I put the effort in and it's something I want to do I will put the effort in. What I've done is, I've looked at my salary, my initial wages through the next seven, say ten years, to be something, not to get a first mortgage and a house and a family with but as something I can use to invest to set me up to a position where I can get a house and a family and still afford to do a lot of other things whereas if I do it all now, then I will never be able to get to that position. So it all fits into a game plan.

It is difficult to know precisely what Bernstein means when he argues that decentred identities are based upon 'local' resources. However, unlike some of our respondents, who saw their future in terms of global travel and international recruitment markets, Peter certainly seems to envisage his identity firmly rooted in his current context:

I: Can I ask you what one of your projects might be?

P: Well it doesn't involve a Securicor van. One of them is, for example, a very good friend of mine, he has a lot of contacts, family friends in the construction field, house renovations and things like that. He also has contacts, he also gets a lot of information about derelict properties – an example being that very recently he was offered the option of buying a house for about £100,000 which in the area it was in and the state, if it was in a good state, would be worth about £220,000. So the problem is that he couldn't get it because he didn't have the money for it. You need 25 per cent deposit for a business loan and he's just not in that position. Ultimately that's one of the projects I want to go down in order to get into that position.

It is important to note that Peter's motivation is not just about money, but about his sense of identity – about being someone who 'operates' in a particular way:

I: Because you'd enjoy it, or more money more quickly?
P: I don't, I'm not, because I'll enjoy it but also because, see, I don't see, getting money doesn't mean that much to be honest but it's what you can do … Having the money will enable me to do the things I want to do, but just having the money is no big deal.

The extent to which consuming becomes a project of individual 'self' is evident in Peter's passing comment:

They make Ferraris … but not everyone drives them.

In line with the dislocation from collective identities, Peter rejects the 'grand narratives' of party politics in favour of a more single-issue approach. When asked about his political allegiances, he responds:

Not so much politics as in 'I side with a particular party', but it's generally specific issues come up. It doesn't matter which side they're on, they're going to find something which you agree with and either side which you disagree with. So not so much particular parties, particular issues maybe.

Conforming to Bernstein's framework, Peter's political orientations are somewhat 'anti-centralist' in stance. In relation to private education, for instance, Peter comments:

I don't agree with this rubbish about just because Fred Bloggs and his kids can't afford to go then we should scrap it for everybody.

Peter describes his political opinions as 'common sense, conservative, progressive'. His regular newspapers are the *Daily Mail, The Sun* and the now-closed *Today*. His favourite authors are fantasy and horror writers (Eric Van

Lustbader and Stephen King) and inspirational business writer Burke Hedges, whose bestselling titles include *The Parable of the Pipeline: How Anyone Can Build A Pipeline Of Ongoing Residual Income In The New Economy* and *You Can't Steal Second With Your Foot on First.* In keeping with his individual-istic and market-driven orientations, the people Peter 'most admires' include Richard Branson. Those most deplored are Saddam Hussein and a Euro MP of the time.

Decentred identities: therapeutic

Here we are looking for someone whose sense of self is introjected rather than projected onto consumables. This kind of identity comes close to the new sense of 'career' among the middle class put forward by Mike Savage (2000). It is worth speculating whether there is a gender dimension to this. Certainly, it was one of our female respondents who came closest to displaying this mode of identity. Louise Boot (St Hilda's School for Girls) provides evidence for this kind of self-projection – rejecting external senses of worth for internal values.

Although her father worked in the economic field as a financial consultant, Louise works in the field of symbolic control. After graduating from St John's College, Cambridge, where she read Economics, Social and Political Sciences, she now works as a political researcher for a Labour MP.

She reads *The Guardian* and the *Financial Times* and cites reading, cinema, seeing friends and travel as her hobbies. Although her reading preferences are distinctly political (Paul Krugman, Will Hutton), and her choices for those she most admires (Gordon Brown and Nelson Mandela) and most deplores (Adolf Hitler and Margaret Thatcher) are somewhat predictable, her relation-ship to her career is more ambiguous. She explicitly rejects conventional notions of success.

I: Do you feel that you are into a successful career now?

L: I don't know – what's a career? And I don't know what the definition of successful would be. So I don't know if I can answer that question. I'm doing something that I believe and like doing, for the moment, but I don't know where it's going, because no-one knows where it's going.

In terms of local resources, it is very much a 'here and now' approach:

> I've got no concrete goal, apart from the fact that I want to do something that I enjoy, and that I'm interested in, and I think I'm going to do well, and contribute something to, and at the moment, what I'm doing fits the bill, but I know it's not going to continue after the next year, and after that, I don't know, I'll wait and see what opportunities arise. Which I hope they will.

While this may at first sight appear to be more to do with inner worth rather than external value, it is quite clear that this kind of construction of self needs to be sustained by material security.

Retrospective identities: fundamentalist

It was in the area of fundamentalist retrospective identities that it was most difficult to find a close match. Bernstein claims that these are most likely to be distributed amongst those who have an entrepreneurial base in the economic field or a threatened base in that field. As noted elsewhere (Power 2000), in terms of Savage *et al.*'s (1992) threefold classification of middle-class assets, our cohort predominantly contains those with organizational and cultural assets – rather than property assets. This itself is likely to reflect the fact that the inclusion of respondents within the sample was based on the identification of early academic promise. It is probable then that the difficulty of finding a match for this mode of identity is a product of the distinctive nature of the cohort (and their relative prosperity).

The only person who came close to constructing their identity around retrospective and collective values was Patricia Woodstock from Nortown High School for Girls, who displayed a strong orientation to the ideal of a stable family. It could be argued that this is a response to the disruption caused by more widespread turbulence in domestic arrangements.

Her recollections of school are largely coloured by the break-up of her parents (both teachers). Her parents separated (and have subsequently each re-married and re-divorced) when she was in her second year at Nortown High (on an Assisted Places Scheme):

> It was a very hard time in my personal life because of my parents getting divorced and such things ... I was very insecure and unhappy at that time in my life because my parents had been rowing for years and I was generally very unhappy with things and insecure. It was turmoil going to the secondary school ... I mean it was very awkward while we were at school because Belinda [sister] and I, obviously we were both at the same school, we were only a year apart and she lived with my mum, I lived with my dad and we never spoke. We didn't talk. I was on Dad's side and she was on Mum's side and it was terrible.

After her A levels, Patricia went to the local university where she studied Pharmacy. At the time of the interview, she had married an engineer and had a 10-month-old daughter. She reads the *Daily Mail* and describes her political opinions as 'tolerant, common sense, conservative, conventional'. She chose not to nominate people she deplored, but identified Princess Diana and Anne Diamond as those she most admired.

Her identity is focused entirely on her desire to provide a stable family life. She works as a pharmacist at the local chemist and was completely adamant that she had no desire to either move 'on' or 'up' (for example, to manage the shop):

> All I've wanted, and this is totally clouded by my childhood, is a secure, stable, reliable life. I want to go to the same job every day, do the same thing. Come home, know where I'm up to, no surprises, no big ambitions because my childhood was totally insecure, never knew where I was up to ... I want to give my family stability.

Retrospective identities: elitist

Surprisingly it was not much easier to identify a retrospective elitist – or at least one which closely matches Bernstein's description. He argues that these are most likely to be distributed in the field of symbolic control – and this may well be the case – but the 'strong classifications' and 'internal hierarchies' on which these identities are constructed are often implicit and are therefore hard to identify in the data. Those respondents that are most explicit in their perceptions of classification and hierarchy are more often in the economic field – which would conform to Bernstein's earlier writings on the 'positional' and 'personal' dimensions of old and new middle-class families.

The implicit and tacit values associated with this type of identity are detectable in our selected 'retrospective elitist' respondent – Hugh Durack. Hugh's parents were both research scientists and, after attending Nortown Grammar, Hugh went to King's College, London, where he read German. His higher education was disrupted by romance and heavy involvement in extra-curricular activities and he eventually completed his degree on a part-time basis at Birkbeck. When interviewed, he was one of our higher-earning respondents and worked as a director of a public relations firm that specialized in political lobbying.

The elitist aspect of his identity is manifest in his general orientation to his career and his work – which displays all the casual offhandedness of the 'elect'. At Nortown, Hugh says he 'was always in the top 25 per cent'. When he slipped, it was 'mainly through laziness'. In terms of his higher education:

> I'm still not entirely sure why I didn't go for Oxbridge. I think part of it was a rebellion in that I just didn't want to follow the line of going to Oxbridge like everybody else did. Part of it was having actually been down to look at Cambridge I think. I actually thought it looks a bit, it doesn't look like there's much going on, I'd rather be in London.

His relationship with his career appears to be one of naturally and inevitably 'falling into place' rather than of effort and application. In his early teens, he wanted to study law. As he reminisces:

It's quite funny actually what I've ended up doing, because one of my clients here is the Bar Council so I've ended up doing public relations for the Bar Council which is quite fun ... I think it was mainly because it seemed like I wanted to do something professional. I wanted to have a career which had some status and which had a definite form to it rather than in Business or something like that. I wanted to have something that was fairly, not so much secure, but defined ... I think probably by 1984 I'd decided that I wanted to be a journalist and given up the idea of Law. I think Law was more like a default setting than anything else and I pretty quickly decided I wanted to go into journalism ... because of an interest in English and writing.

He envisages that in five years' time he will be a New Labour MP and in ten, a minister – possibly in Defence. The 'retrospective' aspect of his identity is also not very explicit, but can be found in his hobbies (which include opera and jazz) and his favourite authors (George Orwell, William Burroughs and Virginia Woolf). It is most revealed though in his selection of 'admired' and 'deplored' people. Hugh's 'most admired' are Tony Blair, Peter Mandelson, Michael Palin and Richard Attenborough – all male and all but one Oxford-educated (Richard Attenborough went to RADA). Hugh's 'most deplored' are Richard Branson, Arthur Scargill, Rupert Murdoch and Tony Banks – all of them to some extent anti-establishment 'self-made men', either through politics and the trade union movement or business.

It may be that New Labour as a party has elements of retrospective elitism that appeal to Hugh. As he comments:

It's amazing, in fact if you look at people my age in the New Labour Party who are the people that supported Blair for the leadership when John Smith died, how many of them actually went to private school. It's quite surprising. It's a majority and it's not the majority of the public. And even those that didn't go to private school, it was very rare to find somebody who isn't university educated.

In terms of education politics, Hugh believes that a high-quality education should be more widely available for all and advocates the implementation of the assisted-places scheme on a much larger scale to achieve this end.

Prospective identities

In contrast, prospective identities seek to draw on new narratives of collectivity. Again, it was difficult to find a close match, but Sian Allan from Moorside does display elements of commitment to new causes and a distancing from current market and therapeutic approaches and retrospective fundamentalism or elitism.

Sian went to Moorside Comprehensive where she claims she was 'emotionally abused' by her fellow students who bullied her because she did not fit in. Her father was the local Anglican vicar. She left Moorside to attend King's College, Cambridge, where she studied Modern Languages.

Her narrative of her identity throughout school and university is one of being an 'outsider' – of being awkward and different and of fighting battles against sexism, racism and homophobia. Although she eventually became engrossed in her work at Cambridge, she wanted to find a more 'authentic' identity:

> The one thing that I did know at the end of my fourth year was that I wanted to get away from Cambridge and that sort of culture for a while, just to check that I wasn't kind of absorbed into it, in a way that wasn't honest and real and so I went to Scotland for a while in the summer and took part in some residential conservation projects and we built a jetty out of Ji-Stone techniques and did some work on sand dunes and that was great.

Since leaving Cambridge, she has not sought out paid employment but undertakes voluntary work on the moors – fencing, heather propagation on areas of bare peat and leading groups of volunteers. At the time of the interview, she was also training to be part of Mountain Rescue.

Her politics are leftist but not easily classified. She does not read the regular daily papers and prefers *The Economist* and the *Big Issue*. She describes her political orientations as 'eccentric, socialist and anarchist!' and prefers green politics to conventional party politics. Her favourite authors are distinctively outside the usual selection – Toni Morrison, Julia Kristeva and the twelfth-century poet Chrétien de Troyes. Something of her distaste for conventional politics in preference for alternative 'crusaders' is evident in those she 'most admires': Kate Adie, Desmond Tutu, Prince Charles and Michel Foucault. Her dislike of popular culture, business and Conservative politics is also evident in her list of those 'most deplored': Michael Portillo, Terry Wogan, Virginia Bottomley and Cedric Brown.

Methodological and theoretical issues

The attempt to use Bernstein's analytical framework to understand better the complexity of identity formation within our cohort of young adults has proved both fascinating and frustrating. It has been fascinating to examine our respondents' narratives from a new perspective of identity construction and, as with so much of Bernstein's work, it has opened up the possibility of making links between the subtle and sometimes apparently trivial differences between individuals and larger social structures and trends. It has been frustrating because of the lack of fit and the slipperiness of the concepts. Some of the frustrations are to do with the nature of the cohort. As mentioned earlier, our cohort has a number of distinctive attributes (largely middle class, white and unrepresentative of entrepreneurial careers) that mean some identities are less likely to be evident than others. It also needs to be noted that the data were not gathered with this analytical framework in mind and therefore the limitations of the application may well be as much to do with the limits of the data.

However, it is probable that some of the frustrations are to do with the methodological and theoretical difficulties of the framework itself. First of all, there is the problem of 'fit'. Although I have identified five students who illustrate the different modes of identity, the connections are often somewhat tenuous and the analysis leaves untouched the overwhelming majority of respondents whom it was impossible to categorize without bending the boundaries too far. This may be related to the problem of 'ideal types' in research generally – and how generalizations and classifications are read off from the messiness of biography. However, it is also related to theoretical issues about the nature, coherency and consistency of 'identity' and its relationship to the social structure.

Bernstein himself is somewhat vague about what he means by the concept of identity, and it is also unclear what is the unit of analysis. In oral presentations of the framework, Bernstein tended to use institutions (and particularly universities) as the unit of analysis. Thus, Oxbridge is typically presented as having a retrospective elite pedagogic identity and a new university is attributed with a decentred instrumental (market) pedagogic identity. However, it is also clear that Bernstein is intending to use the framework to locate *individuals*. But the principles through which you can determine how to classify individuals are somewhat obscure and ambiguous.

There seems to be a tension between how fixed or fluid these identities are. At times, Bernstein seems to favour the fluid approach – the identities are constructed from resources that have been made possible by the disembedding of the old 'fixed' cultural markers. However, at other times, these identities have a strongly determined feel about them. For instance, Bernstein comments that 'These identities, although some share similar features, are mutually exclusive in the sense that the adoption of one excludes the possibility of others' (Bernstein 1996: 79). Of course, it could be argued that individuals can adopt multiple identities selectively – but they cannot simultaneously have more than a single identity. However, this then loosens identity construction from any fixed social and material base. Bernstein is quite clear (as can be seen from the tying of particular modes to particular fields of production) that individuals cannot select multiple identities; but it is unclear what the principle of 'adoption' – or (as Bernstein sometimes puts it) 'distribution' – is. This ambiguity between fixed and fluid, between distribution and adoption, is also evident in the relationship between pedagogic identities and social class.

It has long been recognized that there is some elusiveness in Bernstein's conception of social class (Power and Whitty 2002). Throughout the 1970s, there were criticisms that he ignored issues of conflict and agency (e.g. Rosen 1972) and marginalized power relations (Apple 1979; Bisseret 1979), while others (e.g. Harré 1975) complained that he operated too crude a concept of class domination.

This elusiveness has been increased by Bernstein's incorporation of 'identity' as a unit of analysis within his theories. It is not quite clear what he means by identities or from where they arise. Although he claims these new pedagogic identities can be seen as responses to new times, their relationship with existing structures and inequalities is opaque. The concept of power and struggle has disappeared entirely. Bernstein claims identities are related to social bases (or more precisely 'specialized social bases'), but he does not say what these might be. He suggests that 'social class position may not provide such a base' and that these various identities may well be 'signifiers of class fractions rather than of social classes as such' but the nature and source of the fractions is unclear. In his earlier work on pedagogy and class fractions, there was a clear link between struggles for dominance between two rival fractions of the middle class (new and old) working in the economic field and the field of symbolic control and different forms of socialization. Shadows of this remain in Bernstein's continued reference to these fields, but the connections between new 'transnational' capitalism, changing class fractions and their connection to new forms of identity have disappeared. Thus it is unclear why retrospective elite identities are more likely to be found in the field of symbolic control than in the economic field. It is also unclear how the new collective bases required for the construction of prospective identities relate to social classes or even class fractions.

Conclusion

In pointing out these frustrations with trying to apply the framework to empirical data, I am not trying to say that the theory is unusable. As with so much of Bernstein's writing, his theory of pedagogic identities reveals a recognizable and significant 'truth' about social change. What is needed is greater clarification of the concept of identity, the underlying principles of the distinctions between identities and the development of linkages between identities, class fractions, class interests and new times.

In attempting to clarify principles, it might be fruitful to introduce into the analysis some of Bernstein's key concepts that are strangely absent in this particular exposition. There are clear variations in classification and framing in the construction of these identities. Therapeutic identities might be seen as constructed on tight framing but weak classification. Instrumental (market) identities might be built upon weak framing but strong classification. Clarification of the principles of difference would help in the development of empirical elucidation.

Further clarification of the links with class and class fractions could also be attempted through charting out more systematically the way in which changes in the symbolic and economic spheres are affecting the composition and boundaries (between and within) social classes. How *does* the incorporation of market principles into the public sector and the field of symbolic control actually impact upon socialization practices within the family? Where are the battle lines between the old and the new middle class now drawn – if they exist at all?

As with so many of Bernstein's theories, the frustrations can be many, but the intellectual challenges are important and worthwhile.

Notes

1   Bernstein identifies six further distinctions within the new middle class – each of which has very different attributes: 'regulators' (the legal system, police, prison service, church), 'repairers' (medical/psychiatric services, social services) and 'executors' (civil service and bureaucrats) are likely to be more conservative than 'shapers' (creators of symbolic forms in arts and sciences), 'diffusers' (mass and specialized media) and 'reproducers' (teachers).
2   In subsequent demonstrations of the model, Bernstein used a square diagram. However, the original diagram provides more detail of the modes.
3   Award numbers COO230036, R000235570 and RES000220627. For fuller details of these projects see Edwards *et al.* (1989), Power *et al.* (2003) and Power *et al.* (forthcoming).
4   Based on the Oxford Mobility Study scale.
5   Pseudonyms have been used throughout for schools and individuals.

7   Children's recontextualizations of pedagogy

Gabrielle Ivinson and Gerard Duveen

Recontextualization, in Bernstein's theory, is a form of mediation which points to the transformation of knowledge between sites or groups of people. This chapter focuses on the recontextualization of knowledge that takes place between the education institution and the children within it. A key feature of the theory is that the social organization of the school conceals different approaches to knowledge and to the kind of learner or citizen that the child is expected to become. But competing beliefs about the purpose of education and the relationship between the individual and the state can result in these models of knowledge and its relations with persons becoming highly contested. Social organizations in which the creative impetus of the individual is privileged above state regulation are characterized in terms of weak classification and framing (Bernstein 1971, 1974, 1990, 1996). In this case the recontextualization of knowledge between sites or groups is relatively open and leaves room for negotiation and different points of view. Social organizations in which state regulation is privileged above individual initiative are characterized in terms of strong classification and framing, and the transmission rather than the negotiation of knowledge is paramount. Underlying these opposing pedagogic modes, which in his later work Bernstein (1996: 52) referred to as competence and performance modes, are competing notions of the person and competing notions of the purpose of education.

Pedagogic discourse is not a discourse in its own right, but a 'principle by which other discourses are appropriated and brought into a special relationship with each other' (Bernstein 1996: 47). In the process of recontextualization between sites a gap opens up: a space in which 'ideology can play' (ibid.). All discourses project an interlocutor to whom the discourse is addressed (Bakhtin 1981) and Bernstein refers to the interlocutor projected by pedagogic discourse as the *imaginary subject*. Subsumed within the imaginary subjects projected by teachers' pedagogic discourse are ideological views about who children are and who they ought to become. Bernstein believed that the regulative function of pedagogic discourses dominates the instructional function. However, moral induction is not easy to justify, and different pedagogic modes make the regulative discourses (in comparison to the instructional discourse) more or less explicit. Teachers as well as children are controlled by pedagogic modes, although of course teachers have far greater control than pupils. As teachers construct their imaginary interlocutor, common-sense ideas about childhood are liable to influence them, as well as ideas acquired through their own professional training. It has been suggested that the weak classification of competence modes allows historically rooted social representations of gender, class and age to dominate pedagogic discourse (cf. Sharp and Green 1975; Walkerdine 1988). In performance modes, teachers are constrained by the dominant representations of knowledge that circulate in society and in schools. For example, the literacy and numerous pedagogic strategies in the UK were experienced by some teachers as oppressive (Moss 2004). While teaching involves fostering skills, practices and knowledge, at the same time pedagogic discourse inducts children into becoming particular kinds of moral agents.

The pedagogic device regulates how knowledge is recontextualized as it moves from outside to inside the school. At the level of the classroom, social organization is described in terms of recognition and realization rules, which as well as discourses cover, for example, the punctuation of time, use of space, ability groupings, material culture, text books, forms of assessment and patterns of interaction among peers and between teachers and pupils. Material culture together with discourse constitutes a range of semiotic relays that provide clues about what can legitimately be said, done and produced in a specific classroom context. The control that teachers exert over classroom organization relates to pedagogic modes. However, there is a further level of mediation to which little attention has been paid and that is the constructive activities of children themselves.

Until recently it has been assumed that the constructive activities of children can be explained in terms of socio-linguistic codes relating to social class background. Socio-linguistic codes arise from the conditions of working-class and middle-class family structures, interaction and experiences (Bernstein 1974; Cook-Gumperz and Hymes 1972; Diaz 1984; Holland 1981). If children recognize the specificity of a context, they may or may not learn to produce appropriate texts, while children who do not recognize the specificity of a context have a double burden (Morais and Neves, 2001). Middle-class rather than working-class children are more likely to recognize what is required of them in a school context because pedagogic interactions in schools are closer to the parental–child interactional styles of middle-class rather than working-class families. Research in this area has mapped recognition and realization rules, and the social class background of the child, and investigated comparative levels of understanding using a wide range of approaches such as children's interpretations of wall displays (Daniels 1989), mathematics texts books (Dowling 1998), the production of texts in science (Morais *et al.* 1993), cross-curricular themes (Whitty *et al.* 1994) and mathematical problem-solving (Cooper and Dunne 2000).

We have shown that there are significant differences in the way children recontextualize the curriculum according to pedagogic modality (Ivinson and

Duveen 2005) irrespective of the social class background of the child. Therefore we have shown that pedagogic modes have effects in their own right. Children in classrooms with competence and mixed pedagogic modes were less likely to reproduce knowledge according to disciplinary categories than children in classrooms with performance modes. We found that the effect of pedagogic modes increases across time. In Year 1 there was little to distinguish between children's constructions of the curriculum according to pedagogic modality yet by Year 5 children in classrooms with performance modes had significantly more 'structure' talk[1] than children in classrooms with other pedagogic modes.

We have identified two interrelated levels of mediation; first, the *imaginary subjects* that teachers construct and which relate to pedagogic modalities; and second, the constructive activities of children. Children do not simply internalize the recognition and realization rules available in classrooms; rather, they reconstruct knowledge according to developing socio-cognitive resources. It is thus important to recognize that children are active in the construction of knowledge and that this process of construction reflects their capacity to interpret the recognition and realization rules made available in classrooms.

Our primary interest in this chapter is to investigate the relations between these two levels of mediation. We begin with a review of Bernstein's typology of pedagogic modes. In the empirical study which follows, we first make visible the imaginary subject projected by teachers in schools with different pedagogic modes and, second, investigate how this influenced children by examining talk generated by specially designed research instruments. In conclusion we discuss the relationship between pedagogic modes and the kinds of learners that were being produced in different schools.

Pedagogic modes

Bernstein (1996) defined the kinds of practice projected by two opposing models which represent recontextualized knowledge: a 'competence model' and a 'performance model' (ibid. 58). These two models can be viewed as the 'poles of choice' around which a range of pedagogic practices can be described. Here the important characteristic is that competence is practice which is not constrained by power relationships: 'competencies are intrinsically creative, informally, tacitly acquired, in non-formal interactions' (ibid. 55). Competence relates to behaviour which is manifest in co-operative social relations. Performance, on the other hand, is behaviour shaped by social structures and produced within hierarchical social relations. Features of each model are summarized in Table 7.1.

Broadly, competence models are characterized by weak classification and framing and result in few explicit (instructional) structures. In these contexts teachers are less able to appeal to criteria derived from specialist discourses in their efforts to control children. Children's behaviour and the products of

Table 7.1 Recontextualized knowledge

		Competence models	Performance models
1	Categories space time discourse	weakly classified	strongly classified
2	Evaluation orientation	presences	absences
3	Control	implicit	explicit
4	Pedagogic text	acquirer	performance
5	Autonomy	high	low/high
6	Economy	high cost	low cost

Reproduced from Bernstein 1996: 58

their behaviour – their texts – are more likely to be interpreted as manifestations of inner competence, rather than as manifestations of specialist (disciplinary) discourse.

Performance models are characterized by strong classification and framing. Instructional discourse is relatively explicit and children are expected to reproduce rather than reconstruct knowledge. Surveillance within these contexts focuses on the realization of subject (discipline) criteria. From the child's perspective, the criteria for achieving a legitimate text are made relatively explicit. Success relies less on producing a personal or original text and more on reproducing specialist (disciplinary) criteria. Although fewer of the children's personal attributes, intentions and styles are used as criteria for control, children become easily classified as successful and less successful, precisely because the subject (discipline) criteria are publicly available.

These two models can therefore be seen as two opposing forms of power (classification) and control (framing). Within any school or any classroom we would expect to find a patterning of practice which might tend more towards one of these poles. The theory allows macro relations (social structures) to be recovered from micro interaction (classroom practice) and vice versa. Thus it provides the rules which link descriptions of the surface structure of classroom organization to models of social relations. Children will be controlled in different ways according to which model dominates in a specific classroom.

The study

We chose to work in three types of school that approximated towards a competence model (Copse Junior and Infant Schools), a performance model (Dart Infant and Junior Schools) and a compromise between the two (St Anne's Junior and a feeder school, St Helen's). We mapped and described the recognition and realization rules available in each of twelve classrooms; two parallel Year 5 and two parallel Year 1 classrooms in each school. By mapping classroom practices, we showed how activities and material culture interacted in ways that provided children with different experiences of boundaries, regularities and difference. We also demonstrated that some recognition and realization rules were less salient to younger children than to older children irrespective of pedagogic modality (see Ivinson 1998a and 2000; Ivinson and Duveen 2005). In this chapter we focus first on the imaginary subject projected by teachers' pedagogic discourses in different schools, and subsequently examine how children experienced the regulative control of each pedagogic model.

The imaginary subject and pedagogic modes

Analysis of classroom discourses drawn from across the observational period is presented as a way of describing how the boundary between interiority and exteriority was differentially drawn in different classrooms, legitimating of different imaginary subjects in each school. In Copse School the pedagogic mode tended towards the competence mode (see Ivinson 1998a for a full description of the recognition and realization in this school). The school placed great emphasis on achieving a sense of community, on co-operative work and on sharing activities. Children had no fixed place to sit and were often invited to choose where to sit. Group work was introduced as 'fun' and 'exciting' and children were often asked to work with a friend in order to share ideas. Even the weekly spelling test involved working in pairs. Most of the written work involved sheets of paper and, although children had some identifiable exercise books (for example, for language work), they were not used regularly. Great emphasis was placed on preparing work for display. In the following extract Mr H introduced a creative writing activity to his Year 5 class.

The children were sitting on the carpet area around the teacher's comfortable chair as he explained the value of 'conferencing' which involved discussing ideas for a story with a friend:

Mr H: The first stage then, is just talking about a few ideas ... um ... for the title or for the plot of your story ... and getting some really good ideas. If you've got conference pairs, you've got A and B [gestures – puts his hands out in front of him like puppets]. A and B both want to get a lot out of this little chat, this conference, because at the end of it A wants to go away with some great ideas for a story and B wants to go away with great ideas for a story. Do you think they go away with the same ideas for the story or do they go away with different ideas for a story, or what do you think?

[two boys' and two girls' hands go up]

Mr H: Anthony?

A: Same.

Mr H: You think they can go away with the same ideas. Anybody else got another idea? ... Emma?

E: They go away with different ones.

Mr H: Exactly, you're both right. .. you're both right, Anthony and Emma. You could go away with the same ideas or similar anyway, well not exactly the same, it's impossible to write the same story unless you're actually sitting together ... um ... similar ideas, or completely different.

At the beginning of the extract the teacher asked if the 'conference' pair of children would go away with the same or with different ideas. Even though Anthony and Emma gave him opposing answers he accepted them both, saying 'Exactly, you're both right'. On occasions Mr H explicitly told children not to panic before sending them off to undertake individual work. And while Mr H's comments suggested that both children's ideas were of equal value and therefore each was legitimate, his pedagogic discourse involved a representation of the children as having certain qualities that differentiated them as individuals. A thematic analysis of pedagogic discourses demonstrated that metaphors about the brain, energy and potential were prevalent in Mr H's discourse.

Mr H: I'm interested to know how your brains work, how they work. I'm interested in how you work with each other, you don't scream at each other.

His comment suggests that ideas could be generated as a result of a synergy between two brains, and in the following quotation as a kind of force, which could propel children, 'whizzing up':

Mr H: You have got potential. You have got potential in you, brains to go whizzing up, to go not down but whizzing up, really extend yourself.

The following extracts are from a mathematics lesson in which Mr H tried to grapple with why some children could work things out more quickly than others:

Mr H: I don't understand it. Some people have brains that work things out really quickly and they don't care.

Mr H: Your brains should have thought, well that's strange. It should be a hexagon.

His comments reveal an underlying social representation of the brain as a kind of internal motor that provides the energy for working out problems. Accordingly it would seem that some children naturally have faster brains than others. Brains work things out and children who failed to work things out were accused of being lazy.

The *imaginary subject* projected by this pedagogic discourse is the self-actualizing agent. Interiority was signalled by metaphors of the brain, potential energy and a collaborative synergy. Achievement was viewed as a consequence of the children's ability to access natural energy. During the creative writing lesson, Mr H told children that they could work with a partner to generate ideas and afterwards they would have to split up in order to write. Working individually was presented as a frightening and lonely experience from which the child would be saved by being allowed to return to their partner. Underlying such discourse was a sense that children work best when in community with each other.

In Dart School, knowledge was recontextualized in line with a performance pedagogic mode. Children sat in the same place each lesson and in one classroom the desks were arranged in rows facing the blackboard. Children marked out their place with personal equipment such as pencil holders. The day was divided up into periods of around one hour in length. A timetable displayed when subjects such as mathematics, English, science, religious studies and computer work were undertaken. Each child owned twelve colour-coded exercise books corresponding to curriculum subjects. These books were kept in a drawer below each individual table. There was no group work and children rarely left their designated desk.

During one geography lesson in a Year 5 class the teacher, Mrs S, sat behind her desk instructing the class in map reading. Children sat at their desks with two photocopied maps in front of them. The following extract came near the beginning of the lesson. The names of the places on the map have been changed.

Mrs S: You will see most of this land is in this area ... It has mountains, but not high one ... Close to us are the range of mountains that go just below the river Splash. What is the name printed on the map? ... Oh dear I don't think so. You are not looking at the Splash? ... (ten children have their hands up). Maybe we had better check you know where the river Splash is. Put your finger on the Splash. [Teacher looks round the class to check every child has a finger on the river.] Right, look at the top of the map. Put your finger on Swale. Go out of Flint with your finger. Go round to Ridge and Long. Now transfer your eye from that map to the bottom map. Take your finger and eyes down from the top map to the bottom map. Where is your finger Kevin? You did not do what I asked you to do, did you?

[as the instruction continues a girl comes to the door]

Mrs S: Come in.

G1: Would Adam like to ...

Mrs S: I am sure he would *like* to go. Very much. Off you go, Adam.

Only ten children out of the class of thirty-four put their hands up to answer her question, 'What is the name printed on the map?' Mrs S spent some time giving detailed instructions about how to read the map. Looking round the class she saw that Kevin had his finger on the wrong place and said, 'You did not do what I asked you to do'. The reprimand was direct and made it clear that children were expected to follow her detailed instructions to the letter.

The extract was typical of the teacher's instructional discourse. The extent to which individuality was not tolerated can be illustrated by considering what happened when a girl came to the classroom with a message – she said, 'Would Adam like to go ...'. Mrs S replied by repeating the word 'like'. 'I am sure he would *like* to go'. Her objection to the word 'like' suggested that the girl had attributed more agency to Adam than befitted his role as a pupil. This clash between the teacher and some children's socio-linguistic codes was noticeable in Dart School in both classrooms on a number of occasions. The final extract from the same geography lesson illustrates a similar kind of clash.

Mrs S: What is one thing you can tell me about South East England?
B1:   (a boy gives an answer)
Mrs S: No.
Tom: Is it where we live?
Mrs S: It is. Well done, Tom. That is exactly the answer I wanted, except you should have said, it is the area in which we live, not, is it the region in which we live. I had given you a question. You had to give me an answer.

Mrs S's explanation to Tom about the correct form in which he should reply provides a model of legitimate teacher–child interaction. She said, 'I had given you a question. You had to give me an answer.' Tom's phrase, 'Is it where we live?' implicates the teacher in the construction of the correct answer, and so blurs the teacher–child roles. In contrast, this form of response met with great approval in St Anne's School and Copse School even to the extent of providing one of the markers of the teachers' imaginary subject.

The insistence on rule-following demonstrated that, at this stage in their academic careers, children were expected to reproduce knowledge and con-form to the hierarchical structure of the regulative order. In one lesson Mrs S addressed Sophie on a number of occasions:

> You are doing what you want to do again, Sophie. You will have to learn that sometimes you have to do what everyone else does.
>
> Sophie, you take too much for granted. You are a naughty girl.
>
> If that is what you want to do, you do it. You are saying you are ignoring what is in the book and what I told you, just fine.

In Dart School, in contrast to Copse School, children were expected to learn to follow the rules. There was no expectation that children would produce original work and the emphasis was placed on controlling children's inner force. Typical comments were:

> You were not careful enough. If you had been careful and you followed the instructions properly it will turn out right. If you are not careful, it won't.

> You need to follow instructions carefully, then it will come out right.

> Listen very carefully, because the next part of the afternoon is going to be a bit different. Listen very carefully when you do a … requires a lot of common sense.

Mrs S insisted on conformity. Spontaneity, even in art lessons, was constrained; children's art productions were remarkably similar. The imaginary subject projected by performance modes is an other-realizing agent.

The other schools, St Anne's and St Helen's, reflected a mid-point between competence and performance modes. The morning consisted of structured activities and the afternoon involved project work with more collaborative possibilities. Children were not expected to co-operate with each other and the emphasis was placed on self-organization and independent work. Autonomous decision-making rather than rule-following was encouraged. This is suggestive of a society in which individuals are expected to demonstrate a degree of assertiveness and being articulate is an essential requirement. Children were neither expected to work in natural harmony with peers nor required to be subservient to teachers.

The imaginary subject – summary

In each classroom imaginary subjects projected by each teacher's pedagogic discourse were identified. A distinction between the *self-actualizing* and the *other-realizing* imaginary subjects can be seen to correspond to competence and performance modes of pedagogic discourses respectively. A representation of an imaginary subject as a self-actualizing agent was found in Copse School (competence mode) in which weak classification and framing resulted in an emphasis on individual choice, freedom and movement. The semiotic relays afforded by equipment, space and time signalled communality. In contrast, a representation of an imaginary subject as an other-realizing agent was found in Dart School, which had strong classification and framing. Recognition and realization rules supporting specific subjects were plentiful and the semiotic relays afforded by the material culture of the classroom supported individual work. Underlying Mrs S's pedagogic discourse was a representation of an imaginary subject in which unruly inner forces needed to be suppressed. In these classrooms movement was restricted; teachers demanded subservience and children were expected to reproduce knowledge as well as to conform to a hierarchical social order in which the teacher was the authority. It provided a good example of what Bernstein referred to as a long apprenticeship in a progression from 'concrete local knowledge, to the mastery of simple operations, to more general principles' (1996: 26).

When pedagogic discourse projects a self-actualizing agent, the boundary between the individual and the social privileges the individual initiative. There are two possible ways to imagine the social in these cases. Either the social is represented as ordered and therefore can provide the structuration (in Piaget's sense) from which consciousness will arise, or, as in psychological debates about neoliberalism, ideology has lost faith in the social as a possible source of structure, so placing the burden for producing order on the individual, reflected in prevalent images of the life-long learner surviving independently of state welfare. There is a sense of the individual having to delve deep within to find resources that will compensate for a lack of social or state support. Bernstein identified this identity construction as introjected. He states, 'competence modes are therapeutic and are directly linked to symbolic control' (1996: 68).

Performance modes imply that society is already regulated and children have to learn to recognize and reproduce it. Individual initiative is thought to result in chaotic activity. Here the child is expected to find his or her place within an already existing economic structure. The worker has to follow the rules as in Fordism. Bernstein identified the identity construction of the performance mode as projected. 'Here the performance is dependent upon the economic and the discourse is explicitly applied' (Bernstein 1996: 70).

Children's recontextualizations of knowledge

If the discursive practices of teachers are influenced by the imaginary subjects corresponding to different pedagogic modes, it is then also interesting to explore the ways in which these different patterns of discourse in their turn influence the recontextualization of knowledge by children as they develop their own representations of the curriculum. One of the instruments developed to investigate the ways in which children interpreted the semiotic field of the classroom was a modified version of Kelly's (1955) repertory grid technique. Children were presented with various combinations of subjects in groups of three and were asked to choose which two were similar and which was different. They provided oral justifications of similarity and difference. The task yielded both quantitative and qualitative data. Each child produced twenty-two utterances that were transcribed and coded using a scheme with three main categories of talk: feature, function and structure (see Ivinson 1998 a and b). Feature talk arises when the child is only able to attend to the surface features of subjects such as which books and equipment are associated with them. The relation between the sign – the word naming a subject – and the signifier – the utterance – relied on concrete, context-embedded clues that did not refer to the self.

Table 7.2 Coding scheme with examples of children's talk

Feature talk	
'Cos they both sort of go together, sounds like.	Year 5
Both to do with words.	Year 5

Function	
You can read them all.	Year 5
These are all things that you use for work like pens, and scissors and things.	Year 5

Structure talk	
To do with history. The history book.	Year 5
This is the English group because you've got dictionary, computer, an English board and an English folder. Now English board has got all types of English on, magic, and the computer is mainly used for English.	Year 5

Other talk	
I ain't got nothing for them two.	Year 5
I couldn't find any other reason.	Year 5

In function talk, the self was referred to as the subject in a general classroom activity or in terms of performing functions with the equipment. Descriptions were characterized by action verbs relating to classroom activities, although curricular elements were not named. The self and equipment used were not clearly differentiated, making the relationship between the signifier and the signified context-dependent.

Structure talk used abstract verbs, such as learning, concentrating and practising, indicating that representations had become context-independent. Subjects were named, suggesting that children had acquired categories or signs for them. The relationship between the signifier and the signified was characterized by sign use. Examples are provided in Table 7.2.

One dimension in which children spoke about classroom activities was in terms of an opposition between mobility and stability (Ivinson and Duveen 2005). Stability reflected activities for which they had to sit at a table, on a chair holding a pencil. Mobility reflected activities that afforded relative freedom of movement. Children described when and where they sat, stood, moved and which parts of the body they used to listen, to do art and particularly to do physical education. The first pedagogic regulation is a regulation of the body. While this form of regulation dominated the talk of Year 1 classes in all of the schools we observed, by Year 5 other dimensions appeared in children's talk as differences between pedagogic modes became more important features of these children's utterances. Indeed, by Year 5 children in all the classrooms produced relatively little feature talk, so the rest of this section concentrates on function and structure talk to illustrate how children experienced pedagogic modes.

Function talk

By Year 5 the opposition between stability and mobility had started to become separated from the body and was expressed through functions. Functions were sometimes differentiated by place and movement and these were often related to constraint and autonomy:

> Just sit down and listen to a story. PE you're up on your feet, jump. You can do anything, jump, skip.
>
> (Year 5 Boy, Copse School)

> You're not working hard, writing down on a piece of paper, you're not working for your own.
>
> (Year 5 Girl, Copse School)

Categories do not remain static, they undergo transformation according to the structuration afforded by pedagogic practice and the developing socio-cognitive resources of children. The opposition between work and play became an opposition between activities that were described as relatively open or closed. However, in descriptions that pointed to closure, children often mentioned mental states. In general the activities linked to the body and posture were differentiated from those associated with the mind. One boy described, 'listening with your ears' and 'using your brain for your own things that you're doing' and continued:

> 'cos in story time you're listening again, you're and in English and spelling you're writing down and you're using your brain for your own things that you're doing. Is listening and you're not doing anything the only thing that you're doing is with your ears. You're just listening with your ears. English and spelling, not listening to somebody, you're listening to your brain really and writing down.
>
> (Year 5 Boy, Copse School)

According to some descriptions, learning was associated with being able to re-do something.

> You can learn a lot in PE but you don't. You can fall over in PE but you can do it again. In story time and art if you make a mistake, you can do it again, but you learn it. In PE you just fall over it … you're like you can fall over, you can't really learn not to fall over.
>
> (Year 5 Girl, Copse School)

Falling over did not count as learning because the act has been completely fixed within the here and now of the acting. Subject knowledge was presented as if there was a greater distance between the acting and the consequences of the action, opening up a space for revision, for practice and therefore for re-doing. Repetition meant that you can correct your mistakes and this constituted learning for some Year 5 children. These examples of recognition and realization rules indicate both the functional necessity of classroom life and the beginning of reflective awareness.

Knowledge was represented as gaining distance from concrete, physical activities which could not be re-done. The contrast between the physical, the immediate and the embodied on the one hand and the malleable, flexible properties associated with the mental on the other was reworked and articulated in a variety of ways by children in each of the junior classrooms.

Structure talk

In Dart school, categories became disconnected from the body and started to work as fully symbolic categories that were decontextualized from the local, concrete, here and now of classroom practice. Mastery is achieved through sign use: the ability to name and thus objectify curriculum elements. One of the most sophisticated utterances came from a Year 5 boy in Dart Junior School in his account of the similarities (S) and differences (D) among curriculum elements (each number identifies the specific triad for his utterances). Abstract verbs were taken as one of the indicators of structure talk. In the example below, 'learning', an abstract verb, was used a number of times (turns 3, 4, 5, 14, 17 and 19). Other abstract terms such as 'working things out' (turn 2) and 'create' (turn 3) were also used.

1 S Have to work things out in both of them, experiments, maths.

2 D Writing, doing things, speech, not writing in maths and science, working things out.

3 S About learning things, reading is reading a book, sometimes fictional. Create something from them. Technology, notes, history have to write a whole load from five lines.

4 D Learning things, fictional characters, not reading in real life.

5 S About learning about people things. Geography is all about places and so is music, where instruments come from. Art is just painting, nothing to do with landscapes and people unless you paint people.

6 D Art is about painting fictional things, sometimes paint landscapes, not in school.

14 D About learning about yourself, people, life, what can damage you, smoking, bad pollution, car, people … put up with air.

17 S Technology is making things, not learning (what's) already there.

18 D RE is about learning about faith, people who live in different places. (Mostly) olden days, (faiths) too in RE, could be about Muslims and history could be Muslims, long time ago, them and their (faith).

19 S Learn about things, capitals, speech. RE, real people.

20 D Science is about what can damage you, hurt you. PE learn what
can keep people fit, about people and yourself.

(Year 5 Boy, Dart Junior School)

This boy was able to talk about the disciplinary subjects themselves, differentiating the school context from 'real life' (turn 4). In turn 11 (below), he demonstrated a complex abstract understanding of mathematics when he justified choosing mathematics and technology as similar and PE as different. He suggested that PE was concrete – that it was action-bound – while for him mathematics and technology were in a sense constructive because the basic or raw information 'becomes something bigger than you started from'. This demonstrates an understanding of mental activity. Later, he suggested that technology was not 'learning something' because the (raw material) was already given. Mathematics was about 'working things out' (turn 1) and technology was making things (turn 17). Mathematics was described by this boy as the most 'mental' because information (possibly mathematical symbols) could be 'expanded' beyond what was already there.

Take a bit of information and create something from it. Take, expand it into something that is really. Maths, expand it, create something.

(Turn 11)

In contrast, actions such as running and play remained embedded in the immediate context and did not in some way grow beyond themselves:

Action, run, play. Not like taking information and making it into something much bigger than you started from.

(Turn 12)

Learning was associated with RE (religious education) and English (fictional characters – turn 4) and as something which arose initially from books (turn 3) rather than from 'real life' (turn 4). Art was also considered to be fictional (turn 6) and not to do with real life which was indicated by 'landscapes and people' (turn 5). Art was not to do with things that went on in school (turn 6) but was to do with fiction (not real), the imagination and things found in books (ideas). For this boy, art encompassed literature.

Geography was about 'real people' and about (real) places (turn 5) and so was music (turn 5) which was connected to people and places (humanities or social sciences). PE and science were about diagnosing problems to do with the body (fitness) and the environment (pollution).

Four main distinctions emerged: those which related to construction and working out (mathematics, technology); those which were fictional, imaginative and not real (English, art and religious education); those which were about (real) people and places (geography and music); and those which involved an accumulated body of knowledge and which provided information (science and physical education).

Table 7.3 Number of Year 5 children in each classroom for whom 50 per cent or more of their utterances were coded as 'structure' talk

School	Boys	Girls	Subtotal	Number of children per class
Copse Junior				
C7	3	4	7	20
C8	3	4	7	20
St Anne's Junior				
C9	3	7	10	20
C10	0	1	1	20
Dart Junior				
C11	7	6	13	20
C12	9	8	17	20
Total	25	30	55	120

Structure talk indicates a further qualitative change in the social representation of the curriculum and was found to underlie the talk of children especially from Dart Junior School, demonstrating that they had, in Piaget's terms, 'de-centred' to the extent that all eleven curriculum elements had become objectified. Children who could call upon signification associated with structure talk had an impressive ability to elaborate the differences and similarities between curriculum elements. They used a number of dimensions such as real–imaginary, fact–fiction, working out–learning, linear–multiple forms, generative–static and past–future to describe the curriculum.

While structure talk was most commonly observed in Dart School, it was also present in the talk of children in the other schools, but to a lesser degree (see Table 7.3).

Thirty out of the forty children in Dart School were using structure talk in at least half of their utterances. By contrast, in Copse School only fourteen out of forty children were reaching this level and in St Anne's School it was only eleven out of forty. The influence of differences in pedagogic modes in structuring children's talk is evident from these figures, with structure talk being more closely linked to the performance model of Dart School.

Concluding remarks

The first part of the paper focused on the imaginary subjects projected by pedagogic modes and the recognition and realization rules related to these modes. The second part focused on children's reconstruction of the curriculum by pedagogic mode. The weak classification and framing found in Copse School allowed plenty of scope for children's constructive efforts to be realized. In these classrooms, there was room for children to engage in extensive forms of interaction and negotiation often completely unnoticed by teachers. Indeed, children were observed bartering with goods such as small toys, pencils and picture cards. There was much talk of liaisons with children of the opposite sex, particularly among girls. At times these interactions became overwhelming for some children who were seen running out of the classroom to escape to the toilets, sometimes to cry. The danger in Copse School was that peer-group interaction was consuming a great deal of the children's attention and making it difficult to focus on activities set by the teacher. The self-actualizing that was expected from children in Copse School tended to spill out into peer culture. Peer-initiated power structures were operating strongly in these classrooms, making it difficult for children to find protected spaces in which they could take a break from the need for total self-actualization.

In some respects the control retained by the teachers in Dart School was authoritarian, blocking children's autonomy and self-actualization. Yet on the other hand, once within the protected space of their desk, their books and the imposed curriculum activities, children had the opportunity to escape from peer culture and at times to escape from the regulative gaze of the teacher. Children were being confronted with different subjectivities as well as different social organizations in Dart School. They were developing different forms of categorization. Not only were they learning different forms of knowledge, they were also being encouraged to foster different attitudes towards knowledge.

The strong curriculum structuration in Dart School allowed children to develop more abstract curriculum categories with which to grasp the elements of the curriculum and to become self-reflexive agents. The ability to escape the here and now of classroom life gives children the possibility to recognize the forms of regulation that they are being subjected to, even if they remain relatively powerless to change them. When curriculum experiences remain tied to the body and functional necessities, there is less possibility of children coming to recognize and resist the forms of regulation that they are being subjected to.

We can then draw the threads of this discussion together by adding, as it were, a further line of contrasting characterization to Bernstein's model of the recontextualization of knowledge (see Table 7.1) which refers to the *imaginary subject* constructed by teachers. In the competence model, where there is weak classification and framing, this imaginary subject is constructed as a self-actualizing subject, while under the stronger classification and framing of the performance model, the imaginary subject is constructed as an other-realized subject. These different imaginary subjects inform the pedagogic practice of the teachers in different curriculum contexts, and, as we have seen, thereby also influence the representations of the curriculum which develop among the children, representations which include constructions not only of the form of knowledge legitimated in each context, but equally, of the type of person who is legitimated by the particular form of pedagogic discourse in a classroom.

However, to take a long-term perspective, those children who experience creative self-actualization at some point in their life have it as a pattern that they can draw upon in the future. Those who have only experienced authoritarian regulation have only this to draw upon in later life. While the experience of creative self-actualization may appear chaotic and tight regulation may appear to be authoritarian it is important to consider what each mode is making available to children for imagining future subjectivities.

Note

1　The utterances produced by children in two specially designed tasks – one, a sorting task involving aspects of the material culture from their own classroom, and one based on Kelly's (1955) repertory grid technique – were coded as feature, function, structure and other talk. The coding scheme can be found in Ivinson 1998a, 1998b. Further reports of the two research instruments can be found in Ivinson 1998a, 1998b, 2000; Ivinson and Duveen, 2005).

Part III

Professional knowledge and pedagogic change

8 Languages of description and the education of researchers

Andrew Brown

In the course of his academic career Basil Bernstein was engaged in a wide range of empirical work, often in collaboration with colleagues and research students. Through this work he developed a distinctive approach to social and educational research, which in turn influenced his teaching and research student supervision as well as his critical engagement with empirical work by colleagues, collaborators and others. In his later writing, Bernstein began to explore more explicitly the relationship between his theoretical work and his approach to research, an interest that is evident in the subtitle of his last book: theory, research, critique.

One particular concern for Bernstein was the manner in which the 'new official research economy' was acting both to place limits on the design and conduct of funded research and to reframe the doctorate, with its increasing emphasis on research training, 'as a driving licence rather than a licence to explore' (Bernstein, 1996, p. 135). Research students were, Bernstein argued, increasingly offered a menu of approaches and methods that were abstracted from the practice and process of doing research, thus rendering research as a set of technical choices or procedures. His concern was that choices of procedure would ultimately be determined by the economic context in which the research is positioned, rather than the 'necessity of the research' itself. The economic pressures on funded research were seen as limiting the time available to researchers, which in turn limited the approaches and methods that could be adopted. Similar limitations were seen as being placed on research students by conceiving of the doctorate as principally a professional training programme, the content of which was in danger of rendering research in predominantly technical terms and the scope of which placed limits on the time available for research and thus limited the form that doctoral research could take. It was against this background that Bernstein (1996, pp. 134–144), in the paper 'Research and Languages of Description', elaborated the notion of research as the development of languages of description, an idea that had been implicit in his earlier writing, and explicit in his teaching and work with doctoral students and colleagues (see also Dowling, 1998; Moss, 2001). The process of analysis was presented as the construction of translation devices that both highlight and attempt to traverse the discursive gap between the 'internal' models and descriptions derived from theory and the 'enactments' of the researched, with the consequent potential for transformation of theory and ability to accord 'respect for the researched'. Bernstein presented this conceptualization of research as generally applicable to a range of modes of enquiry, from experimental research to ethnography, and gave examples of its application. This approach, however, is a time-consuming process that requires extensive, and thus expensive, engagement with empirical texts, which Bernstein somewhat gloomily concludes is likely to come at too great a cost for the strictures of new research economy.

In this paper I want to explore some of the changes that have taken place in the education of researchers in the ten years since Bernstein's paper. Whilst the PhD has, in this period, become ever more strongly identified with the training of new generations of researchers, with increasing emphasis on explicit acquisition and assessment of generic and transferable skills, this has clearly generated a number of tensions in the field of educational research that have yet to be resolved. The steadily growing interest in 'mixed methods' research has, in particular, had an impact on doctoral education, including a perceived need for broad-based education in research that encompasses the collection and analysis of both qualitative and quantitative data. Alongside this there has been growth in 'professional doctorates' (principally, in the field of education, the Doctor of Education (EdD) degree), which has signalled a shift in both the sites and agents of the production of knowledge. Doctorates have thus become a means for the education of both professional researchers and researching professionals. These tensions and developments open up new challenges and possibilities for 'research education' (a term I am using in preference to 'research training'). In exploring these I will return to, and illustrate, the potential of the approach to social research advocated by Bernstein, not only for the conduct of social and educational research per se, but also for learning and teaching research and for the establishment of a productive relationship between research and professional practice.

Broad-based training and generic skills

In the UK, the Economic and Social Research Council (ESRC), the government agency responsible for funding social research, has increasingly presented the PhD as a means of training successive generations of professional researchers. The most recent postgraduate research training guidelines (ESRC, 2005) follow earlier editions in placing heavy emphasis on transferable skills, stating that:

> Whatever career paths research students may follow, there are clear advantages to students if they have acquired general research skills and transferable employment-related skills.

(p. 18)

The generic skills listed thus have a strong professional orientation and include language, teaching, bibliographic and computing skills and familiarity with legal, ethical and intellectual property rights issues. They further mark out a range of personal development and employment-related skills, such as communication, management and team-working skills. The generic research skills cover the design, conduct and dissemination of research and include specific items on research design and the collection and analysis of data. Students are required to understand the rationale for and relationship between qualitative and quantitative work and to understand alternative epistemological positions and approaches to research. All students, whatever the form and focus of their research, are required to become competent in specific techniques of data collection and of both qualitative and quantitative data analysis. The subject-specific education guidelines follow the same general approach, stressing the need to develop a facility with a 'range' of approaches, strategies, designs and methods (ESRC, 2005, pp. 36–37).

The guidelines operate within a training paradigm. The skills and competences are to be acquired through a structured programme, and programmes are required to indicate how acquisition is formally assessed. A range of approaches is marked out and content is delineated with varying degrees of specificity. The skills and understandings associated with these approaches are underpinned by a set of generic skills that enable individuals to operate effectively as professional researchers and to move into other domains of practice. This approach implies a fragmented curriculum with strong insulation between individual elements (in order that they may be distinguished and recognized) and clear specification of the criteria for the evaluation of acquisition (in order that students can be judged to have acquired the skills). Although elements can be combined, the danger here is that the resulting programme will lack coherence. Methods become easily reduced to tools (as they are frequently described in the guidelines) and their utilization a matter of technique. Research consequently runs the risk of collapsing into pastiche. Skills and understandings that might be seen as being tacitly acquired through the process of engaging with and doing research become prerequisites for competent researchers, and thus the explicit focus of research training programmes.

Mixing methods

In a consultation exercise to ascertain the professional development needs of researchers and identify specific areas for capacity building, key stakeholders representing the major constituencies of educational research in the UK expressed concern about the poor quality of much educational research (Taylor, 2002). They also stated that researchers appeared to lack skills in both qualitative and quantitative research, that research training was lacking in breadth and that there was a tendency for researchers to adopt relatively narrow fixed 'methodological identities' that act to stifle debate and limit the form, scope and relevance of the research conducted. Prominent amongst the areas identified for the professional development of researchers was being able to combine qualitative and quantitative approaches and to develop and use new methods.

As Tashakkori and Teddlie (2003), editors of the *Handbook of Mixed Methods in Social and Behavioral Research,* have observed, the insulation of qualitative from quantitative research is also being challenged in the US and elsewhere. They note that an:

> intense demand originating from applied research for the professional development and preparation of researchers competent in both areas is gradually changing the way people think about and teach research methods.
>
> (p. 63)

They define the mixed-method approach as:

> the type of research in which a qualitative and a quantitative data collection procedure (e.g. a personality inventory and focus group interview) or research method (e.g. ethnography and field experiment) is used to answer the research questions.
>
> (p. 62)

Accordingly, the research training programme they present covers a wide range of data collection techniques and approaches to the analysis of both qualitative and quantitative data. One of the difficulties of programmes of this kind is that they lack coherence, as methods are presented as theoretically and methodologically neutral and thus, like the menu of methods that concerned Bernstein, become unrelated elements in a collection of possible research tools. Tashakkori and Teddlie (2003, p. 74) attempt to achieve coherence in their mixed-methods programme by adopting a 'pragmatist approach'. The programme is organized around the principle that the selection of methods to address a given research question is a matter of fitness for purpose. Here the research question dictates the choices subsequently made by the researcher.

At the very beginning of their training programme they consider 'the paradigm wars and their dénouement through the use of the pragmatist philosophy' and subsequently champion 'the dictatorship of the research question' (Tashakkori and Teddlie, 2003, p. 65). They are clearly aware of the possibility that a mixed-methods course, conceived of as the presentation of a range of disconnected methods or tools for the collection and analysis of data, will collapse into a technical enterprise with little conceptual coherence. However, the recourse to a particular philosophical perspective, in this case pragmatism, alienates alternative positions. The desire to move beyond warring paradigms to create the possibility of reduced insulation between approaches and the development of new methodological configurations, whilst imposing a particular epistemological framework, leads to a new form of agonistic relation and the reinforcement of epistemological boundaries.

Epistemological oppositions

There is a countervailing tendency amongst educational researchers, which is also evident in the ESRC guidelines. This emphasizes the importance of:

> understanding the significance of alternative epistemological positions that provide the context for theory construction, research design, and the selection of appropriate analytical techniques.
>
> (ESRC, 2005, p. 23)

Similarly, in mapping the specific requirements for educational researchers it is stated that students 'should have training in philosophical issues in educational research' and that this should include 'epistemological and ontological issues in the philosophy of social science and the philosophical underpinnings of educational theories' and 'the philosophical assumptions underlying different methods of empirical enquiry' (ESRC, 2005, p. 36). This interest in the epistemological foundations of different approaches sits uneasily with technical or pragmatist orientations. Furlong (2003) takes up this issue and argues that for educational research to reach maturity, it is necessary to 'recognize the richness and diversity of the research community, tolerate differences and contradictions and promote dialogue' and 'insist that each different subcommunity engages in its own robust review of what quality is and how it can be promoted' (Furlong, 2003, online). Like Tashakkori and Teddlie (2003), Furlong acknowledges the harm done to educational and social research by earlier 'paradigm wars'. Epistemological debate, Furlong argues, is in principle healthy, but becomes damaging when researchers trivialize what they see as opposing positions, refuse to recognize the complexity of the issues in question and slide into personal attack and acrimony. He states that educational researchers 'must, as a community, rise above such divisions, recognize our differences but also the potential contributions of different research traditions' (Furlong, 2003, online).

With the shift to a research training paradigm this position also becomes problematic. It is difficult to see how, with the demand that research students become competent in a comprehensive range of approaches, induction into these traditions, with a full appreciation of the foundations of each approach, can take place. Furthermore, educational researchers rarely follow a tidy pathway from undergraduate study in education to postgraduate to research degree to research career (Taylor, 2002). Rather, they are likely to come from diverse disciplinary backgrounds, sometimes relating not to social science but to the subject they teach or their area of professional expertise and experience.

Education could more appropriately be seen, in Bernstein's (1996) terms, as a region of knowledge rather than a discipline. Educational research provides a space for the concurrence of a range of disciplinary perspectives, sometimes working together in an interdisciplinary manner, sometimes providing different perspectives on areas of common interest, sometimes producing critical commentaries on each other. This space also holds the potential for new perspectives and new forms of research. In order to realize this potential, researchers have to have both an understanding of a range of approaches and forms of research and some sense of their own specialized knowledge. The research education provided does have to give the opportunity both to develop a sound understanding of a wide range of approaches and perspectives and to gain specialized knowledge and skills. Here, however, a distinction is being made between a form of educational research literacy, which allows access and informed participation to the general field of educational research, and specialized induction into a particular community or communities of research practice.

Diversification of doctoral studies

It may be that the impact of technically oriented research training approaches will ultimately be limited. In the UK, the diversification of forms of doctoral level study could be one factor in this. For instance, the PhD Plus, initiated by the government higher education funding council and billed as 'a doctorate for the 21st century', takes the idea of a doctorate as training for a research career in a different direction by incorporating into the programme a one-year research-based internship in a professional research setting. This begins to acknowledge that developing research practice in context might, as theories of cognition in practice and situated learning suggest (Rogoff and Lave, 1984; Lave, 1988; Lave and Wenger, 1991; Wenger, 1998), be more effective than decontextualized training. This form of professional research apprenticeship is clearly very different from the type formerly offered by working intensively, and almost exclusively, with a thesis supervisor, and will induct research students into a very different form of practice.

The NewRoutePhD™, another recent government-sponsored initiative, presents a further challenge to dominant notions of doctoral and research education. Claiming to recast the UK doctorate to meet the demands of the global knowledge economy, it focuses on the development of broad-based transferable skills in relation to business, rather than academic or research, practices.

> The NewRoutePhD™ is a PhD with real added value and will have a broad appeal to those professionals and business people who want to spearhead progress in the 21st century information economy. The programme is fully equivalent to the highly regarded traditional PhD and combines a specific research project with a coherent programme of formal coursework. This seamless programme of research methods training,

taught subject specific modules and inter-disciplinary studies will both broaden and deepen students' subject knowledge and extend their expertise in new directions.

(Online, http://www.newroutephd.ac.uk, accessed 1 August 2005)

It is difficult to know how these initiatives will develop as they are relatively new and are aimed very much at recent graduates looking at a doctorate as a preliminary step in their career development.

Possibly of greater significance in terms of research student numbers is the growth of professional doctorates (Bourner *et al.,* 2001; Lunt, 2002). These programmes are aimed at people who are already well established in a particular professional domain and who see doctoral level study, with the acquisition of advanced research skills and the opportunity to carry out their own professionally relevant research, as advancing their own professional practice and development. It is the focus on professional work that is the defining feature of this form of doctorate, reflecting a recognition that work-based learning should be extended to the highest level of academic award. A report by the UK Council of Graduate Education (UKGCE), for example, suggests that:

> the aim of the 'professional doctorate' is the personal development of the candidate coupled with the advancement of the subject or the profession. They include a substantial taught component and one or more practice-based research projects which result in the submission of a thesis or portfolio of projects which has to be defended by oral examination. The degrees are equivalent in standard to the PhD but different in their approach to the achievement of 'doctorateness'.
>
> (UKGCE, 1998, p. 6)

The research carried out in these programmes is predominantly workplace based and takes an aspect of professional practice or a professionally relevant problem as its focus. This casts research training in yet another light. Individuals, sometimes sponsored by their employers, are making a substantial investment in their own professional development. That the research skills developed and the research conducted need to be professionally and personally relevant militates against a discipline-oriented notion of 'comprehensiveness' of training, or a skills-oriented curriculum driven by national research priorities.

The development of professional doctorates constitutes yet another pressure for different forms of research education. Research questions are generated and addressed within the field of professional practice, marking the shift from Mode 1 to Mode 2 knowledge production suggested by Gibbons *et al.,* (1994). As a recent study of UK professional doctorates in engineering, business and education has demonstrated (Scott *et al.,* 2003, 2004), this challenges the established relationship between the university, knowledge production and professional practice, and raises fundamental questions about what the university brings to this relationship and, as different areas of professional practice themselves encompass diverse sets of values and conceptions of knowledge, who legitimizes knowledge and the practices of knowledge production. This is not an insubstantial challenge. Whilst some academics in education might have doubts about the status of the EdD, professional doctorates in other fields, notably engineering, have become the preferred route for professionals wishing to develop a research-driven career (Scott *et al.,* 2004).

The pedagogic potential of languages of description

Bernstein's concern in the mid-1990s was that decisions relating to the processes of research were increasingly made on economic grounds, and that this was acting to limit what form of research was possible within the context of both funded projects and research degrees. Subsequent developments in research and the education of research students in the field of education, some of which are discussed above, indicate that this concern was well founded, both in terms of funding at the level of the state and choices made at the level of the individual. The demand for accountability regarding the use of public funds for research has influenced how the quality of research is judged and how the outcomes of research are mediated to users, as well as placing time pressures on researchers and research students which, through the need to manage risk at institutional and personal levels, attenuates the willingness to adopt more open and exploratory research strategies. Of particular concern to Bernstein in this respect was the time-consuming, and risky, nature of rigorous qualitative research, which in his view required engagement with extensive, complex and multi-layered texts for which there are no appropriate routine analytical procedures or 'quick fixes'. Whilst 'botanical garden' research methods courses, in which items are 'nicely domesticated and epistemologically labelled' (Bernstein, 1996, p. 135), clearly do not provide appropriate preparation for this, it is difficult to see from Bernstein's discussion what the alternative might be. Bernstein's own teaching and supervision tended strongly towards an apprenticeship mode. For instance, presented with data collected by a student he would set to work on it, exemplifying, but not imposing, the strategies he had developed in his own work (Brown, 2001). This is an approach that relies heavily on the inspiration of the supervisor (abundant in Bernstein's case) and the time to work in a collaborative and dialogic manner, which is clearly in tension with the strictures of the new research economy.

   With more explicitly pedagogic goals in mind, Brown and Dowling (1998) address this by presenting a framework for both engaging with (reading) research and the processes of designing, conducting and disseminating (doing) research, from a position that 'understands research as a particular coherent and systematic and reflexive mode of interrogation' (p. 4). The framework acts to provoke questions about, and an active engagement with, research and helps organize a critical account of both one's own work and that of others. The approach developed is designed to allow for, indeed encourage, diversity in approaches to educational research and is motivated by the need for frameworks for inducting postgraduate students into the practices of rigorous social research. Central to this is the promotion for coherence and transparency in accounts of research. Whatever theoretical or methodological position one is adopting, the articulation of the theoretical perspective adopted and the empirical sites being investigated has to be made clear. The researcher is thus adopting a pedagogic relationship with their readership with respect to the process and products of the research. The development of the details of the design and conduct of a research study occurs through a process of empirical localizing (from a broadly defined empirical field to particular settings and methods to specific outcomes), which takes place in dialogue with a process of theoretical specializing (from a broad theoretical field to relevant research and writing to a specific research question). It is these processes and relationships that need to be uncovered in our reading of research and to be made clear in our own accounts in order to speak to, and be heard by, researchers and practitioners who perhaps do not share our, often implicit, assumptions. In doing this we also generate texts that can be used in more explicitly pedagogic contexts, to exemplify and induct practitioners and researchers, whatever professional route they are following, into the range of ways of working within education as a field of research.

It could be argued, in the current climate, that the kind of rigorous, explicit and non-circular forms of analysis promoted by Bernstein are more vital than ever. In order to counter the lack of confidence expressed in educational research, it is necessary to demonstrate that research, of whatever scale or approach, can be rigorous, illuminative and trustworthy. One part of this is to be able to make visible the process of analysis and the articulation between the empirical and the theoretical, and to open this to the critical scrutiny of others. This is particularly important if educational researchers are to manage the diversity of perspectives and approaches and to reach the necessary maturity of mutual understanding identified as a key objective by Furlong (2003). With the increase in workplace-based research conducted by practitioners working towards professional doctorates, this explicitness and transparency helps to clarify what precisely the university brings to these emerging partnerships in the production of professionally relevant knowledge. More specifically, the development of a language of description allows the possibility of integration of different approaches to research and of qualitative and quantitative data and forms of analysis in a coherent manner, which is clearly evident in Bernstein's own empirical work.

Pedagogically, the approach offers a means for induction of research students into the process of analysis by making clear how researchers have moved, in a principled manner, between theory and data. Research of this form can contribute to a growing bank of work that can be used both to illustrate the process of analysis and to provide a context for critical engagement with research, alongside the development of students' own research studies.

The process of analysis

In order to unpack the notion of analysis as the production of a language of description, and to illustrate and explore the issues relating to research and research education raised above, I am going to present, in compressed form, an example taken from a study of my own. This research was conducted as one component of a part-time PhD study (Brown, 1999). The study combines a range of forms of data and methods of data collection and employs qualitative and quantitative data analysis techniques and modes of representation. The aim of the study was to explore the socially differentiating effects of parental partic-ipation in schooling and to understand the processes underlying these effects, an interest that relates directly to my own professional background and experi-ence as a primary school teacher. The form of the study was guided by a sociological interest in the relationship between social class, orientation to schooling and pedagogic practice, and, in terms of theory, was inspired by crit-ical engagement with the work of Bernstein, Bourdieu and Foucault. The empirical focus of the study was a national (and later, international) primary school initiative to involve parents in the mathematical education of their chil-dren. This initiative, the IMPACT project (see Merttens and Vass, 1990, 1993), provided banks of mathematical activities for children and parents to do together in the home, which teachers could incorporate into their schemes of work. The study was organized as a number of interrelated pieces of research, which included: an initial ethnographic style study designed to better under-stand the culture of the project and the practices of participants; an analysis of booklets and tasks produced by teachers for parents; interviews with parents and teachers from schools with different social class intake characteristics.

The particular component of the study considered here focused on the home/school diaries completed by parents each time they carried out one of the mathematics tasks with their child. A sample of parent diaries was col-lected from schools with distinctively different intake characteristics in terms of social class (278 diaries in total, each covering one school year). The aim of the analysis was to describe the characteristics of the messages that were relayed from home to school by parents and thus look at how the parents from different social class backgrounds positioned themselves in relation to the school, teachers and school mathematics.

The idea that empirical research is centrally concerned with the produc-tion of languages of description was helpful in creating a context for the coherent and meaningful use of a range of approaches to data collection and in making explicit the processes of analysis and the relationship between theory and empirical data. Bernstein makes the distinction between internal lan-guages of description (L^1) and external languages of description (L^2). Internal languages relate to the development of conceptual frameworks; external lan-guages enable internal languages to describe phenomena beyond the internal language itself. The development of an internal language thus concerns the production of a coherent and explicit system of concepts.

Whilst these internal languages produce descriptions of empirical phenomena, and are frequently judged in terms of the adequacy of the descriptions that they produce, they do not engage in a systematic and principled manner with the empirical. In the production of social theory, for example, theorists might, in the construction of networks of concepts, evoke phenomena external to their language as exemplars, illustrations or critical cases. If we look, for instance, at the work of Anthony Giddens (for example, Giddens, 1991), we see the highly productive incorporation of references to global trends, specific events and reference to published empirical research (produced by others) into the production and elaboration of a general theory of, for example, social relations in late modernity. The aim of such theorizing is not to produce a strong set of principles for the recognition of relevant empirical phenomena, nor to develop strong principles of description of empirical phenomena. The theory produces, rather, a systematic orientation towards the empirical, a potential for movement away from general description to empirical specifics, an explanation of the empirical, but not an unambiguous specification of the principles of its description.

Internal languages will clearly vary with respect to their degree of development. A highly developed internal language will enable the production of tightly specified hypotheses or models that are open to empirical investigation. Less developed languages will produce general orientations towards the empirical and, perhaps, provide a collection of potentially productive but weakly associated concepts.

Researchers engaged in empirical investigation will bring to the field some understanding of the phenomena they are investigating. They thus bring with them some form of internal language. This might be implicit or explicit, highly developed or weakly defined. In the case of the research presented here, I came to the design and conduct of the study with both a set of professional concerns (relating to my work as a mathematics educator) and a range of theoretical (sociological) orientations. Both have played a part in the development of the problem being addressed (through a process of theoretical specialization) and the selection of specific empirical settings within which to address the problem (through a process of empirical localization). My professional concerns have been dominant in the initial selection of home–school relations and primary school mathematics as empirical fields (though this selection is mediated by my sociological concern with the (re)production of social relations in and through schooling), whilst my sociological perspective has been dominant in the conceptualization of pedagogy, home–school relations and of primary school mathematics (though the development of my accounts of these has been in dialogue with my professional understandings and concerns). In the light of these initial theoretical orientations, consideration of the contemporary relations between parents/home and teachers/school, in general, and the particular form of intervention that takes place within the IMPACT project, has given rise to a number of empirical questions and has enabled me to identify apposite empirical sites. Rather instrumentally adopting a number of high-level structuring concepts drawn from various forms of social theory, I established a dialogic relationship between theory (specialized to the particular phenomena in which I am interested) and empirical investigation (localized to particular aspects, participants and forms of data within the IMPACT project). The production of a specialized language of description of the empirical phenomena I am addressing is as much an outcome of the research as the generalized statements made on the basis of the analysis of the empirical data. The purpose of the study is both theoretical development and empirical illumination, recognizing that there cannot be one without the other.

In the presentation of the research I have attempted to be as explicit as possible in describing the movement between theory and data. In the development and presentation of my external language of description, I have been careful to elaborate terms, to give criteria for categorization of data and to provide examples. The ultimate test of a language is clearly to gauge the extent to which it can be acquired and used with a minimal level of ambiguity. Acquirers have to be able to both recognize and produce legitimate statements with a high degree of reliability. In the studies of the parent diaries and of parents' discussion of activities, the language developed is presented as a system of conceptually consistent categories organized in the form of a network (see discussion of networks below). In both cases the language is tested by training other people in its use and testing the level of agreement in both the recognition of codable units and in the actual coding of units of data according to the network. The importance here is to stress that the approach being taken seeks to make the process of movement between data and analytic statements as rigorous and explicit as possible. It attempts to establish a relationship between empirical work and theory that is non-circular and thus avoids the dominance of high-level structuring concepts. Being explicit about the treatment of data ensures that the research is open to the critical scrutiny of other researchers. Ensuring the testability of language further strengthens the statements that can be made on the basis of the analysis and maximizes the possibility of the development of a language that can be adapted and applied in other contexts. In this way it is hoped to be able to illustrate one way in which the claims for qualitative research can be strengthened. The nature of the analysis carried out in this study also enables some degree of quantification and thus blurs the customary distinction between qualitative and quantitative research.

Moving between qualitative and quantitative analysis

The entries in the parent diaries, and later sections of the parent interviews, were analysed by developing analytic networks. These were used as a device to produce a language, in the form of a system of interrelated concepts, to translate the qualities of the writing and speech of parents into theoretically recognizable terms. The networks resemble the form of semantic network developed and used in systemic functional linguistics by Halliday and colleagues (see Halliday,

1985b) and employed, in the context of sociological analysis, by Bernstein and colleagues (see Bernstein and Cook-Gumperz, 1973). In this research the networks are not used to describe language, as they are in systemic functional linguistics, but to read and render the language of parents in sociologically recognizable and meaningful terms.

With respect to the diaries, my interest is to examine *what* is relayed from home to school through the comments made by parents and *how* it is relayed. In order to explore this, I analysed diaries from schools with different intake characteristics. The process adopted in the analysis of the diaries was to work through a cross-section of the diaries and draw up a network for the classification of the responses. This network must aspire to account for all the text and be sensitive enough to address the central issues of this research. The process of analysis is dialogic, with constant movement between theory and the empirical data by means of the development of a theoretically motivated system of distinctions. In practice this involves the intensive and time-consuming process of shuttling back and forth through the diaries, adapting the analytic network, redefining distinctions, finding examples and counter-examples, coding and recoding. Once the network was stable and able to account for the comments made, all the diaries were analysed. In its final form, this network represents a system of semantic possibilities that can be used to describe the comments made by parents in the diaries. Explicit and detailed description of distinctions made in the networks also makes it possible to teach others the 'language' developed and test its application.

An initial distinction is made, with respect to the focus of each comment, between comments that relate to the acquirer and those that relate to the task. The acquirer-focused comments are subdivided into those that refer to the competence of the child (for instance, 'she was able to add the small numbers together') and those that refer to their dispositions (for example, 'John likes cutting and sticking activities'). The task-focused comments are divided into those that focus on the realization of the task (for example, 'we made a ruler from card') and those that focus on evaluation of the task (for instance, 'this was a good activity'). This gives four subsystems, differentiated in terms of the focus of the statement being described (see Figure 8.1).

The subsequent levels of the network address the form of the comment and share the same structure. A distinction is made initially between comments that are task-dependent, that is comments that refer directly to the activity of doing the task, such as 'she did some good colouring' or 'it was fun', and task-independent comments, that is those that pass beyond the context of the specific task and make more generalized statements, such as 'she knows her multiplication tables'. Task-dependent statements are then divided into those that are specific, that is they make reference to a particular aspect of the task, its realization, the child's performance and so on, and those that are unspecific. Specific comments are further divided into those that explicitly index an element of school mathematics (mathematical comments) and those that do not (non-mathematical comments). Finally, a distinction can be made between

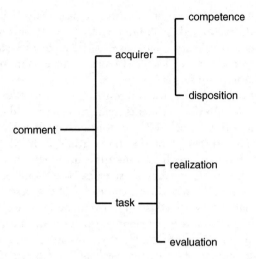

Figure 8.1 Initial levels of the diary coding network

positive and negative comments. This generates the subsequent levels of the network. Figure 8.2 shows the continuation of the network from the upper track of Figure 8.1, that is, following the acquirer competence route. The complete network is constructed by appending the additional levels shown in Figure 8.2 to each of the terminal points of the network in Figure 8.1.

In reporting the research, every distinction made has been tightly defined and examples given (see Brown, 1999). All the diaries have been analysed and all the comments made in them have been coded. Within any given diary it is possible to look at the focus and form of the comments made, and tendencies,

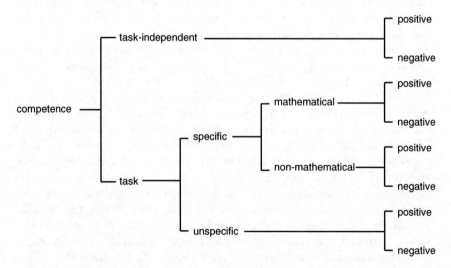

Figure 8.2 The acquirer competence subsystem

patterns and relationships within the diary. It is also possible to count incidences of particular kinds of comment and to make comparisons, for instance, between schools in terms of the social class characteristics of the intake. The distinctions made in the network are theoretically informed. The distinction between task dependence and task independence, and the relationship of this distinction to orientations towards meaning, pedagogy and social class, for instance, relate to Bernstein's theories of social class and pedagogic discourse (Bernstein, 1977, 1990, 1996). The theory informs the development of the networks, but cannot directly describe, prescribe or predict the comments of the parents in the diaries. The dialogic development of the networks enables the language of enactment to be understood in terms of the initial theory, whilst creating the potential to challenge, transform, develop or extend the theory. The potential for quantification has value in enabling a researcher to bring a greater proportion of the data explicitly into the analysis presented. The weight of evidence and argument is not held entirely by illustrative extracts, though these continue to be important in exemplification and in exploring the dynamics of particular cases. To give a simple example, parents who make context-independent comments, I have called *generalizers*. Context-independent comments say something about the child or the task that is independent of the details of the realization of the task, and as such they resemble the kinds of assessments made by teachers. Parents who do not make these kinds of comments, I have called *localizers*. Once we can define and identify generalizers and localizers through the use of the networks in coding diary entries, it is possible to make comparisons between schools. Table 8.1 summarizes the analysis by comparing the numbers of localizer and generalizer parents for classes of similar-aged children in the school with the most middle-class intake (East Wood) and the school with the most working-class intake (Chambers).

The statistically significant difference between the schools in the numbers of generalizers and localizers here suggests a possible relationship between localizing/generalizing and social class, which can be exemplified and further investigated by going back to the diary entries and the network. Similarly, it is possible to explore the volume of positive and negative comments made about the competence of the children by different groups of parents, the relative emphasis they give to the realization and the evaluation of the activities, the extent to which they draw on specialized mathematical discourse in their

Table 8.1 Distribution of generalizers and localizers amongst parents at East Wood and Chambers Schools

	East Wood	*Chambers*	*Total*
Generalizers	28	6	34
Localizers	28	48	76
Total	56	54	110

$(\chi^2 = 17.970, df=1, \text{significant at } p<0.01)$

diary comments, and so forth. A productive relationship can thus be established between qualitative and quantitative forms of data via a theoretically informed analytic framework. This form of quantification allows the outcomes of the analysis of large amounts of data to be meaningfully summarized and presented. It also paves the way for further quantitative, as well as qualitative, studies. Rather than having what, in much 'mixed method' research, are essentially two or more studies running alongside and in dialogue with each other, and operating according to their own possibly conflicting principles (see argument presented by Nash, 2002), this is an attempt to integrate methods, at the levels of both data collection and analysis, in a manner that is explicit, rigorous and open to interrogation.

Conclusion

It is clear that the context within which researchers in education, and the social sciences more generally, are educated is in a state of flux. This is a response to and reflection of changing expectations at the level of individuals embarking on research degrees, and public and private institutions engaging with research and the state. Economic factors, of the kind considered by Bernstein in 1996, are undoubtedly a major influence on practice. So, too, are shifts in the legitimation of knowledge and modes and agents of knowledge production, and stakeholder confidence in the quality and value of research. These changes are evident in the increasing variety of forms that a doctorate can take, and the diversification of people studying for doctorates, which are increasingly associated with particular career or personal trajectories and identities.

These developments have created new possibilities and challenges. Professional doctorates, and other innovative forms of doctorate, keep open questions of what is gained from a doctorate for individuals and institutions, what form of knowledge is produced and how this relates to professional and academic practice, who produces knowledge, where and how? In view of this, it is clear that the time is not right, in a fragmented field such as education, to fall back into 'paradigm wars' and other disputes that might act to undermine the credibility and strength of the field and its research community. Under these conditions, a broad-based education has to be very broad indeed, to allow for the breadth of understanding and conditions for robust critique that are necessary to maintain dynamism and innovation. It also has to be open, transparent and inclusive.

Bernstein's notion of analysis as the development of languages of description is thus apposite. It establishes a dynamic relationship between theory, empirical research and practice, and fosters an openness and transparency in presentation of the analysis of data that facilitates both induction into the practices of analysis and critical engagement with processes and products of research. It also accommodates a wide range of forms of research and allows for the integration of diverse methods, forms of data and modes of analysis, including the integration of qualitative and quantitative research. With respect to how doctoral students learn to do research, Bernstein (1996, p. 135) suggested that rather than focus in on the specificities of methods and techniques, we should 'view research procedures from a wider perspective'. The greater openness to critique and transformation of the approach advocated here has the potential not only, as Bernstein claimed, to accord respect to the researched, but also, through more transparent modes of analysis and research education, to accord respect to the researcher, however they are positioned and wherever they are located.

9 Teachers as creators of social contexts for scientific learning

New approaches for teacher education

Ana M. Morais and Isabel P. Neves

The increasing attention now being paid internationally to professional development reflects the need for teachers with a sound scientific and pedagogical background who are also able to implement teaching–learning processes that take into account the sociocultural diversity that is part of our schools. Wilson and Berne (1999) believe that there is progress towards achieving a consensus about the aims of teacher education. However, what we know about teachers' learning remains fragmented and disconnected. Many teacher education activities contain an evaluation process (mostly focused on what teachers have enjoyed), but efforts to measure what teachers learn and its relation to change in their pedagogic practice have not been part of typical evaluations. What the knowledges are that teachers acquire through these activities and how they influence their practice are questions that still demand an answer.

On the basis of recent research, some (e.g. Driel *et al.* 2001) have suggested that there are radically distinct conceptions of teachers' knowledge and that teachers' performance requires a clear definition of relevant concepts. We believe that a fundamental aspect that should be present in all teacher education is a sound evaluation of performance in order to promote professional growth. This implies the development of instruments of analysis designed to explore, in precise and detailed ways, the reasons for teachers' difficulties in planning and implementing pedagogic practices that promote effective learning by all their students.

The present study is based on research into teacher education by the ESSA Group (Sociological Studies of the Classroom) (e.g. Rocha and Morais 2000; Rosa 2002; Morais *et al.* 2005). Bernstein's (1990) theory of pedagogic discourse provided the main conceptual framework. The concept of specific coding orientation (recognition and realization rules) was used to evaluate the professional development of teachers in in-service training programmes using an action–research approach. The aim of this chapter is to present work on teachers' professional performance and development, in terms of specific coding orientations in relation to contexts of pedagogic intervention. We discuss the meaning of that relation and the potentialities and limitations of the methodological instruments which have been used.

Teacher performance and specific coding orientation

We started from the idea that, as *student* performance in specific learning contexts presupposes a given coding orientation to these contexts, *teachers'* performance in specific teaching contexts also presupposes a given coding orientation to these contexts. It is, then, possible to use the same kind of conceptualization that has been used in the analysis of students' learning in the analysis of teacher performance. The assumption is that teachers' pedagogic practices may be analysed as texts (instructional and regulative) and that these texts may represent various levels of teacher performance; that is, various levels of specific coding orientation to the implementation of pedagogic practices with given sociological characteristics. The external language of description which has been developed at the micro level is then transferred to the meso level of the educational system.

For Bernstein, the acquisition of a specific coding orientation, that is the acquisition of recognition and (active and passive) realization rules for a given context, is fundamental to the success of acquirers in that context. However, Bernstein argues that for the subject to produce the legitimate text in a given context, s/he should also have the *socio-affective* dispositions favourable to that context: the aspirations, motivations, values and attitudes adequate to the production of that text (Figure 9.1).

According to the model, having a specific coding orientation to a given pedagogic practice means that *teachers* possess:

(a) *recognition rules* which allow the recognition of the specificity of the context of that pedagogic practice, in its multiple aspects, distinguishing it from other contexts of pedagogic practice;
(b) *passive realization rules* which allow the selection of meanings/justifications appropriate to that context of pedagogic practice;
(c) *active realization rules* which allow the production of the text required by implementing in the classroom a pedagogic practice with the proposed characteristics.

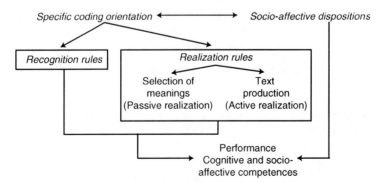

Figure 9.1 Specific coding orientation, socio-affective dispositions and performance in specific learning contexts (Morais and Neves, 2001)

According to Bernstein's model of pedagogic discourse, since any pedagogic practice may be characterized in terms of the various social relations
(between subjects, discourses and spaces) which define its instructional and
regulative dimensions, teacher performance may have different levels according to the specific coding orientation to each one of these dimensions and
relations. This means that the possession of recognition and realization rules
(both passive and active) should not be evaluated in terms of the global context of the pedagogic practice, but rather in terms of each of the social
relations which characterize its instructional and regulative dimensions.

The differentiation that is usually made between what teachers think and
what teachers do may, in our model, be seen in sociological terms as having a
broader meaning and higher conceptual and discriminative power. First, the
ideas/representations may be distinguished by taking as analytical components those ideas teachers have about the characteristics of the pedagogic
practice which may be more favourable to the learning of all students (recognition rules) and, also, the ideas they have about how these characteristics can
be met and the pedagogic principles in which they are grounded (passive realization rules). Second, at the level of practice, a further distinction is possible
by taking as components of analysis the instructional and regulative contexts
of the pedagogic practice and, within each context, the multiple social relations which define that context. When directed to these various aspects of the
pedagogic practice, the active realization represents a deeper and more subtle
analysis of distinct teacher practice in the classroom.

Furthermore, the fact that the analysis of the various rules (recognition
rules and passive and active realization rules) is centred on the same social
relations and the fact that the same concepts (classification and framing) are
used to analyse these relations, allows better, theoretically grounded and more
conceptually consistent, comparisons between what teachers think and what
teachers do. Figure 9.2 shows these relations.

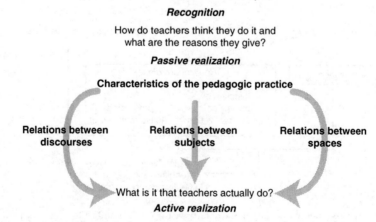

What is it that teachers think they do?

Recognition

How do teachers think they do it and
what are the reasons they give?

Passive realization

Characteristics of the pedagogic practice

**Relations between   Relations between   Relations between
discourses   subjects   spaces**

What is it that teachers actually do?

Active realization

Figure 9.2 Teacher pedagogic practice – specific coding orientation

In a study of physics and chemistry teachers of eighth and ninth grades (14–15 year olds) (Matos and Morais, 2004), we used the concepts of classification and framing to develop a comparative analysis of, respectively, the ideas and the practices of teachers when conducting experimental work in the classroom. The practices were analysed using an instrument which characterized the modalities of pedagogic practice; the ideas were analysed through interviews which had, as a starting point, the actual classroom occurrences. In this way, it was possible to appreciate, for each one of the various characteristics of the pedagogic practice, the extent to which the values of classification and framing of each teacher's *practice* were similar to or different from the value of classification and framing they indicated in the interview. Although in this study, the two components (ideas and practices) of teacher performance were analysed within the same conceptual framework, teacher performance was not conceptualized in terms of specific coding orientation. Thus, the data about the characterization of the practice were not transformed into degrees of active realization and the ideas shown in the interviews were not analysed in terms of recognition and passive realization.

The analysis of teacher performance and professional development in terms of the concept of specific coding orientation was initiated in a study, carried out by the ESSA Group, which focused on the relation between distinct modalities of pedagogic practice and the learning of a specific regulative text by primary school children (Rocha and Morais, 2000). This study involved teacher training within an action–research framework and was intended to encourage teachers to implement, at the level of classroom regulative context, a modality of pedagogic practice with successful characteristics (see Tables 9.1 and 9.2). Since this modality of practice was taken as the legitimate text to be produced by teachers, different levels of performance in relation to that text were taken as different levels of specific coding orientation to the context under analysis (see instruments of analysis). The data about active realization were obtained through an instrument (see instruments of analysis) constructed to characterize teacher performance in

Table 9.1 Characteristics of a mixed pedagogic practice: instructional context

Relation between subjects teacher–student (Ci Fi)					Relation between discourses (Cie Fie)		
Power relations (Ci)	Control relations (Fi)				Inter-disciplinary knowledge (Ci)	Inter-disciplinary knowledge (Ci Fi)	Academic/non-academic knowledge (Ce Fe)
	Discursive rules SIP						
	Selection	Sequence	Pacing	Evaluation criteria			
C⁺	F⁺	F⁺	F⁻⁻	F⁺⁺	C⁻⁻	C⁺F⁻	C⁺F⁻⁻

(Adapted from Morais *et al.* 2005)

Table 9.2 Characteristics of a mixed pedagogic practice: regulative context

Relation between subjects (CiFi)				*Relation between spaces (Ci)*	
Teacher–student		Student–student			
Power relations (Ci)	Control relations (Fi) Hierarchical rules	Power relations (Ci)	Control relations (Fi) Hierarchical rules	Teacher–student space	Student–student space
C^+	F^{--}	C^{--}	F^{++}	C^-	C^{--}

(Adapted from Morais *et al.* 2005)

the classroom in terms of the various characteristics of the pedagogic practice. The data about recognition and passive realization were obtained through discussions during the training process, without the direction of a specific instrument.

This study constituted the starting point for the construction of the initial instruments designed to analyse recognition and passive realization rules, in order to discriminate the various components of the specific coding orientation. The aim was to make it possible to understand the meaning of the various teacher levels of performance and their interrelation. It is possible that different levels of teacher performance may represent not only differences in the range of social relations of the pedagogic practice in which the teacher possesses the coding orientation, but also differences in the degree of coding orientation with respect to each one of the sociological characteristics used to define the pedagogic practice.

Let us begin with the modality of pedagogic practice that studies carried out by the ESSA Group have shown to be favourable to the learning of all students (e.g. Morais and Neves, 2001; Morais *et al.* 2004). This modality of practice, implemented by teachers as a result of their training process, was a mixed pedagogic practice – that is a practice with strong or weak classifications and framings according to specific aspects of the teaching–learning context (Rocha and Morais, 2000; Rosa 2002; Morais *et al.* 2005). Tables 9.1 and 9.2 show the characteristics of this modality of mixed pedagogic practice, in both instructional and regulative dimensions, where the scale of classification and framing is referred to four degrees (C^{++}, C^+, C^-, C^{--}; F^{++}, F^+, F^-, F^{--}).

In the context of this modality of mixed pedagogic practice, let us consider teacher performance when analysed in terms of specific coding orientation with reference, for example, to *selection* (see Table 9.1). According to this modality of pedagogic practice, selection should be characterized by a strong framing (F^+), that is the teacher should have control over the macro selection but s/he should also give the students some control over the micro selection. If the teacher recognizes that this characteristic is to be valued in his/her pedagogic practice, s/he demonstrates possession of the recognition rules for selection in the teacher–student relation. If the teacher is also able to tell what should be done to meet that characteristic and to explicate the foundational principles underlying the selection of that characteristic, s/he also demonstrates passive realization for the same characteristic. If, when acting in the classroom, the teacher implements a pedagogic practice where this characteristic is present, s/he can also demonstrate active realization for that characteristic.

Instruments of analysis

This section starts by presenting some general aspects of instrument construction, followed by specific aspects referring to recognition and (active and passive) realization rules.

General aspects

As a result of the constructive methodology used in this study, which is based on the dialectical relation between the theoretical and the empirical, we have developed an external language of description for the analysis of teacher performance and professional development where the concept of specific coding orientation, that is part of the internal language of description, was the theoretical reference, and the 'texts' produced by teachers in both interview situations and classroom contexts were the main empirical data. The construction of the instruments started with the definition of indicators which, in empirical terms, would correspond to the various components of the specific coding orientation, that is to the recognition and (active and passive) realization rules, and to indicators which would be used to characterize the various social relations of the instructional and regulative contexts of a given pedagogic practice.

In order to co-ordinate, at both the conceptual and the empirical levels, the various components of specific coding orientation (recognition rules and active and passive realization rules), we needed to start by defining the social relations which would be the object of the analysis of teacher performance. These are relations which are part of instruments constructed for various studies (e.g. Morais and Neves, 2001) with the aim of characterizing the pedagogic practices implemented by teachers at various levels of schooling (see these relations in Tables 9.1 and 9.2). The instruments contained, for each relation, a set of empirical indicators[1] and, for each indicator, descriptors corresponding to degrees indicated on a classification and/or framing scale. Thus, the sociological relations and the concepts of classification and framing we used to characterize teachers' pedagogic practice in the classroom context (and which gave us the performance in terms of active realization) were also used to evaluate the possession of recognition and passive realization to the context under study.

Recognition and passive realization rules

Data about recognition and passive realization have been obtained through semi-structured interviews with primary school and kindergarten teachers within various action–research projects (Rosa, 2002; Morais *et al.* 2005). Both models of interviews, conducted so far, were structured around a series of questions, each of which centred on one of the social relations which define the instructional and regulative contexts of any modality of pedagogic practice. For each one of the relations, situations were given which illustrated modalities of practice with distinct characteristics. Teachers were asked to indicate a situation or situations which they would value (recognition) and to justify their choice (passive realization).

It is important to notice that, in these studies, our appreciation of passive realization was limited to the reasons teachers gave for privileging specific characteristics. The other dimension of passive realization, i.e. what should be done to meet those characteristics (Figure 9.2), was not considered in these analyses.

Although the two types of interview followed the same conceptual pattern, there were differences in their structures. In one type, the alternative is expressed in just one sentence and in the other it is expressed under the form of two hypothetical situations of pedagogic intervention. Below, we illustrate the two types of interview for the discursive rule *selection:*

Interview 1
What should teacher–children relations be like within the classroom?
Do you think that children should help to choose the content to be studied and the materials to be used?
Or do you think that it is the teacher who should select the content and materials? Why?

Interview 2
Imagine the following two situations related to the teaching–learning process in the classroom:
Situation *A* – Activities related to living things, namely to animals, are taking place. In the course of the talk between two children a problem arises – 'Are plants living things or not?' Children ask the teacher who did not give an immediate answer. The teacher thought that the problem should be discussed in the groups, this theme becoming scientific content to be studied by all children. On the following day, some children brought in materials which helped them study the subject. Teacher and children together decided to develop further activities related to plants.
Situation B – The theme/project chosen by the teacher is related to animals. Children ask questions, some of them referring to birds. The teacher, who is concentrating on mammals, ignores the children's questions, telling them that this will be studied later. It is the teacher who chooses the activities related to animals and does not use materials brought by children into the classroom but only materials she has selected. She is the only person who manipulates the material.
Which of these situations would you value? Why?

In these examples, there is an alternative between a situation where some control over selection is given to the child (second question in Interview 1 and Situation A in Interview 2) and a situation where selection is controlled by the teacher alone (third question in Interview 1 and Situation B in Interview 2). Although, in either of the two cases, there is evidently a dichotomy between a set of characteristics representing very strong framing (teacher's control) and a set of characteristics representing very weak framing (child's control), the interview was conducted in such a way that the teacher's choice was not limited to that dichotomy, but could also combine characteristics of the two situations. For example, in this particular case of selection of curricular content, the answers could be of a kind that showed that the control might be exclusively centred on the teacher in some cases, but also centred on the child in some others.[2]

In order to analyse the possession of recognition and passive realization rules by teachers, we constructed instruments on the basis of the interview responses. Considering the dialectical relation between the concepts which guided the analysis and the empirical data obtained from the various answers, we defined the main categories[3] to be included in these instruments.

Tables 9.3 and 9.4 show the instruments of analysis of recognition and passive realization rules respectively. Each instrument is followed by excerpts from the interviews which illustrate one characteristic of the pedagogic practice – *hierarchical rules* (teacher–children relation). It is important to note that the analysis of the answers takes as reference the characteristics of the practice to be implemented by teachers as a result of the training they received. The examples refer to a pedagogic practice defined by very weak

Table 9.3 Instrument for analysing recognition rules and examples of interview excerpts concerning hierarchical rules (teacher/children relation)

Instrument of analysis – Recognition rules (RC)			
Indicator	*Does not have RC*	*May have RC*	*Has RC*
Characteristics of pedagogic practice	Characteristics indicated are different from/ opposed to those of the theoretical model	Characteristics indicated are ambiguous/not clear	Characteristics indicated are similar to those of the theoretical model

Examples of excerpts of interviews – hierarchical rules (teacher/children):

Does not have RC – Sometimes I listen to their [the children's] reasons, but my present children enjoy talk a lot and sometimes I have to tell them that we cannot talk too much and I get cross with them to make them shut up, and I tell them that we are wasting our time ... I am unable to make them understand that we should not have too much talk ...

May have RC – This situation did not occur.

Has RC – For example, I had given them [the children] some work to do and the time had run out, and I would try to lead them to understand that the time had run out and that next time they should have to keep more quiet [...] because the time would run out and the work was not done.

(Adapted from Morais *et al.* 2005)

Table 9.4 Instrument for analysing passive realization rules and examples of interview excerpts concerning hierarchical rules (teacher/children relation)

Instrument of analysis – Passive realization rules (RLp)

Indicator	Does not have RLp	May have RLp	Has RLp
Reasons given for pedagogic practice chosen	Reasons given are different from/ opposed to those of the theoretical model	Reasons given are ambiguous/not clear or no reasons are given	Reasons given are similar to those of the theoretical model

Examples of excerpts of interviews – hierarchical rules (teacher/children):

Does not have RLp – The teacher did not give any justification [the teacher started by showing herself not to have recognition rules – see example for *Does not have RC*].

May have RLp – The teacher did not give a justification for the characteristic she chose and which corresponded to the theoretical model.

Has RLp – I think it is very important to call their [the children's] attention [...] that the work was not properly done, they will be at a loss when they leave primary school[4] [...] they are accustomed to keep things going without bothering with the time they are spending! This is not going to happen later on, therefore we have to call their attention so that they are prepared ... it's a way of getting the habit of doing things properly.

(Adapted from Morais *et al.* 2005)

framing at the level of the hierarchical rules in the teacher–child relation (see Table 9.2).

Both instruments were used to guide the analysis of the data obtained in either of the two models of interviews. However, some adjustments in the analysis were needed, as a consequence of the specificity of each study. For example, at the level of the primary school, we had a considerable amount of data from classroom observations. For that reason, we used the possession of active realization rules as one more category to indicate the possession of passive realization and recognition rules. Thus, whenever, for a given characteristic of the pedagogic practice, the interview data was not clear about the possession of recognition and/or passive realization but the teacher's practice in the classroom clearly showed the presence of that characteristic, we assumed that the teacher would not only possess an active realization rule, but also recognition and passive realization rules. This is a consequence of the fact that, theoretically, the possession of active realization assumes necessarily the possession of recognition and passive realization.

The analysis of the interviews in the kindergarten study was different in that data about active realization was obtained from more limited and less diversified classroom interventions. For that reason the possession of active realization was not used as an indicator of recognition and passive realization. Instead, the possession of passive realization was taken as an important indicator in deciding about the possession of active realization. Thus, we considered that the teacher would only possess active realization if, together with a practice in the classroom which had the sociological characteristics favourable to children's learning, she had demonstrated in the interview that she had passive realization for these characteristics. We considered that acting in the classroom according to the model proposed, but in ways that were inconsistent or even contradictory in relation to the justifications given in the interview to explain those actions, might not indicate the possession of active realization. We thought that this ambiguous situation did not offer any guarantee that the practice implemented was based on pedagogic principles internalized by teachers – that is, that the practice implemented corresponded to a consistent pedagogic intentionality.

However, it is possible to accept that the inconsistencies sometimes witnessed between the interview data and the data based on classroom observation are a consequence of the way in which the instrument of analysis of recognition and passive realization was constructed and applied. We believe that, for example, the way passive realization was analysed was incipient, centring on a somehow restrictive aspect of this component of the specific coding orientation. According to the theoretical model (Figure 9.1), to possess passive realization means to select the meanings relevant to the context. In our interviews, the meanings to be selected corresponded to pedagogic principles which grounded given characteristics of the practice for successful learning by all children. However, following the model of Figure 9.2, we should consider another level of passive realization, according to which the meanings to be selected may also correspond to forms of acting in the classroom.

Let us again take *selection of curriculum content* (see above) as a reference. If (as in the interviews) we take the *principles* in which the pedagogic practice is grounded as the indicator of passive realization, teachers' answers should, then, refer to features such as the importance of children's interest, motivation and involvement, and their participation in the choice of some aspects related to the learning process (micro selection), but not others such as choice of the themes to be studied, given that children do not yet have the knowledge to choose an option relevant to their learning needs. However, if the indicator is *forms of acting* in the classroom which bring about successful practice, then teachers' answers should refer to features such as the teacher selecting the themes and sub-themes and then allowing the children to put questions and raise problems, or letting the children participate in the selection of materials previously chosen by the teacher. We believe that this new mode of empirically analysing passive realization needs further thought so that it can be used to substitute for the previous one or complement it. These are two alternative ways of looking at the empirical manifestation of passive realization. They appear to us at this moment as complementary forms which can give the analysis of passive realization greater powers of discrimination which, in turn, can give rise to a more comprehensive theoretical conceptualization of passive realization.

Analysis of recognition also requires improvement. We believe that we need to use a more diversified number of situations in order that answers are not conditioned by dichotomies which, to a certain extent, may indicate the choice valued by the interviewer. Although the interview questions were intended to be only guidelines for dialogue, so that choice was not necessarily limited by the dichotomy contained in the situations, the application of these models by other researchers may put in question the objectives of the interview. On the other hand, we believe it would be important to try to devise interview situations where it was possible to conduct a better exploration of the relation between possession/absence of recognition and passive realization rules. For example, in the models previously constructed, the absence of recognition appears associated with the absence of passive realization. As it stands, situations may occur where there is recognition and not passive realization, but there is no possibility of a situation where there is no recognition but there is passive realization (one of the indicators of the absence of passive realization is the absence even of recognition). To avoid this, a moment should be created in the interview where, in the absence of recognition rules, these would be given to the teacher. This procedure was part of interviews conducted with children to appreciate their specific coding orientation (e.g. Câmara and Morais, 1998) and which has given to the analysis of children's performance a greater explanatory power of differences encountered.

Active realization rules

The instruments employed to analyse active realization rules are the instruments we have used to characterize pedagogic practice in the classroom. These instruments have been subjected to successive reformulations and adaptations in order to achieve a higher level of significance of indicators and the empirical relations that define the contexts under study. We have sought a fine and rigorous analysis of teacher performance in the classroom and their professional development and, for this reason, we have been concerned with the selection of indicators that can cover a diversity of situations of that performance and with the specification of those situations through descriptors containing increasing powers of explication and discrimination.

As indicated above, the instruments used to characterize the pedagogic practice consider various social relations that define the instructional and regulative dimensions of teaching–learning contexts. The instruments contain a set of indicators applicable to each one of those relations and they contain the descriptors for each indicator which correspond to various degrees on the classification and/or framing scale.

Although following a similar pattern, the instruments may differ in the indicators selected for each one of the sociological characteristics under analysis and in the classification and framing scales. These differences are a function of the specificity of the contexts under study, the depth of the analysis and the scope of the research.

The indicators correspond to real situations in the pedagogic contexts under analysis, that is they are defined on the basis of situations previously observed in the classroom and which were found to be the most representative of what happens in those contexts. Thus, for example, 'Planning/doing experimental work' and 'Observing/interpreting and concluding in experimental work' are indicators only used in contexts of scientific learning where experimental work occurs and 'Presenting team work' is an indicator that is only relevant when students work in groups. The degrees of classification and framing represent, in any instrument, relative and not absolute values – each degree referring to a given form of teacher action in the classroom.

As in the case of recognition and passive realization rules, the possession of active realization rules has been analysed in reference to each one of the social characteristics of the pedagogic practice. The observation of classroom activities and the transcription of tape and video recordings gave us the basis for analysing teacher performance, by taking as reference the 'type-behaviours' indicated in the instruments. For each one of the indicators of each sociological relation, the teacher's 'behaviour' is signalled, attributing to it one of the four degrees in the classification and framing scales. The 'behaviours' are registered on tables and the distribution of signals for the set of indicators of each characteristic of the pedagogic practice gives the trend of teacher action with reference to that characteristic. This procedure was completed by using the researchers' field notes. The final characteristic of teacher practice was a compound of both procedures.

Teacher performance, in terms of active realization, is evaluated with reference to the characteristics of the practice which are taken as the legitimate text of the pedagogic context under study. If we take as reference the modality of pedagogic practice that we have led teachers to implement in recent studies of our action–research projects (see Tables 9.1 and 9.2), to possess active realization means to create a performance in the classroom which has the characteristics of that practice.

For example, according to that practice, possession of active realization for the evaluation criteria would be shown by a very strong framing (F^{++}) and for pacing and hierarchical rules (teacher–student) by a very weak framing (F^{--}). For some other characteristics, like selection and sequence, the possession of active realization would be shown by a strong framing (F^{+}), as a result of a very strong framing at the macro level and very weak framing at the micro level.

In order to make clear how active realization was evaluated, we show in Table 9.5 an example of one indicator of the instrument we constructed for analysing teacher pedagogic practice with reference to hierarchical rules (teacher–children). This is followed by two examples of classroom interactions, one of which indicates the possession of active realization for the characteristic under analysis.

When defining the indicators to evaluate the possession of active realization, we have recently considered new criteria. In order to discriminate between the macro and the micro levels of analysis, we have grouped indicators into two categories. These criteria were first used in the case of discursive rule selection to lead to the differentiation between macro selection and micro selection and are now being applied to the various characteristics of pedagogic practice (Silva *et al.* 2003). This distinction is related to the fact that some indicators are more associated with the general aspects of syllabuses whereas

Table 9.5 Extract of the instrument for analysing active realization rules and examples of transcripts concerning hierarchical rules (teacher/children relation)

Instrument of analysis – Active realization rules (Rla): Excerpt

Indicator	F''	F'	F⁻	F⁻⁻
when addressing children	The teacher does not give any reason, using the imperative control	The teacher uses positional control, giving reasons related to school/ classroom rules	The teacher uses personal control, appealing to her own reasons	The teacher uses personal control, appealing to children's personal attributes

Examples of transcripts:

Fi'' *Child* – Teacher, may I drink some water?
   Teacher – Talk less and you won't need to drink so much – *Does not have RLa*

Fi⁻ *Teacher* – [...] respect for others so that nobody is disturbed [...] and now you are going to look at your worksheet, do what is indicated [...] cooperating with each other, waiting for your turn, right? And, keeping your voice down, for the group only, right. – *Has RLa*

(Adapted from Morais *et al.* 2005)

others are more related to specific aspects of pedagogic relations. For example, in the case of the indicators of the discursive rule selection, 'Themes/scientific contents' is an indicator of the macro level whereas 'Answers to children's questions/comments' is an indicator of the micro level. Grouping indicators in these two categories accords more rigour to the analysis of active realization and, in future, will also accord more rigour to the construction of instruments of analysis of recognition and passive realization.

The fact that teacher performance is viewed as a consequence of their specific coding orientation for a given context of the pedagogic practice means that distinct levels of performance correspond to distinct levels of specific coding orientation. Figure 9.3 shows schematically the empirical relation

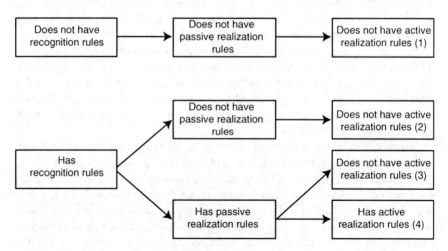

Figure 9.3 Levels of teachers' specific coding orientation

which was made between recognition, passive realization and active realization rules, in order to give to each one of the characteristics of the pedagogic practice implemented by the teacher, different levels of specific coding orientation (1, 2, 3, 4) and therefore different levels of performance.

The transcripts that follow exemplify the level of coding orientation (level 3) which turned out to be the most frequent in a study carried out at the primary school level (Morais *et al.* 2005) when we looked at teacher performance with regard to the relations between discourses (intra-disciplinary, inter-disciplinary, academic/non-academic knowledges). The transcripts are part of the interviews and classroom observation.

Intra-disciplinary relations

What teacher Dulce tells us she does and why she does it [Interview responses]:

'[The scientific contents] are studied in an interlinked way' – HAS RECOGNITION.
'Because we cannot put them [the scientific contents] in separate compartments and that relation favours learning and makes it useful' – HAS PASSIVE REALIZATION.

What teacher Dulce does [Classroom observation]:

The teacher asks children for examples of state of matter changes which occur in the outside world. One of the children observes that when one places sea water under the sun, we will obtain salt instead of water. The teacher analyses the child's example in terms of state of matter changes and says that: 'The salt was dissolved in the water', but she does not indicate any relationship between this issue and the study of the dissolution of substances – DOES NOT HAVE ACTIVE REALIZATION.

Inter-disciplinary relations

What teacher Céu says she does and why she does it [Interview responses]:

'I relate science subjects to other subjects' – HAS RECOGNITION.
'Because in this way I can lead the child to develop a broader reasoning and that certain children can more easily apply the knowledge acquired in sciences to other areas and vic.e-versa' – HAS PASSIVE REALIZATION.

What Teacher Céu does [Classroom observation]:

Together with children, the teacher discusses the results obtained through the evaporation of alcohol and acetone. When comparing the initial and

final levels of those liquids, some children observe that the level of the alcohol lowered 1 mm. A child asks: Is it millimetre or millilitre [that should be written to indicate the lowering of the level of a substance]?
'He wrote millimetre. He wrote an *m* and not an *l*', said the teacher. Children and teacher continue to discuss what happens to the alcohol and acetone without any reference to unities of length/volume, which is the content of Maths – DOES NOT HAVE ACTIVE REALIZATION.

Academic–non academic knowledge

What teacher Rita says she does and why she does it [Interviews' responses]:

'Yes, yes [I relate scientific knowledge to everyday knowledge]' – HAS RECOGNITION.
'[Because] it helps them to understand better the subject they are learning and helps them to understand what surrounds them ... those things they sometimes do not understand and that they can be helped to understand with the knowledge we give to them [...] it is easier to understand' – HAS PASSIVE REALIZATION.

What teacher Rita does [Classroom observation]:

Children were studying air constituents, that 'air' is different from 'oxygen' and that oxygen is used up in given phenomena, for example combustion. A child says that when she is in the classroom or in the car, 'she also feels without air' and 'she must fully open the car window'. The teacher listens to the child but does not explore her intervention in terms of what they had been studying in sciences, and she goes on by giving a new worksheet – DOES NOT HAVE ACTIVE REALIZATION.

One further significant aspect that should be considered in the analysis of teacher performance and professional development is the possession of socio-affective dispositions favourable to the pedagogic practice to be implemented (Figure 9.1). In the studies done so far, we have explored this, but not with the depth it deserves. The absence of socio-affective dispositions favourable to that characteristic may constitute a limiting factor in teacher performance. Future studies should explore combinations between specific coding orientation and socio-affective dispositions.

Conclusion

Productive discussion of new approaches to teacher professional development implies careful and sound evaluations, based on instruments that can be applied to the various contexts of initial and in-service teacher training and to various contexts of pedagogic intervention, in distinct levels of schooling.

The main purpose of this chapter was to reflect on new paths for researching and analysing teacher performance by explaining what we have been doing and what we intend to do.

The analysis of teachers' professional development requires that what is going to be analysed is made clear and that appropriate instruments to be used for that analysis are constructed. In the research we have carried out, we structured and applied interview guidelines and instruments to characterize teachers' practices in order to analyse teacher performance in terms of specific coding orientation.

The level of depth and conceptual power of the model of analysis of teacher performance in terms of the specific coding orientation offers the possibility of making fine and detailed analyses of that performance and as such gives a better understanding of teacher difficulties in implementing pedagogic practices which have the potential to be successful. This is a crucial aspect for teacher training as it permits us to know with greater precision which are the components of teacher performance that teachers experience greater difficulties with. For example, it has been possible to distinguish teachers' difficulties at the level of their ideas/representations about the practices – when discriminating between those ideas in terms of their possession of recognition and passive realization. It has also been possible to distinguish teacher difficulties at the level of their practices in the classroom by distinguishing between those practices in terms of the instructional and regulative contexts and within these in terms of various levels and various indicators of each one of the social characteristics of the pedagogic practice.

It would be possible, in the future, to accord a higher degree of accuracy to the analyses we have conducted. Although the structure of our interviews was organized to make possible the articulation of data about recognition and passive realization rules with data related to active realization rules, that articulation needs to be worked out more fully. We believe that a strong aspect of that structure is the fact that the interviews contained questions directed to each one of the social relations which have been the object of analysis when characterizing pedagogic practice in the classroom. This is an aspect which gives consistency to the analysis of the specific coding orientation, in terms of its various components. However, whereas for recognition and passive realization the analysis has been directed to the whole of each one of the relations, the analysis of active realization has considered each one of the indicators which together define each relation under analysis. In order that the analysis of teacher performance in terms of specific coding orientation increases in consistency and explanatory power, it is important that future instruments of analysis of recognition and passive realization include questions that give more precision to the evaluation of teachers' ideas/representations, with reference to the set of indicators selected for the analysis of each one of the sociological characteristics of the pedagogic practice. It is also important to distinguish, at the level of passive realization, two levels of ideas – the foundational principles which justify the valuing of given characteristics of the practice and the ways of acting to meet those characteristics.

We consider that the procedures we have followed to analyse teachers' professional development make a contribution to this field. We analyse this development in terms of the acquisition by teachers of recognition and realization rules and, in doing so, the studies suggest a methodological approach which gives the possibility of discriminating between specific components of teacher performance. However, in contrast with student learning where we have already conducted various studies leading to greater rigour of the instruments of analysis, the studies of the same kind at the level of *teacher* learning represent only a first step. We believe that considerable investment is needed in this area.

Notes

1   The following are examples of indicators for the discursive rule selection which were used in studies carried out in the science primary school contexts (Morais *et al.* 1997): exploring/discussing themes under study; doing activities; selecting materials; using models/schemes; planning/doing experimental work; using children's spontaneous selections; observing, interpreting and concluding in experimental work; answering children's questions; presenting group work; looking for information in books/journals/newspapers; finishing and recapitulating themes.

2   Answers of this kind would be in accordance with research results about the characteristics most favourable to children's learning which suggest that selection should be regulated by strong framing as a result of very strong framing at the level of the macro selection and weak framing at the level of the micro selection.

3   The whole system of categories used to evaluate teachers' possession/absence of the recognition rules and of the passive realization rules can be seen in Morais *et al.* 2005.

4   In Portugal, children leave primary school when they are ten years old and they enter elementary school, distinct in every aspect from primary school.

Acknowledgements

The authors acknowledge the financial support given to this study by the Foundation for Science and Technology, the Gulbenkian Foundation and the Institute for Educational Innovation.

10 Activity, discourse and pedagogic change

Harry Daniels

In this paper, I wish to explore the extent to which two approaches to the social formation of mind are compatible and may be used to enrich and extend each other. These are: activity theory as derived from the work of the early Russian psychologists, Vygotsky and Leontiev, and the work of the sociologist Basil Bernstein. The two styles approach a common theme from different perspectives. In the case of Vygotsky, the unit of analysis was word meaning, and in the case of Leontiev, it was the activity system in which the individual was located. In their attempt to develop an account of social formation the Russians' gaze fell first on the individual in dialogue or the object-oriented activity system. The notion of the object of activity – the problem space or raw material that is being worked on in an activity – is central to the work of Leontiev. Bernstein developed a theory with a language of description which allowed researchers to move from a gaze which lighted first on the social and cultural, and permitted a trace to be drawn through principles of regulation at the social organizational level through principles of regulation in and through discourse to possibilities for individual thought and action. The rules of cultural historical formation rather than the object of activity are the focus. It is, as it were, that they were starting from opposite 'ends'. To some extent both attempt to account for cultural historical formation at ontogenetic and cultural levels.

A focus on the rules which shape the social formation of pedagogic discourse and its practices employed by Bernstein (2000) will be brought to bear on those aspects of psychology which argue that object-oriented activity is a fundamental constituent of human thought and action (Cole, 1996). The institutional level of analysis was all but absent in much of the early Vygotskian research in the West (see Daniels, 2001). There was no recourse to a language of description that permitted the analysis of object-oriented activity in terms of the rules which regulate the microcultures of institutions. Recent developments in post-Vygotskian theory and activity theory have witnessed considerable advances in the understanding of the ways in which human action shapes and is shaped by the contexts in which it takes place (Daniels, 2001). They have given rise to a significant amount of empirical research within and across a wide range of fields in which social science methodologies and methods are applied in the development of research-based knowledge in policy-making and practice in academic, commercial and industrial settings (e.g. Agre, 1997; Cole *et al.* 1997; Engeström and Middleton, 1996; Daniels, 2001; Lea and Nicoll, 2002; Wenger *et al.* 2002). The paper is comprised of three sections. In the first, I will trace the development of Russian social theory through the current manifestation of activity theory. In the second, I will provide a very brief outline of Bernstein's work on the sociology of pedagogy. I will subsequently argue that these two theoretical developments may be brought into productive relation with one another.

The development of activity theory

Vygotsky provided a rich and tantalizing set of suggestions that have been taken up and transformed by social theorists as they attempt to construct accounts of the formation of mind which, to varying degrees, acknowledge social, cultural and historical influences. His is not a legacy of determinism and denial of agency – rather he provides a theoretical framework which rests on the concept of mediation. The means of mediation which have tended to dominate recent discussions are cultural artefacts such as speech or activity. These semiotic and activity-based accounts may be seen as referring to different levels of emphasis within a single process. Wertsch (1998) advances the case for the use of mediated action as a unit of analysis in social–cultural research. Engeström points out the danger of the relative undertheorizing of context: 'individual experience is described and analyzed as if consisting of relatively discrete and situated actions while the system or objectively given context of which those actions are a part is either treated as an immutable given or barely described at all' (Engeström, 1993: 66). Activity has developed in response to the challenge embedded in this statement. I will now outline the three generations of activity theory which mark the developments since the work of the early twentieth century, and will follow this with a brief account of relevant aspects of Bernstein's thesis.

The first generation

This first approach drew heavily from Vygotsky's concept of mediation (see Figure 10.1). This triangle represents the way in which Vygotsky brought together cultural artefacts with human actions in order to dispense with the individual/social dualism. During this period, studies tended to focus on individuals.

The second generation

Here Engeström advocates the study of artefacts 'as integral and inseparable components of human functioning' but he argues that the focus of the study

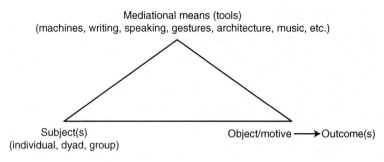

Figure 10.1 The first generation of activity theory

of mediation should be on its relationship with the other components of an activity system (Engeström, 1999: 29).

In order to progress the development of activity theory, Engeström expanded the original triangular representation of activity to enable an examination of systems of activity at the macro level of the collective and the community in preference to a micro level concentration on the individual actor or agent operating with tools. Here the work of Leontiev was influential. Vygotsky was more a semiotician than an analyst of activity. Despite appeals to a broader conception of social formation, much of Vygotsky's theory remains an analysis of semiotic mediation in small-scale settings. This expansion of the basic Vygotskian triangle aims to represent the social/collective elements in an activity system, through the addition of the elements of community, rules and division of labour while emphasizing the importance of analysing their interactions with each other. In Figure 10.2 the object is depicted with the help of an oval indicating that object-oriented actions are always, explicitly or implicitly, characterized by ambiguity, surprise, interpretation, sense making, and potential for change (Engeström, 1999). At the same time, Engeström drew on Ilyenkov (1977) to emphasize the importance of contradictions within activity systems as the driving force of change and thus development.

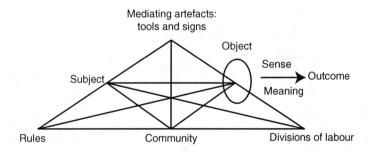

Figure 10.2 The structure of a human activity system in the second generation of activity theory

The third generation

Engeström (1999) sees joint activity or practice, not individual activity, as the unit of analysis for activity theory. He is interested in the process of social transformation and includes the structure of the social world in analysis, taking into account the conflictual nature of social practice. He sees instability (internal tensions) and contradiction as the 'motive force of change and development' (Engeström, 1999: 9) and the transitions and reorganizations within and between activity systems as part of evolution; it is not only the subject but also the environment that is modified through mediated activity. He views the 'reflective appropriation of advanced models and tools' as 'ways out of internal contradictions' that result in new activity systems (Cole and Engeström, 1993: 40).

The third generation of activity theory as proposed by Engeström intends to develop conceptual tools to understand dialogues, multiple perspectives, and networks of interacting activity systems. He draws on ideas on *dialogicality* and *multivoicedness* in order to expand the framework of the second generation. The idea of networks of activity within which contradictions and struggles take place in the definition of the motives and objects of the activity calls for an analysis of power and control within developing activity systems. The minimal representation which Figure 10.3 provides shows but two of what may be a myriad of systems exhibiting patterns of contradiction and tension.

Activity theory (AT) provides a means of studying learning understood as the expansion through change and development of the objects of activity. This is undertaken through a critical consideration of contradictions within and between activity systems. It lacks a sophisticated account of the regulation of subject–subject relations (and thus social positioning) and of the production, and to some extent the structure and function of the cultural artefacts (such as discourse) which mediate subject–object relations. As

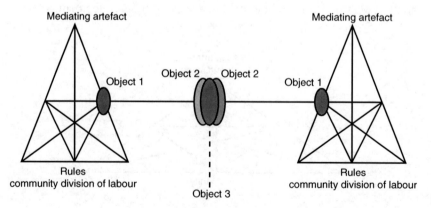

Figure 10.3 Two interacting activity systems as a minimal model for the third generation of activity theory

Engeström and Miettinen have noted: 'the integration of discourse into the theory of activity has only begun' (Engeström and Miettinen, 1999: 7).

An overview of relevant aspects of Bernstein's thesis

Bernstein's work on analysis and description focuses upon two levels: a structural level and an interactional level. The structural level is analysed in terms of the social division of labour it creates and the interactional level with the form of social relation it creates. The social division of labour is analysed in terms of strength of the boundary of its divisions, that is, with respect to the degree of specialization. The interactional level emerges as the regulation of the transmission/acquisition relation between teacher and taught: that is, the interactional level comes to refer to the pedagogic context and the social relations of the classroom or its equivalent. The interactional level then gives the principle of the learning context through which the social division of labour, in Bernstein's terms, speaks.

It becomes possible to see how a given distribution of control and principles of control are made substantive in agencies of cultural reproduction, e.g. families/schools. The form of the code (its modality) contains principles for distinguishing between contexts (recognition rules) *and* for the creation and production of specialized communication within contexts (realization rules). The analysis can be applied to different levels of school organization and various units within a level. This allows the analysis of power and control and the rules regulating what counts as legitimate pedagogic competence to proceed at a level of delicacy appropriate to a particular research question.

Bernstein (1990: 13) used the concept of social positioning to refer to the establishing of a specific relation to other subjects and to the creating of specific relationships within subjects. As Hasan (2002a, 2002b) notes, social positioning through meanings is inseparable from power relations. Here the linkage is forged between social positioning and psychological attributes. This is the process through which Bernstein talks of the shaping of the possibilities for consciousness. This form of analysis allows for the refinement of Engeström's (1999) suggestion that the division of labour in an activity creates different positions for the participants and that the participants carry their own diverse histories with them into the activity. Where Vygotsky speaks of mediation and Leontiev of activity systems with a division of labour which sets up different subject positions in relation to an object, Bernstein provides a more detailed analysis of subject positioning which is ultimately grounded in an analysis of power and control.

> The dialectical relation between discourse and subject makes it possible to think of pedagogic discourse as a semiotic means that regulates or traces the generation of subjects' positions in discourse. Within the Bernsteinian thesis there exists an ineluctable relation between one's

social positioning, one's mental dispositions and one's relation to the distribution of labour in society.

(Hasan, 2004: 4)

Here the emphasis on discourse is theorized not only in terms of 'the shaping of cognitive functions but also, as it were invisibly, in its influence on dispositions, identities and practices' (Bernstein, 1990: 3).

Bernstein (1990: 16–18) postulates pertinent concepts to show how this comes about. Socially positioned subjects, through their experience of and participation in code-regulated dominant and dominated communication, develop rules for recognizing what social activity a context is the context for, and how the requisite activity should be carried out.

In this way Bernstein's work provides a means of translating principles of power and control into principles of communication and through an account of social positioning within pedagogic discourse theorizes the distribution of forms of pedagogic consciousness. As it stands this approach is not well placed to study the emergent objects of human activity through time. This is something which activity theory has, in its more recent incarnations, sought to establish.

The potential for progress in the development of Bernstein's work

I will now discuss those aspects of Bernstein's work which may be open to development and synthesis with the post-Vygotskian account.

Organizational practices

The organizational dimensions of social practice are provisionally sketched in AT but lack a sophisticated account of the way in which a dominating distribution of power and principles of control generate, distribute, reproduce and legitimize dominating and dominated principles of communication such as that to be found in Bernstein (2000).

Engeström talks of the division of labour in terms of the horizontal division of tasks between the members of the community and of the vertical division of power and status. Engeström's notion of rules refers to the explicit and implicit regulations, norms and conventions that constrain actions and interactions within the activity system.

Bernstein uses the concept of classification to determine the underlying principle of a social division of labour and the concept of framing to determine the principle of its social relations and in this way to integrate structural and interactional levels of analysis in such a way that, up to a point, both levels may vary independently of each other.

Classification

Classification is defined at the most general level as the relation between categories. The relation between categories is given by their degree of insulation. Thus where there is strong insulation between categories, each category is sharply distinguished, explicitly bounded and having its own distinctive specialization. When there is weak insulation, then the categories are less specialized and therefore their distinctiveness is reduced. In the former case, Bernstein speaks of strong classification and in the latter of weak classification. Classification may also be discussed in vertical and horizontal dimensions. For example, the strength of the boundary/distinction between subjects in the curriculum may be described in terms of a horizontal dimension (how different they are) or a vertical dimension (how important they are).

Framing

The social relations are generally those between parents/children, teachers/pupils, doctors/patients, social workers/clients, but the analysis can be extended to include the social relations of the work contexts of industry or commerce. Bernstein considers that from his point of view all these relations can be regarded as *pedagogic.*

> Framing refers to the control on communicative practices (selection, sequencing, pacing and criteria) in pedagogical relations, be they relations of parents and children or teachers/pupils. Where framing is strong the transmitter explicitly regulates the distinguishing features of the interactional and locational principles which constitute the communicative context ... Where framing is weak, the acquirer is accorded more control over the regulation.

> Framing regulates what counts as legitimate communication in the pedagogical relation and thus what counts as legitimate practices.
>
> (Bernstein, 1981: 345)

Bernstein also provides an account of external framing which refers to the control over communication outside the context of concern. Here is the parallel with the AT notion of community. Crucially, Bernstein allows us to move beyond questions concerning who is a member of the community to questions of relations of control within that community. Above all, this form of analysis permits the move between organizational structure and the structure of the discourse.

> Classification refers to what, framing is concerned with how meanings are to be put together, the forms by which they are to be made public, and the nature of the social relationships that go with it.
>
> (Bernstein, 2000: 12).

In that the model is concerned with principles of regulation of educational transmission at any specified level, it is possible to investigate experimentally the relation between principles of regulation and the practices of pupils. Relations of power create and maintain boundaries between categories and are described in terms of classification. Relations of control revealed in values of framing condition communicative practices. It becomes possible to see how a given distribution of power through its classificatory principle and principles of control through its framing are made substantive in agencies of cultural reproduction, e.g. families/schools. The form of the code (its modality) contains principles for distinguishing between contexts (recognition rules) *and* for the creation and production of specialized communication within contexts (realization rules).

> Through defining educational codes in terms of the relationship between classification and framing, these two components are built into the analysis at *all levels*. It then becomes possible in one framework to derive a typology of educational codes, to show the inter-relationships between organizational and knowledge properties to move from macro- to micro-levels of analysis, to relate the patterns internal to educational institutions to the external social antecedents of such patterns, and to consider questions of maintenance and change.
>
> (Bernstein, 1977: 112, emphasis added)

The analysis of classification and framing can be applied to different levels of school organization and various units within a level. This allows the analysis of power and control and the rules regulating what counts as legitimate pedagogic competence to proceed at a level of delicacy appropriate to a particular research question.

In AT the production of the cultural artefact, the discourse, is not analysed in terms of the context of its production. It is in Bernstein's work. The language that Bernstein has developed, uniquely, allows researchers to take measures of institutional modality. That is, to describe and position the discursive, organizational and interactional practice of the institution. Through the concepts of classification and framing Bernstein provides the language of description for moving from those issues that activity theory handles as rules, community and division of labour to the discursive tools or artefacts that are produced and deployed within an activity.

Culture and language

Hasan (1992a, 1992b; 1995) and Wertsch (1985; 1991) note the irony that whilst Vygotsky developed a theory of semiotic mediation in which the mediational means of language was privileged, he provides very little if anything by way of a theory of language use. In an account of the social formation of mind there is a requirement for theory which relates meanings to interpersonal relations. The absence of an account both of the ways language serves to regulate interpersonal relations and of how its specificity is, in turn, produced through specific patterns of interpersonal relation and, thus, social regulation, constitutes a serious weakness. This absence in the post-Vygotskian work does constitute a significant part of Bernstein's project. He seeks to link semiotic tools with the structure of material activity. In Engeström's (1996) work within activity theory the production of the outcome is discussed but there is less emphasis on the production and structure of discourse itself. The challenge is to theorize the Vygotskian tool, or cultural artefact, as a social and historical construction.

Bernstein (1996) refined this discussion through making a distinction between instructional and regulative discourse. The former refers to the transmission of skills and their relation to each other, and the latter refers to the principles of social order, relation and identity. Whereas the principles and distinctive features of instructional discourse and its practice are relatively clear (the what and how of the specific skills/competences to be acquired and their relation to each other), the principles and distinctive features of the transmission of the regulative are less clear as this discourse is transmitted through various media and may, indeed, be characterized as a *diffuse* transmission. Regulative discourse communicates the institution's public moral practice, values, beliefs and attitudes, principles of conduct, character and manner. It also transmits features of the institution's local history, local tradition and community relations. Pedagogic discourse is modelled as one discourse created by the embedding of instructional and regulative discourse.

Bernstein (1999b) provides a further refinement in that he distinguishes between vertical and horizontal discourse. Horizontal discourse arises out of everyday activity and is usually oral, local, context-dependent and specific, tacit, multilayered and contradictory across but *not* within contexts. Its structure reflects the way a particular culture is segmented and its activities are specialized. Horizontal discourse is thus segmentally organized. In contrast, vertical discourse has a coherent, explicit and systematically principled structure which is hierarchically organized or takes the form of a series of specialized languages with specialized criteria for the production and circulation of texts. Bernstein (1999b: 159) suggests that Bourdieu's notion of discursive forms which give rise to symbolic and practical mastery respectively and Habermas's reference to the discursive construction of life worlds of individuals and instrumental rationality both refer to parts of a complex field of parameters which, in turn, refer to both individual and social experience and relate to the model of horizontal and vertical discourse which he seeks to develop. He offers an initial set of contrasts and indicates that many more exist (see Table 10.1). His lament is for the lack of a language of description of these forms which can serve to generate and relate the possibilities for difference (see Chapter 2, this volume).

Bernstein's (1999a) paper serves as an important reminder that the theoretical derivation of 'scientific and everyday' in the original writing was

Table 10.1 A comparison of the two fundamental forms of discourse: vertical and horizontal

	Horizontal discourse	*Vertical discourse*
Evaluative	spontaneous	contrived
Epistemological	subjective	objective
Cognitive	operations	principles
Social	intimacy	distance
Contextual	inside	outside
Voice	dominated	dominant
Mode	linear	non-linear
Institutional	gemeinschaft	gessellschaft

(After Bernstein 1999b: 158)

somewhat provisional. For example, the association of the scientific with the school does not help to distinguish those aspects of formal instruction that merely *add* to everyday understanding without fostering the development of scientific concepts. The association also suggests that the development of scientific concepts must take place in the school and not outside it. Bernstein's analysis is suggestive of a more powerful means of conceptualizing the forms which Vygotsky announced.

It may be as a consequence of the dualist perspective, which remains so powerful, that the emphasis on the interdependence between the development of scientific and everyday concepts is also not always appreciated. Valsiner (1997) distinguishes 'dualisms' from 'dualities'. He argues that the denial of dualism of the inner and outer world in appropriation-based models of learning with their emphasis on appropriation of knowledge through participation, leads to a denial of the dualities which are the constituent elements in dialectical or dialogical theory. This echoes the Marxist notion of internal relationship in which two elements are mutually constitutive (see Valsiner, 1997 for an extended discussion). Vygotsky argued that the systematic, organized and hierarchical thinking that he associated with scientific concepts becomes gradually embedded in everyday referents and thus achieves a general sense in the contextual richness of everyday thought. Vygotsky, thus, presented an interconnected model of the relationship between scientific and everyday or spontaneous concepts. Similarly he argued that everyday thought is given structure and order in the context of systematic scientific thought. Vygotsky was keen to point out the relative strengths of both as they both contributed to each other.

Social positioning

Leontiev used the term 'activity' in which subject, object, actions and operations are mutually present:

Activity is the minimal meaningful context for understanding individual actions ... In all its varied forms, the activity of the human individual is a system set within a system of social relations ... The activity of individual people thus *depends on their social position,* the conditions that fall to their lot, and an accumulation of idiosyncratic, individual factors. Human activity is not a relation between a person and a society that confronts him ... in a society a person does not simply find external conditions to which he must adapt his activity, but, rather, these very social conditions bear within themselves the motives and goals of his activity, its means and modes.

(Leontiev, 1978: 10, emphasis added)

Whilst Engeström acknowledges that the division of labour in activity results in the creation of possibilities for social position, the implications of Leontiev's account are not fully developed in modern AT. Bernstein's account of social positioning within the discursive practice that arises in activity systems, taken together with his analysis of the ways in which principles of power and control translate into principles of communication, allow us to investigate how principles of communication differentially position subjects acting within particular activity settings. As Hasan (2004) notes, there exists a clear relation between one's social positioning, one's mental dispositions and one's relation to the distribution of labour in society. The 'same' context could elicit different practices from persons differently positioned. Socially positioned subjects through their experience of and participation in pedagogic practice, mediated by pedagogic discourse, develop rules for recognizing what social activity a context is the context *for,* and how the requisite activity should be carried out (Hasan, 2004). Subject–subject and within–subject relations are under-theorized in AT. The challenge is to develop Bernstein's account of social positioning to allow for the analysis and description of complex activity formations as they change through time.

Contradiction and change in transmission practices

The focus of AT is on instability (internal tensions) and contradiction as the 'motive force of change and development' (Engeström, 1999: 9) and the transitions and reorganizations within and between activity systems as part of evolution. It is not only the subject, but also the environment, that is modified through mediated activity. Rules, community and division of labour are analysed in terms of the contradictions and dilemmas that arise within the activity system specifically with respect to the production of the object. Activity systems do not exist in isolation – they are embedded in networks which witness constant fluctuation and change. Activity theory needs to develop tools for analysing and transforming networks of culturally heterogeneous activities through dialogue and debate (Engeström and Miettinen, 1999: 7). Bernstein's work has not placed particular emphasis on the study of change (see Bernstein, 2000). The introduction of the third generation of AT initiated the development of conceptual tools to understand dialogues, multiple perspectives on change within networks of interacting activity systems, all of which are under-developed in Bernstein. The idea of networks of activity within which contradictions and struggles take place in the definition of the motives and object of the activity calls for an analysis of power and control within and between developing activity systems. The latter is the point at which Bernstein's emphasis on different layers and dimensions of power and control becomes key to the development of the theory. The minimal representation in Figure 10: 1 shows but two of what may be a network of systems exhibiting patterns of contradiction and tension.

Lemke (1997) suggests that it is not only the context of the situation that is relevant, but also the context of culture when an analysis of meaning is undertaken. He suggests that 'we interpret a text, or a situation, in part by connecting it to other texts and situations which our community, or our individual history, has made us see as relevant to the meaning of the present one' (Lemke, 1997: 50). This use of notions of intertextuality, of networked activities, or of a network of connections provides Lemke with tools for the creation of an account of ecosocial systems which transcend immediate contexts. Engeström and Miettinen (1999) recognize the strengths and limitations of this position. They imply a need for an analysis of the way in which networks of activities are structured – ultimately for an analysis of power and control:

> Various microsociologies have produced eye-opening works that uncover the local, idiosyncratic, and contingent nature of action, interaction, and knowledge. Empirical studies of concrete, situated practices can uncover the local pattern of activity and the cultural specificity of thought, speech and discourse. Yet these microstudies tend to have little connection to macrotheories of social institutions and the structure of society. Various approaches to analysis of social networks may be seen as attempts to bridge the gap. However, a single network, though interconnected with a number of other networks, typically still in no way represents any general or lawful development in society.
>
> (Engeström and Miettinen, 1999: 8)

Leontiev (1981) explored this issue from the perspective of development through time. He suggested that in the study of human ontogeny, one must take account of the ordering of categories of activity that corresponds to broad stages of mental development. According to Leontiev:

> In studying the development of the child's psyche, we must therefore start by analyzing the child's activity, as this activity is built up in the concrete conditions of its life ... Life or activity as a whole is not built up mechanically, however, from separate types of activity. Some types of activity are

the leading ones at a given stage and are of greatest significance for the individual's subsequent development, and others are less important. We can say accordingly, that each stage of psychic development is characterized by a definite relation of the child to reality that is the leading one at that stage and by a definite, leading type of activity.

(Leontiev, 1981: 395)

This analysis of development in terms of stages characterized by particular dominant activities is often associated with the work of Elkonin. In the terms of contemporary AT, this account is one of progressive transformation of the object through time. This could be called a *horizontal analysis*:

when we speak of the dominant activity and its significance for a child's development in this or that period, this is by no means meant to imply that the child might not be simultaneously developing in other directions as well. In each period, a child's life is many-sided, the activities of which his life is composed are varied. New sorts of activity appear; the child forms new relations with his surroundings. When a new activity becomes dominant, it does not cancel all previously existing activities: it merely alters their status within the overall system of relations between the child and his surroundings, which thereby become increasingly richer.

(Elkonin, 1972: 247)

This concern for the analysis of 'leading' activity is also to be found in the work of Norman Fairclough (1992, 2000):

Social practices networked in a particular way constitute a social order ... The discourse/semiotic aspect of a social order is what we can call an *order of discourse*. It is the way in which diverse genres and discourses and styles are networked together. An order of discourse is a social structuring of semiotic difference – a particular social ordering of relationships amongst different ways of making meaning, i.e. different discourse and genres and styles. One aspect of this ordering is dominance: some ways of making meaning are dominant or mainstream in a particular order of discourse, others are marginal, or oppositional, or 'alternative' ... The political concept of 'hegemony' can usefully be used in analyzing orders of discourse (Fairclough, 1992, Laclau & Mouffe, 1985) – a particular social structuring of semiotic difference may become hegemonic, become part of the legitimizing common sense which sustains relations of domination, but hegemony will always be contested to a greater or lesser extent, in hegemonic struggle. An order of discourse is not a closed or rigid system, but rather an open system, which is put at risk by what happens in actual interactions.

(Fairclough 2004: 2, emphasis added)

Griffin and Cole (1984) noted that in the course of a single session of an after-school activity designed for 7–11-year-olds, there could be fluctuations in what activity seemed to be 'leading'. This could be termed a *situated* analysis. In Figure 10.4 an analysis of a particular moment in time (A or B or C) would consider the network of activity systems in which subjects were located and seek to discern the shifts in dominance that take place in short periods of real time in a particular context. For example, at time A activity 1A assumes dominance whereas at time B activity 2B is represented as dominant or leading. This analysis could be pursued through the application of Bernstein's model to several activity systems (rather than the one which is usually referenced) and also seek to apply his analysis of power and control to the emergence of dominance (1A vs. 2A vs. 3A). This situated analysis would combine the strengths of AT, with its emphasis on networks of activity and the formation of objects of activity, with the analytical power and descriptive elegance of Bernstein's work. The implications of different social positions would have to be taken into account, as would the recognition that activity systems may be invoked in the absence of the physical presence of all the actors involved (Vygotsky, 1978). The analysis is thus one in which the relational interdependence of individual and social agencies is recognized. The historical analysis would focus on the transformation of dominance through time.

The historical background of much of what is now termed activity theory posits 'networks' of activity systems, in which dominance arises at particular moments in both long and short periods of time. I have placed inverted commas around the word networks because I am wishing to signify a resistance to

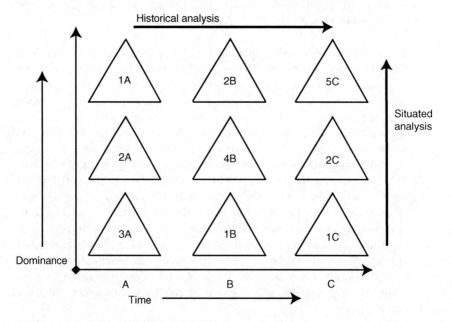

Figure 10.4 Dominance in networks of activity systems through time

the notion of network as a connected system within which component parts share some function. Here I am concerned with the existence of multiple activity systems which may supplant each other and may be mutually transformed. By way of illustration I offer this rather crude example: suppose a person is both a care-giver to their own child as well as a professional teacher. If that teacher has a need to collect their child from a nursery at the end of the school day, then the way that they might respond to class disruption close to the final bell of the day may be very different to the way in which they might respond earlier in the day. Here two activity systems assume a different relationship to one another at particular times of the day. These pulsations in dominance are rarely subjected to rigorous empirical scrutiny. Much of the empirical work which is conducted under the 'label' of AT seems to constrain its analysis to one activity system rather than a network of activity systems and rarely strays into the analysis of shifts in dominance. Taken together the implications of the work of Griffin and Cole (1984), Fairclough (1992), Lemke (1997) and Leontiev (1978, 1981) suggests that such an analysis should be deployed at the levels of both long-term ontogenesis as well as short-term or even micro analysis. Makitalo and Saljo argue that it is through the analysis of categories that 'people draw on the past to make their talk relevant to the accomplishment of interaction within specific traditions of argumentation' (2002: 75). They note, along with Sacks (1992), that categories are activity-bound and that their use is inextricably bound up with a particular interactional and moral order (Jayyusi, 1984: 2). Such analyses would share the concern to explore the way in which subjects are shaped by fluctuating patterns of dominance from the perspective of those actors. However, the emergence of categories is not explored in relation to the principles of regulation of the social setting in which they emerge. The strengths of the language of description within the sociology of pedagogy developed by Bernstein is that it explores possibilities for the individual from the direction of an analysis of the rules regulating social circumstances. I want to suggest that there may be some benefit in pursuing the Bernsteinian perspective in the context of the analysis of fluctuating patterns of dominance within networks of activity systems within this framework, but from the point of view of the pathway of the object through networks of activity.

Conclusion

In order to refine an understanding of organizational, discursive and transmission practices in such situations, new theories of concept formation which emphasize the complex nature of concepts will need to be deployed. There is a need to develop current work on the predictive relationships between macro structures and micro processes. An important part of the challenge is to show how written and spoken hybrid discourse arises and to investigate the consequences of its deployment. In response to this challenge an understanding of discursive hybridity (Sarangi and Roberts, 1999) may provide an important opening for the development of an understanding of changes in discursive practice as different activity systems are brought into different forms of relation with each other. Research in this field requires a unified theory that can give rise to a coherent and internally consistent methodology rather than a collection of compartmentalized accounts of activity, discourse and social positioning which have disparate and often contradictory assumptions.

Consider the situation in which several professionals meet to discuss a supposedly common issue, so for example a psychologist, a teacher, a social worker and a mental health worker meet to discuss the education and care of a young person who has been excluded from school. We can analyse the historical formation of the professional identities of each actor. They will all have been children, pupils, students, trainees and moved through professional structures. A historical analysis of the transformations that take place in activity systems could be brought to bear on the formation of dispositions and identities in each of their career trajectories. A situated analysis would need to pursue the ways in which each subject moved (and was able to move) through a short negotiation of possibilities for action as they attempted to understand and work within or impose professional codes. It is here that Bernstein's work on horizontal and vertical structures and pedagogic discourse as an embedded discourse is important. He provides the language of description and the theoretical basis from which to analyse the emergence of the 'leading' or most powerful activities. Engeström has rightly pointed to the need to analyse contradiction within and between activity systems and Bernstein provides the theoretical tools with which to empirically investigate such phenomena in that he connects the analysis of the organizational, discursive and psychological aspects in a coherent language of description.

In order to make progress in such empirical work, there is a need for theoretical and methodological development which allows us to identify and investigate:

- the ways in which objects of activity are transformed within the networks of activity systems in which subjects participate;
- the circumstances in which particular discourses are produced;
- the modalities of such forms of cultural production; and
- the implications of the availability of specific forms of such production for the positioning of subjects in social space.

Part IV

Policy innovation, discourse and educational reform

11 'Directed time'

Identity and time in New Right and New Labour policy discourse

John Beck

'Directed time', at least in England and Wales, is a term which has become familiar to teachers since the imposition in 1987 of a requirement for teachers to work a stipulated number of hours per year performing contractually specified duties (Tomlinson 1993: 58).[1] As Leaton Gray (2004) has suggested, the notion of 'directed time' has metaphorical resonance far wider than teachers' contracts. First, this regulation of teachers' time-management was a symbolic marker of the new regimes of performativity and audit that began to be imposed in the 1980s. Second, 'directed time' points to the fact that educational time itself can be variously punctuated and periodized, oriented to past or future, accelerated or slowed, according to the requirements of different policy discourses and agendas. This chapter offers a tentative exploration of contrasting orientations to time associated respectively with the political and educational priorities of New Right Conservatism and New Labour in Britain. It will seek to relate these orientations to official attempts to shape new educational and citizen identities.

Basil Bernstein suggested that a key part of the state's reassertion of control over education in England and Wales in the last three decades of the twentieth century involved efforts to project new 'official' educational identities – pupil and (future) citizen identities, and teacher identities. Briefly, he argued that a 're-centred state' was attempting to manage educational change in a context of new economic, cultural and moral challenges, by reasserting centralized control, with the explicit aim of reshaping the pedagogic identities of pupils and teachers in determinate ways (2000: 66–8). Bernstein identified two contrasting types of such 'centred' identities, 'retrospective' and 'prospective', and it is the latter that will mainly concern us here. Prospective identities are *future*-oriented – incorporating a specification of the person as a particular kind of economic producer, consumer and citizen. But with characteristic perceptiveness, Bernstein stressed that these identities are not purely future-oriented. Rather, they are formed by 'recontextualizing selected features of the *past* to stabilize the future through engaging with contemporary change' (ibid. 68, original italics deleted, my italics inserted). Consequently, the shaping of such identities involves both reconfiguring the past (as well as the past's relation to the present) and also projecting a version of the future that is consistent with this imaginary past. Although Bernstein offered brief sketches of the prospective identities projected respectively by 'Thatcherism' and by 'Blair's New Labour' (ibid. 67–8), he did not elaborate them. In what follows, I shall attempt to 'fill in' these outlines and explore some of the ways in which such identities incorporate particular orientations to *time*, within and beyond education.

'Thatcherism' and New Right prospective identities

Several commentators have argued that 'Thatcherism' should be seen 'as an alliance of disparate forces around a self-contradictory programme' rather than as an ideologically unified and coherent political phenomenon (Jessop *et al.* 1984: 38). Similarly, the New Right educational agenda in the period between 1979 and 1997 has also been viewed as an attempt to unite two contradictory projects – those of neo-conservative 'cultural restoration' (Ball 1990; Wexler and Grabiner 1986) and the marketizing, privatizing concerns of neo-liberalism. Although certain of these apparent contradictions may not really have been as fundamental as they at first seemed (see Whitty 1990), it is nevertheless hard to disagree with David Marquand's observation in *The Guardian* that:

> The global market place which the new-style Tories celebrate is cold and hard; in a profound sense, it is also subversive. It uproots communities, disrupts families, mocks faiths and erodes the ties of place and history. It has created a demotic global culture contemptuous of tradition, hostile to established hierarchies and relativist in morality.
>
> (Marquand 1995)

These considerations, however, suggest something problematic when we turn to consider the forms of identity which, if Bernstein is right, successive New Right administrations sought to project. How could a coherent identity grow from such forked roots? Admittedly, post-structuralists remind us that subjectivities are normally fragmented. Nevertheless, attempts to project 'official' identities presuppose an endeavour to shape something possessing some degree of coherence. How might this have been accomplished? Interestingly, several writers use the term 'fusion' to explain this. For example:

- Ken Jones began his book *Right Turn* as follows: 'Conservative education policy, Janus-headed, *fuses* the archaic and modern, mixes nostalgia with technology ...' (1989: 1, my italics).
- Bernstein himself, in his brief sketch of the prospective pedagogic identity projected under Thatcherism, suggests that 'a new collective social base was formed by *fusing* nation, family, individual responsibility and individual enterprise' (2000: 68, my italics).

This language of 'fusion' does intuitively grasp something central to the Thatcherite project of identity formation but it is more than a little inexplicit. It could, variously interpreted, imply aggregation, coalescence, or reduction to an underlying essence.

A fruitful approach to unravelling these issues can be found in social anthropologist Marilyn Strathern's *After Nature* (1992). Strathern's overall concern in this text is to analyse the conditions that made possible the changing ways in which the English middle classes, across more than two hundred years, imagined themselves and their relationships – to one another, to convention, to family and to society. One section of the book deals directly with 'Thatcherism' and here Strathern's point of departure is Thatcher's assertion that: 'There is no such thing as society. There are individual men and women and there are families' (ibid. 158).

Against those who homed in on the supposed absence of morality and the 'sheer selfishness' implied in this claim, Strathern's interest is in how something that was a morality – a morality apparently independent of society – came to be constructed as a possible discursive object. She poses the question 'So where, then, does the morality now come from, how can it be seen?' (ibid. 159). She suggests that a key 'strategy' involved was one of dislocating the individual from society by depicting collectivism, especially state-sponsored collectivism, as something 'artificial' and alien to British instincts. This was counterpointed within Thatcherite discourse, by a 'naturalism' in which morality is installed as an inherent property of 'responsible' individuals who simply 'know' how to conduct themselves. Strathern speculates that:

> Perhaps that possibility draws on the ease with which the English have in the past personified convention: the 'forces' or 'principles' for morality, good conduct and the rest can be apostrophized as existing of themselves, so that people can respond to those forces without the intervention of (contrived, collectivist) human institutions. Morality is set free from such institutions. ... People, we are told by the Government, do not need government to tell them what to do. Since ideas and values are seen to exert an influence by themselves, they do not have to be mediated by others, but can be taken for granted in the minds of right thinking individuals. All that individuals have to do is manage their lives properly ... What displaces the plurality of other persons who might be held to 'make society' is the single individual with means. 'Society' thereby becomes unimaginable.
>
> (Ibid. 160–1)

Two crucial consequences of this are first, that 'it becomes impossible to invoke selfishness with the same axiomatic condemnation; attention to one's own interests is now a virtue' and second, 'since morality is within, then it must necessarily take the form that in turn typifies the individual: the capacity to exercise *choice*' (ibid. 161, my italics).

In all this, something rather strange and paradoxical happens to time. The naturalizing move seems to cancel temporal referents by eternalizing certain dispositions as natural properties of individuals per se. Yet, this turns out to be not just any individual but rather one who is somehow innately 'British'. John Quicke, for example, has drawn attention to the significance in New Right discourse of recourse to certain 'givens' supposedly 'lodged in the British Personality' (1988: 18). Strathern makes a similar connection: 'that people know what is right is taken for granted, rather like the stereotyped English gentleman who knows his duty even if he cannot say what it is until the moment is upon him' (1992: 159). Strathern is referring here to a lecture series delivered in 1929 by a certain Professor Dixon, concerning the 'English Genius'. Dixon suggested not only that the Englishman is typically an individualist but also that the Englishman's sense of duty is at once unreflective but instinctively sure – issuing in appropriate *action*:

> What is English here is the sense of conduct as the test of a man. Not what he thinks or feels. ... Let others judge by the state of their emotions or of their minds ... Brushing all these aside as irrelevant, the Englishman judges simply by the act ...
>
> (Dixon 1938: 78–80)

Or as Strathern satirically glosses this, 'the Englishman does his duty without quite knowing what it is', adding: 'this 1930s evocation of individual motivation anticipates a most interesting feature of the (neo-conservative) active citizen: that he or she is their own source of right acting' (1992: 153).

This analysis suggests that the construction of time in these discourses involves an amalgam of contradictory but efficacious fictions. On the one hand, time is cancelled by the appeal to naturalism. But it is enabled to reappear by associating this 'natural' individualism with a conception of national character – one which in one sense is also 'eternalized' as the unchanging instincts of the Englishman, but that in another sense is necessarily 'historical', incorporating a vision of the national past. Here, perhaps, is a key element of the 'fusion' of conflicting elements that has been seen as a hallmark of Thatcherism. The values which motivate this individual are at once purely individual and also 'timeless' because natural, but at the same time they are historical because inseparable from a rugged but rooted Englishness. The consequences are significant. On the one hand, the resonance of this individualism with so-called Victorian values comes to appear self-evident as an expression of authentic English character in the past and thus also of 'tradition'. But at the same time, what is licensed and legitimized is the innately 'morally responsible' individual whose primary moral responsibility is to seek the good of themselves and their family through the exercise of marketized choices and enterprising behaviour.

The extent to which and the ways in which education (and more specifically pedagogic transmissions) may have contributed to a similar shaping of such 'dissociated' individualism is not easy to assess. Bernstein argued explicitly that the prospective pedagogic identity projected under Thatcherism was designed to shape 'what were considered to be appropriate attitudes, dispositions and performances relevant to a market culture and reduced state welfare' (2000: 68) and (as we have seen) he suggests that this involved an attempt to create a 'new collective social base ... formed by fusing nation, family, individual responsibility and individual enterprise' (ibid.). The resonances with Strathern's analysis are clear. However, curricular constructions of the nation's past, even when surrounded by restorationist rhetoric, cannot be easily shaped to simply reinforce the sort of potent but unreflective common sense Strathern describes, especially where the curriculum takes the form of a 'collection code' (Bernstein 2000: 10–11) which supports academic virtues such as respect for evidence and the importance of weighing competing interpretations of issues and events. Recognizing this tension, a number of other commentators have highlighted the significance of the role of the hidden curriculum as possibly a stronger influence on identity formation than either the content or pedagogy of the overt curriculum. For example, Whitty and Power have commented: 'while the content of lessons emphasizes heritage and tradition, the form of their transmission is becoming increasingly commodified within the new education marketplace' (2002: 103). And Bernstein himself similarly suggested that context was likely to outweigh content in this contradictory pedagogic transmission:

> The culture of the pedagogic discourse of schools is retrospective, based on a past narrative of the dominance and significance of disciplines, whereas the management structure is *prospective,* pointing to the new entrepreneurialism and its instrumentalities. The state has therefore embedded a retrospective pedagogic culture into a prospective management culture. However, the emphasis on the performance of students and the steps taken to increase and maintain performance, for the survival of the institution, is likely to facilitate a state-promoted instrumentality. The intrinsic value of knowledge may well be eroded even though the collection code of the curriculum appears to support such a value.
>
> (2000: 61)

If this analysis is persuasive, 'Thatcherite' conservatism sought to both project and ratify a new–old British identity centred in ostensibly self-made and self-supporting individuals and their families who had an intuitive sense of their links to a heritage of robust national and individual independence. This identity was thus able to combine a strong sense of continuity with a shared (if highly fictitious) national past which was also the foundation of a 'realistic' orientation to a future in which markets and individual effort would rightly allocate resources and opportunities in an increasingly competitive world. The individual's sense of moral obligation towards the welfare of others would be expressed in voluntary effort rather than mediated by enterprise-sapping statist provision.

New Labour's modernizing agenda and new prospective identities

Before embarking on a discussion of identity formation under New Labour, it is worth recalling that Bernstein's analysis of identity was grounded in a broadly Durkheimian view that individual identity must be rooted in a 'collective social base'. It follows that any endeavour to construct identities therefore requires the parallel or prior construction of such a social base. In the case of New Labour's attempts to project centred prospective identities, what was explicitly foregrounded in contrast to Thatcherism was social belonging – linked, however, to strong notions of individual enterprise and responsibility. The social base of these centred identities was thus:

> An amalgam of notions of community (really communities) and local responsibilities to motivate and restore belonging in the cultural sphere, and a new participatory responsibility in the economic sphere.
>
> (Bernstein 2000: 68)

In his broader discussion of pedagogic identities, however, Bernstein emphasized that at any historical moment, no one identity-project was likely to be hegemonic. And in his analyses of social and educational change in late-twentieth-century Britain, he saw the co-existence of contradictory forms of identity as characteristic of the period, in particular, the tension between centred identities projected by government and 'de-centred market' identities arising from the effects of market forces. For our purposes, it is significant that Bernstein did not examine in any detail the temporal aspects of the various forces that were reshaping identity as the twentieth century moved towards its close. In this section, therefore, I shall tentatively explore some of the ways in which New Labour has sought to construct a new version of the past's relation to the present, as a basis for an agenda of urgent 'modernization'.[2]

In repositioning itself in the political landscape, it is significant that New Labour chose to re-brand itself by employing two key descriptors – 'New' and 'modernize'. Such terms are examples of what Bill Readings (1996) calls 'dereferentialization', i.e. words which are relatively content-less, but which for that very reason can be mobilized to support whatever more specific goals an organization's current agendas may require. Readings cites the example of 'excellence' as used in mission statements and the like (but see also DfEE 1997a, 1997b, 1999 and DfES 2003). 'New' and 'modernize' are not, of course, wholly content-less. Both have a clear temporal reference: together they signify a future that will be radically different from the past, though still linked to it: what was good will be conserved and the bad abandoned. In some respects, of course, the party leadership was content with nothing short of rupture – most clearly in expunging the old Clause 4 from the party's constitution. But for the most part, the 'modernizing' initiatives have involved retaining both terminology and organizational forms from the past, whilst radically changing and sometimes inverting their meaning.

It will clearly not be possible to examine here the whole of New Labour's political or even educational discourse. Rather, I shall focus on just two areas of educational policy: first, the 'modernization of the teaching profession', and second, the intensification of the 'standards agenda'. In each case, the discussion will draw mainly on education policy documents from a variety of sources. I shall also refer to a number of secondary commentaries.[3]

The modernization of the teaching profession

The 2001 Green Paper *Schools: Building on Success* (DfEE 2001) felt able to celebrate the progress already achieved in 'modernizing' the teaching profession:

> The changing economy is increasingly placing new demands on professionals in every field. In the 20th Century, the professional could often expect to be treated as an authority, whose judgment was rarely questioned and who was therefore rarely held to account. Despite this ... particularly in the public sector, services were arranged to suit the producer rather than the user.

> Teaching, by contrast is already in many ways a 21st century profession. More perhaps than any other, the teaching profession accepts accountability, is open to the contributions that others can make and is keen to seek out best practice ... Growing acceptance of accountability means that the relationship between teachers and Government can build more than ever before on trust ... In this climate, in partnership with teachers, we will take forward the agenda of reform ... and complete the modernization of the teaching profession.
>
> (DfEE 2001, paras. 5.4, 5.5. and 5.6)

It is instructive to set this alongside a recent speech by Michael Barber, formerly the director of the DfES Standards and Effectiveness Unit and currently head of the Prime Minister's Delivery Unit:

> Until the mid-1980s what happened in schools and classrooms was left almost entirely to teachers to decide ... Almost all teachers had goodwill and many sought to develop themselves professionally, but, through no fault of their own, the profession itself was uninformed ... Under Thatcher, the system moved from *uninformed professional judgement* to *uninformed prescription*.
>
> (Barber 2001, cited in Alexander 2004: 15–16, Barber's italics)

Such statements are examples of a discursive strategy that seeks to construct an imaginary version of the past in an effort to shape conditions for a new consensus between teachers and government, and also to shape the identities of 'modern' professionals. This strategy employs a dichotomous periodizing of educational time in order to create a pathological past set against an 'enlightened' present. A pervasive feature of the discourse is its tendency to present highly contestable claims as if they were unquestionable truths. Older forms of professional organization in which professions enjoyed greater autonomy are pathologized not merely as self-serving and unaccountable but also as professionally 'uninformed'. As Alexander has trenchantly remarked:

> Note how heavily professional ignorance features in this professional pathology, and how it is presented as an inevitable concomitant of professional autonomy. To be free to decide how to teach is to be uninformed.
>
> (Alexander 2004: 16)

He adds: 'it sets things up nicely, of course, for the transformation achieved by New Labour and the Utopia which is now in sight' (ibid.).

A related characteristic of the discourse is that it presents a range of crucially significant concepts as if they had only one legitimate interpretation. Thus we are told, baldly, that the modernized teaching profession 'accepts accountability' – as if there was only one concept of accountability possible. It is ironic that those who accuse others of being uninformed can so conveniently overlook the debates of the 1980s on competing conceptions of accountability – for example, Bailey's discussion of the professional responsibilities of liberal educators (1984: 236–40), or the work of the Cambridge Accountability Project (Elliott *et al.* 1981). By being positioned on the 'wrong' side of the historical divide between pathology and enlightenment, such work is consigned to oblivion by the new modernizers, whose instrumental training schedules allow no time for teachers to think in an informed manner about such issues. In these ways, the scope of professional debate is drastically narrowed and the professional conversations of the past are written out of history.

Pathologizing the past is, however, only half the story. Its counterpart is the deployment of a would-be inclusive language that seeks to co-opt teachers (and other professionals) as 'modern' professionals. Here, 'modernization' reveals its versatility. It cannot only signal the new but also suggest continuities with the past. The message is that teachers have always been in certain respects professional and now they are being 'helped' to become more so. Here, a further periodization becomes significant: between a Thatcherism that castigated teachers for their alleged inadequacies, replaced by a stance that recognizes teachers' long-standing professional commitment and seeks 'partnership' with them. The new language of 'shared vision', 'trust', 'goodwill', 'partnership' and 'dialogue' is increasingly prominent in recent documents. Even where teachers are judged inadequate, e.g. by virtue of being 'uninformed', they are reassured that this was *through no fault of their own* (Barber 2001, cited in Alexander 2004: 16, my italics). This ostensibly 'post-Fordist' turn in official discourse has helped New Labour to present its overall project as one of *re*-professionalization, not *de*-professionalization.

This invitation to partnership has been linked to a further claim: that New Labour's reforms have raised the status of the profession. The 2002 DfES document *Time for Standards,* under a sub-heading 'Teaching – A High Status Profession', claimed:

> In talking about what our best teachers are doing, we are describing a profession that is on the move ... We hope that teaching will emerge as the most admired profession of the 21ˢᵗ century, and the one young people are keenest to join ... Together, we can create a new and thoroughly deserved image for ... teachers as mind-shapers and not child-minders.
>
> (DfES 2002: 17–18)

Such rhetoric risks imploding into its own vacuity. Nevertheless, it signals a significant discursive shift from a 'culture of blame', to a culture of 'partnership' and *'earned* autonomy'. This presages a whole new 'era':

> The 1997–2001 Blair Government inherited a system of *uninformed prescription* and replaced it with one of *informed prescription* ... The White Paper signals the next shift: from *informed prescription* to *informed professional judgement* ... The era of informed professional judgement could be the most successful so far in our educational history ...
>
> (Barber 2001, cited in Alexander 2004: 16)

At the heart of 'informed professional judgement' is the idea of 'evidence-based teaching and learning'. Thus a 2002 DfES paper confidently declares:

> Our best teachers are already using informed professional judgement. They are creating an evidence-based body of knowledge about teaching and learning. Establishing such a body of knowledge has always been a crucial step in marking out the top professions in our society. It will provide working models that other teachers will adopt and ensure that teaching is acknowledged for what it is: an innovative and expert profession.
>
> (DfES 2002: 12)

Once again, the language of the discourse is as revealing as the content. It is 'our' best teachers who have created this body of knowledge – though, of course, crucially 'enabled' by government. And, in an appeal to those older models of professionalism that the government is in other respects so keen to discredit, we are told that teaching may advance to the rank of a 'top profession' by virtue of being based on such 'expert' knowledge. What is more, teaching will win further recognition of its status through disseminating such 'proven best practice'. So far, so simplistic! It is ironic that what is being celebrated is *professional judgement,* when what is occurring is the narrowing of the scope of autonomous judgement about education and pedagogy in favour of a state-imposed technicism.

The creation (significantly by government itself) of the General Teaching Council for England in September 2000 was intended to be a key symbol of the claimed re-professionalization of teaching. The GTC is, in the words of its first chief executive, a body which has been given 'responsibility for advising the government and other bodies on education policy' and which has taken on certain functions of traditional professional associations including 'developing a code of professional practice with the full involvement of the profession' and also the regulation of professional misconduct (Adams 2000). On closer analysis, however, this professional re-empowerment turns out to be remarkably circumscribed. The GTC may *advise* on educational policy but it is government and its agencies that continue to operate the levers of power. Symptomatically, government spokesmen when addressing the public at large remain unabashed in declaring that it is *they* who are in charge and are 'driving through necessary change'. Thus Andrew Adonis could write in 2001: 'We have *imposed* a new national curriculum for initial teacher training, setting out the standards and content of training courses, which all providers *must* follow' (Adonis 2001, quoted in Alexander 2004: 17, my italics), while Education Secretary David Blunkett declared 'I make no apologies for the *prescription* in the literacy and numeracy strategies; we had to deal with the failure of teacher training over decades' (2001: 7, my italics). The italicized imperatives here provide a discordant counterpoint to the themes of trust and partnership so prominent elsewhere. As Alexander succinctly summarizes the situation:

> it is clear that in the post-2001 era of 'informed professional judgement', to be 'informed' is to know and acquiesce in what is provided, expected and/or required by government and its agencies ... no less and, especially, no more.
> (2004: 17)

Making up for lost time: accelerating the 'standards agenda'

Although New Labour may allow itself some celebration of progress, there is no room (or time) for complacency. The latest imperative is to *accelerate* the pace of change. Michael Barber again:

> Our vision is of a world-class education service: one that matches the best anywhere ... We want to see it achieved ... as soon as possible within the decade that has just begun. Our sense of urgency comes ... from the belief that time is running out for public education to prove its worth.
> (Barber 2003)

Again, the discourse presents a set of speculative and contentious claims as unarguable imperatives. Thus, in a passage that directly follows that quoted above:

The danger is that ... more and more people will see private education for their children as a rational lifestyle option. If this were to occur, they would become less and less willing to fund public education, which would become ... a poor service for poor people ... Only if public education delivers, and is seen to deliver real quality, can this unwelcome prospect be avoided; ... successful reform is possible ... and ... need not take forever.

And a little later:

In the modern world ... electorates are fickle and impatient ... They ... will not wait patiently for five or ten years to see if it delivers. They want immediate evidence that it is on the way.

The 'clincher' follows:

Hence the central paradox facing education reformers in a democracy – a long-term strategy will only succeed if it delivers short-term results.

(Ibid.)

As well as anxious parents and impatient electorates, contemporary education is also depicted as beset by inexorable globalization seen as shaping an economic environment in which educational institutions and national economies alike face a stark choice: adapt or perish. As David Blunkett (2000) put it: 'Universities need to adapt rapidly to the top-down influences of globalization and the new technologies', adding menacingly that 'the "do-nothing" universities will not survive – and it will not be the job of government to bail them out'. Barber extends this diagnosis, employing further specious periodization, to announce the inevitability of *educational* globalization:

Just as financial services globalized in the 1980s and media and communications in the 1990s, so in this decade we will see education reform globalizing ... We, in England, will want to be sure that our 14-year-olds are as well educated as students in the USA, Germany or Singapore, not least because they will ultimately be competing in a global job market.

(Barber 2003)

What is perhaps most striking about such claims (and they are legion – reiterated in almost every major government education policy document) is that 'no alternative is conceived, except that we, as a nation, might fail to keep up' and that 'few ends are considered for the nation and its education system, other than meeting the challenge and adapting' (Ahier *et al.* 2003: 82). In reality, however, globalization is not an unquestionable fact: rather, it is a contested concept where definition and effects are vigorously disputed (see, for example, Beck 2002; Callinicos 2001; Gray 1999; Held and McGrew 2002; Hirst and Thompson 1996).

New Labour's enthusiasts for change, however, are in no mood to allow mere academic arguments to impede the 'essential' task of further and faster modernization. We must, we are urged, be decisive, innovative and pragmatic in dealing with these pressing challenges. Moreover, we must not cling to 'outdated' delivery mechanisms:

> We must ask ourselves from where the energy, knowledge, imagination, skill and investment will come to meet the immense challenge of education reform over the next decade. For most of the 20th century, the drive for educational progress came from the public sector ... Towards the end of the 20th century, as frustration with existing systems grew, this legacy was challenged by a growing vibrant private sector ... The challenge for the 21st century is surely to *seek out what works*. The issue is not whether the public, private or voluntary sector alone will shape the future but what partnerships and combinations of the three will make the most difference to student performance.
>
> (Barber 2003, my italics)

Yet again we encounter a pathologized past (of public provision) counterposed to a glowing future (of 'vibrant' private sector leadership and 'partnership'). And once more, complex issues of political philosophy and value are overridden by the supposed pragmatic imperatives of adopting whatever 'delivery systems' work best and quickest. Even issues as complex and controversial as expanding the provision of faith schools can, in this hurrying discourse, be treated almost entirely instrumentally – as little more than pragmatic mechanisms to help deliver the really important goal: driving up 'standards':

> We are intentionally breaking the mould in our relationships with the voluntary and religious sectors, by, for example, providing for the first time, state funding for Muslim, Sikh, and Seventh Day Adventist schools ... The central challenge is to build social coalitions in the drive for higher standards and radical reform. It is clear in Hong Kong and elsewhere that the business and religious sectors are strong allies. This is true in the USA too where ... the churches provide real energy and drive for educational progress ... Each a different combination, each fit for purpose ...
>
> (Ibid.)

Let us now consider the implications for identity of this headlong instrumentalism and pragmatism. They seem to point towards what Bernstein saw as a new sort of identity – whose most striking characteristic was that it was socially empty. Marketization and managerialization of education, he suggested, were likely to promote, at least in certain parts of the education system, *'generic' pedagogic modes*:

based on a new concept of 'work' and 'life' which might be called *'short-termism'*. This is where a skill, task, area of work, undergoes continuous development, disappearance or replacement; where life experience cannot be based on stable expectations of the future and one's location in it.

(Bernstein 2000: 59, my italics)

In such circumstances, Bernstein argues, a new kind of ability comes to be seen as particularly desirable: *'trainability'* – the capacity to accept and (ideally) embrace 'continuous pedagogic re-formations' requiring 'an ability to respond effectively to concurrent, subsequent, intermittent pedagogics'. Unlike more stable bases of identity formation, however, the identity produced by this combination of short-termism and trainability is intrinsically 'socially empty': 'there seems to be an emptiness in the concept of trainability, an emptiness which makes the concept self-referential' (ibid.). It denotes, precisely, a vacant space waiting to be filled with whatever temporary contents market, or institutional, or governmental imperatives may dictate.[4]

A similar substantive emptiness seems to lie at the heart of New Labour's agenda of accelerating modernization. What is most striking about the modernizers' 'machismo' – that there is no alternative but to respond to 'the challenge ahead' through '"step change", "tough", "new", "tough new", "world class", "best practice", "delivery", and so on' (DfEE 2001, cited in Alexander 2004: 14) – is precisely that it too is so empty of principled or grounded educational content, largely as a result of being pragmatically orientated to short-term instrumental goals and adaptive responses. It is no less noteworthy that this change agenda is permeated with attempts (both discursive and practical) to reconfigure relationships between past, present and future, and that it seeks to do this in ways that would, if successful, render much of the past inaccessible and therefore unavailable as a basis for identity formation. In New Labour's rhetoric of adaptation and modernization, it is increasingly the case that those parts of the past that do not fit are either repudiated or repressed:

• repudiated as irrelevant because they offer no guide to challenges which are, by definition, unprecedented as well as pressing;
• repudiated as in various ways pathological and dysfunctional – a place of self-indulgence, or at best of well-intentioned but inadequately informed practice;
• repudiated as the site of discredited and inefficient forms of 'statist' provision;
• repressed by attempts to silence discourses critical of current policy and dismantle or restructure the organizational forms that carried them.

Recent reforms of initial teacher training in England display both these tendencies.[5]

Conclusion

This orientation to the past by the party of government may be both an effect and a cause of what some have seen as a more general phenomenon of our times. As Eric Hobsbawm expressed it:

> The destruction of the past, or rather of the social mechanisms that link one's contemporary experience to that of earlier generations, is one of the most characteristic and eerie phenomena of the late twentieth century. Most young men and women at the century's end grow up in a sort of permanent present lacking any organic relation to the public past of the times they live in.
>
> (Hobsbawm 1994: 3)

Such reflections return us to the theme of emptiness. As Bernstein saw it, something would be necessary to fill the empty identity-space produced by short-termism and 'trainability': 'If the identity produced by "trainability" is socially "empty", how does the actor recognize him/herself and others?' His answer was: 'by the materialities of consumption ... the products of the market relay the signifiers whereby temporary stabilities, orientations, relations and evaluations are constructed' (2000: 59). If this analysis is persuasive, it may not be entirely far-fetched to suggest that New Labour's modernizers are tapping into but also shaping something that may indeed be an emergent socio-cultural reality: an historically dissociated 'middle England' in which identity is increasingly centred in consumerist signifiers of value and personal worth. The tragedy (but paradoxically also the success) of New Labour may be that it so assiduously promotes this emergent sensibility, rather than doing anything to question or challenge it.

Speaking out in this way against current shibboleths carries a certain risk. As Frank Kermode put it in relation to his own critical comments on 1960s literary modernism:

> To speak clearly on these issues is to attract the charge that one is simply no longer young enough or bright enough to grasp the exciting things that are going on.
>
> (Kermode 1966: 123)

However, academics of a certain age may take some comfort from Kermode's affirmation: 'The critics should know their duty' (ibid. 124).

Notes

1   The imposition of new statutory pay and conditions of service requirements under the Teachers' Pay and Conditions Act of 1987 followed 'a prolonged and bitter dispute between the DES, teachers' unions and LEAs' between 1984 and 1987 (Tomlinson 1993: 49). The School Teachers' Pay and Conditions Act 1991 modified the statutory framework in various

ways. In addition to 'directed time', teachers' contracts also contained provision for 'additional contractual obligation time' and a much smaller element of 'self-directed time' (Tomlinson 1993: 58).

2 This chapter will not attempt to assess the extent to which this was accomplished. The discussion is mainly concerned with analysing educational and other discourses rather than estimating their effectivity.

3 I have, in particular, made extensive reference to Robin Alexander's paper 'Still No Pedagogy?' (2004), in which he developed a trenchant critique of the Government's 2003 Primary Strategy via a detailed analysis of the DfES document *Excellence and Enjoyment: a Strategy for Primary Schools* (DfES 2003).

4 Although generic modes are treated by Bernstein as linked to 'de-centred market' identities (Bernstein 2000, Chapter 3), we need to remind ourselves that he recognized that in reality, more hybrid forms are encountered. It certainly seems plausible that under New Labour, hybrid identities of this kind are being shaped and that they are the product not only of direct market imperatives but also of 'centred' (i.e. governmental) initiatives intended to 'functionalize' the education system to more effectively meet perceived market demands. Centrally imposed reforms of teacher training, under both Conservative and Labour governments since the 1980s, have arguably resulted in a significantly stronger emphasis on 'trainability' (see Beck 2002; Beck and Young 2005).

5 It was Moore and Jones who first drew attention to the ways in which the introduction of competency-based paradigms into teacher training in England in the 1990s threatened to deny 'trainees' access to more critical kinds of academic discourse, notably insights developed within the philosophy and sociology of education. As these writers also pointed out, competency-based training tended to conceal its own grounding in theoretical knowledge (mainly in behaviourist psychology), and it did this by representing itself as simply 'common sense' and thus as an alternative to what the Secretary of State for Education at the time, Kenneth Clark, memorably called 'barmy theory' (Jones and Moore 1995).

12 Toward a sociology of educational change

An application of Bernstein to the US 'No Child Left Behind' Act

Alan Sadovnik

The No Child Left Behind Act (NCLB 2002) is a landmark and controversial piece of legislation that may have far-reaching consequences for education in the United States. Already there is talk of spreading similar accountability efforts to higher education in the next re-authorization of the Higher Education Act. And, of course, state governments have been busily pushing accountability requirements for K-12 (Kindergarten through grade 12, the last year of high school) and higher education for years now. No Child Left Behind is the centerpiece of President George W. Bush's educational policy. A logical progression of the standards movement initiated in 1983 by *A Nation at Risk* (NCEE 1983) and in federal legislation under Presidents G.H.W. Bush (*America 2000;* see Cross 2004: 100) and W.J. Clinton (*Goals 2000;* 1994), NCLB is the most comprehensive federal legislation governing state and local educational policies in US history.

No Child Left Behind represented a logical extension of a conservative standards movement that tossed the left's critique of US education back on itself. Based on the critique that US education has historically underserved low-income and minority children through curriculum tracking and poor instruction and low-quality teachers in urban schools, NCLB mandates uniform standards for all students in order to reduce and eventually eliminate the social class and race achievement gap by 2014. Given the importance of NCLB, it is imperative that legislators, policy-makers, educators and parents have objective, data-driven, theoretical and non-ideological information and analyses to guide decision-making and policy debates. Unfortunately, the discussion of NCLB has too often been ideological, rhetorical, and lacking in data about the law and its effects.

Much of the public debate about NCLB has been political and ideological with little light shed on the effects of the law on the organizational contexts of schools. As a discipline, sociology has much to say about key concerns of NCLB assessment, instructional improvement, teacher recruitment and professional development, and school choice. However, the discourse on NCLB has been dominated by educational psychology and economics, with insufficient regard to the issues of stratification processes, organizational dynamics and institutional structure that sociology would illuminate. Within these contexts, sociological analyses can examine the effects of NCLB on different groups of students and schools and the ways in which school organization and structure affect achievement. Further, sociologists of education will provide much-needed data-driven analyses of the law's components and their effects on children, teachers, parents and schools. Finally, sociological analysis will provide an understanding of how the organizational and interactional processes within schools may change to respond to the specific mandates of the law.

Although much of this work is being carried out by US sociologists of education, the work of Basil Bernstein is absent from these endeavors. Often deemed too theoretical and not applicable to the analysis of educational policy and its effects, US sociologists of education have failed to draw on the important theoretical and empirical insights of Bernstein's work for the purpose of understanding educational policy in general and NCLB in particular. The purpose of this paper is to apply the sociology of Basil Bernstein to an analysis of NCLB. Using Bernstein's theories of pedagogic practice and discourse developed in *Class, Codes and Control, Volumes 3, 4 and 5* (Bernstein 1977 Ch. 6; 1990 Ch. 2, Ch. 3, Ch. 5; 1996 Ch. 2), this paper will demonstrate how NCLB can be understood within the larger contexts of debates about visible pedagogy (VP) and invisible pedagogy (IP) and the role of the state in mediating conflicts between two forms of visible pedagogy, market dependent visible pedagogy (MVP) and autonomous visible pedagogy (AVP). Further, using Bernstein's analysis of the pedagogic device (1996 Ch. 2), the paper will analyze the ways in which NCLB is related to instructional and regulative discourse and their distributive and evaluative rules, as well as the role of the state in privileging some forms of evaluative rules over others. The paper will then analyze how Bernstein's theories enable us to understand the evolution of the standards movement in the US and the effects of NCLB on different schools and different groups of students, especially with respect to race, social class, ethnic and gender differences. Within this context, the paper will analyze how NCLB has attempted to reduce the achievement gaps by equalizing classification, distributive and evaluative rules, while at the same time leaving the framing rules of pedagogic practice and discourse open to individual schools. Drawing upon research on the effects of different pedagogic practices for different groups of students in the US (Sadovnik 1991, 1995; Semel 1995; Semel and Sadovnik 1999), the paper will provide a Bernsteinian analysis of the social class basis of educational inequality and conservative attempts, at least in principle, to reduce them, as well as liberal and radical criticisms that such efforts simply mask the overall goals to privatize US education.

Finally, using Bernstein's analysis of educational change, the paper concludes that over the past twenty years, the state has responded to powerful conservative groups to eliminate the progressive pedagogies of the past and replace them with more traditional forms of curriculum and pedagogic practices. Within this context, the state has implemented strong evaluative rules to effect radical educational change and to weaken the classification between schools, businesses and religious institutions. Although based on an egalitarian call for equity, the evidence suggests that NCLB is an ambitious attempt to privatize education and to provide publicly funded vouchers for private and religious schools. Bernstein's theories present an important conceptual tool for understanding the dynamics of this form of educational change.

'No Child Left Behind' legislation

Unlike the UK and other nations with centralized national control of educational policy, the US has no history of federal control. The US constitution does not explicitly mention education as a federal role, and therefore, under its tenth Amendment, control of education is delegated to the individual states. Federal involvement in education began in the post-Second-World-War years, with legislation such as the GI Bill in 1945, the Elementary and Secondary Education Act in 1965, the Education for Children with Disabilities Act in 1975 and the Individuals with Disabilities Act in 1996, and with landmark Supreme Court decisions on desegregation in *Brown* v. *Board* in 1954, *Swann* v. *Charlotte-Mecklenberg* in 1971 and *Milliken* v. *Bradley* in 1974 (see Patterson 2002 for details on these cases). However, the federal government did not begin to set educational standards until the 1990s, specifically with *America 2000* and *Goals 2000*. NCLB, which was passed as part of the reauthorization of the Elementary and Secondary Act in 2001, for the first time set specific standards for schools and their students and penalties for not meeting these standards. Although states are still able to set their own curriculum and assessment standards, leaving the US without a national curriculum and assessment system like in the UK, states that do not comply with the federal standards are ineligible for millions of dollars in federal Title I monies for disadvantaged students, as well as other federal educational aid.

The key components of NCLB are:

* Annual testing of students in Grades 3–8 in reading and math plus at least one test in Grades 10–12; science testing to follow. Graduation rates are used as a secondary indicator for high schools.
* Require states and districts to report school-by-school data on student test performance, broken out by whether the student is African-American, Hispanic, Native-American, Asian-American, White non-Hispanic, Special Education, Limited English Proficiency (LEP), and/or Low Income.
* States must set 'adequate yearly progress' (AYP) goals for each school. In order to meet AYP, not only must each subgroup make progress in each year in each grade in each subject but there must be 95 per cent participation of each subgroup as well. The increments in AYP should be arranged so that 100 per cent of students reach proficiency by 2014.

- Schools that don't meet AYP for two years are labeled 'In Need of Improvement' (INOI). Initially, this means that schools must offer students the option to go to another public school and/or to receive federally funded tutoring. Monies would also be made available for teacher professional development. In the absence of meeting future AYP targets, schools would be subject to 'restructuring' (firing teachers and principal; state takeover; private company takeover; etc.).
- Schools must have 'highly qualified' teachers for the 'core academic subjects' (English, reading or language arts, math, science, foreign languages, civics and government, economics, arts, history and geography) by 2005–6.

With respect to the school choice provision, although capacity is not supposed to be used as an excuse, in urban areas with large numbers of low-performing schools and low numbers of successful schools there is little capacity for public school choice and neighboring suburban districts rarely permit urban-to-suburban transfers. In some states such as Florida, where there are public voucher programs for low-income families for use in private and religious schools, families are permitted to use vouchers if there are no public transfers available. Some critics of NCLB argue that President Bush, who supported a voucher provision in the original legislation but was thwarted by a Democratic Congress opposed to vouchers, supported choice language in NCLB that would result in the creation of state-wide charter programs.

Advocates of the legislation, including progressive organizations such as the Education Trust, argue that its annual testing and disaggregation requirements will force states to ensure that low-income students who continue to lag far behind higher-income students will meet the same standards, and thus reduce the achievement gap by 2014. Critics from both the academic and political worlds argue that however noble the goal of eliminating the achievement gap, the Bill does not provide sufficient funds to improve failing schools and, more importantly, is heavy on punishment and light on building school capacity. More radical critics (Anyon 2005) argue that NCLB fails to acknowledge the social and economic foundation of unequal schooling and is a backdoor to the implementation of publicly funded school vouchers and the dismantling of public education in the US. Finally, assessment experts (Dworkin 2005) argue that since the types of tests and definitions of adequate yearly progress vary by state there is no uniform definition of proficiency and since the assessments evaluate schools rather than students, schools with high mobility rates are punished for such a high turnover, which most of the time is outside of their control. In addition, since the assessments are based on a zero-sum definition of proficiency rather than a value-added one, schools whose students show significant progress but are still below proficiency are labeled as failures rather than rewarded for their progress. Although sociologists of education have devoted considerable attention to NCLB,[1] none of the papers have included an application of the work of Basil Bernstein, despite the fact that his work provides an important theoretical lens for viewing US federal educational policies.

Bernstein's theory of pedagogic practice and discourse

Beginning with the third volume of *Class, Codes, and Control* (1977), Bernstein developed code theory from its sociolinguistic roots to examine the connection between communication codes and pedagogic discourse and practice. In this respect, code theory became concerned with the processes of schooling and how they related to social class reproduction. Bernstein's quest for understanding the processes of schooling led him to continue to pursue the fruitful avenue of inquiry developed in his article 'Class and Pedagogies: Visible and Invisible' (1977 Ch. 6). In that article, Bernstein analyzed the differences between two types of educational transmission and suggested that the differences in the classification and framing rules of each pedagogic practice (visible = strong classification and strong framing; invisible = weak classification and weak framing) relate to the social class position and assumptions of the families served by the schools. (For a detailed analysis of this aspect of Bernstein's work, see Atkinson 1985; Atkinson *et al.* 1995; Sadovnik 1991, 1995.) The article clearly demonstrated that sociologists of education had to do the difficult empirical work of looking into the world of schools and of linking educational practices to the larger institutional, societal and historical factors of which they are a part.

The concept of classification is at the heart of Bernstein's theory of pedagogic discourse and practice. Classification refers to 'the degree of boundary maintenance between contents' (Bernstein 1971/1973a: 205; 1971/1973b: 88) and is concerned with the insulation or boundaries between curricular categories (areas of knowledge and subjects). Strong classification refers to a curriculum that is highly differentiated and separated into traditional subjects; weak classification refers to a curriculum that is integrated and in which the boundaries between subjects are fragile. Using the concept of classification, Bernstein outlined two types of curriculum code: collection and integrated codes. The first refers to a strongly classified curriculum; the latter, to a weakly classified curriculum. In keeping with his Durkheimian project, Bernstein analyzed the way in which the shift from collection to integrated curriculum codes represents the evolution from mechanical to organic solidarity (or from traditional to modern society) (see Walford and Pickering 1998), with curricular change marking the movement from the sacred to the profane.

Whereas classification is concerned with the organization of knowledge into curriculum, framing is related to the transmission of knowledge through pedagogic practices. Framing refers to the location of control over the rules of communication and, according to Bernstein (1990 Ch. 3: 100), 'if classification regulates the voice of a category then framing regulates the form of its legitimate message'. Furthermore, 'frame refers to the degree of control teacher and pupil possess over the selection, organization, pacing and timing of the knowledge transmitted and received in the pedagogical relationship' (1973b: 88). Therefore, strong framing refers to a limited degree of options between teacher and students; weak framing implies more freedom.

Bernstein developed this approach into a systematic analysis of pedagogic discourse and practices. First, he outlined a theory of pedagogic rules that examines the 'intrinsic features, which constitute and distinguish the specialized form of communication realized by the pedagogic discourse of education' (1990 Ch. 5: 165). Second (1990 Ch. 2), he related his theory of pedagogic discourse to a social class base and applied it to the ongoing development of different educational practices.

The concept of code was central to Bernstein's sociology. From the outset of its use in his work on language (restricted and elaborated codes), code refers to a 'regulative principle, which underlies various message systems, especially curriculum and pedagogy' (Atkinson 1985: 136). Curriculum and pedagogy are considered message systems, and with a third system, evaluation, they constitute the structure and processes of school knowledge, transmission, and practice. As Bernstein (1973b: 85) noted: 'Curriculum defines what counts as valid knowledge, pedagogy defines what counts as valid transmission of knowledge, and evaluation defines what counts as a valid realization of the knowledge on the part of the taught.' Thus, his theory of education must be understood in terms of the concepts of classification, framing and evaluation, and their relationship to the structural aspects of his sociological project.

Following this earlier work on curriculum and pedagogic practice was a detailed analysis of pedagogic discourse (1990 Ch. 5) that presented a complex analysis of the recontextualization of knowledge through the pedagogic device. Bernstein's work on pedagogic discourse was concerned with the production, distribution and reproduction of official knowledge and how this knowledge is related to structurally determined power relations. What is critical is that Bernstein was concerned with more than the description of the production and transmission of knowledge; he was concerned with its consequences for different groups.

Bernstein's analysis of pedagogic practice looked at the process and content of what occurs inside schools. His theory of pedagogic practice and discourse examined a series of rules and considered both how these rules affect the content to be transmitted and, perhaps more importantly, how they 'act selectively on those who can successfully acquire it' (1990 Ch. 2: 63). From an analysis of these rules, Bernstein examined 'the social class assumptions and consequences of forms of pedagogic practice' (1990 Ch. 2: 63). Finally, he applied this theory to conservative/traditional versus progressive/child-centered practices. He differentiated between a pedagogic practice that is dependent on the economic market – that emphasizes vocational education – and another that is independent and autonomous of the market – that is legitimated by the autonomy of knowledge. Bernstein concluded that, despite their claims to the contrary, both would not eliminate the reproduction of class inequalities. Through a consideration of the inner workings of the types of educational practice, Bernstein contributed to a greater understanding of how the schools reproduce what they are ideologically committed to eradicating – social class advantages in schooling and society.

Bernstein's analysis of the social class assumptions of pedagogic discourse and practice is the foundation for linking microeducational processes to the macrosociological levels of social structure and of class and power relations. His thesis was that there are significant differences in the social class assumptions of visible and invisible pedagogy and, despite these differences, there may indeed be similar outcomes, especially in the reproduction of power and symbolic control. In *Pedagogy, Symbolic Control and Identity* (1996) Bernstein elaborated his concept of the pedagogic device and related it to a theory of educational change. Building upon his analysis of pedagogic discourse (Bernstein 1990), which emphasized 'that this device provides the intrinsic grammar of pedagogic discourse through *distributive rules, recontextualizing rules and rules of evaluation*' (Bernstein 1990: 180), Bernstein argued that the recontextualization of knowledge since the 1960s shifted from competence models to performance models. In the UK, for example, this meant the increasing power of the state in the recontextualization of knowledge through the National Curriculum and an emphasis on sophisticated evaluative rules through a system of national tests. Bernstein argued that this resulted in the return to a strong classification system in order to transmit a collection code, but weaker framing to accommodate increased school autonomy over delivery systems. Through the embedding of a regulative discourse (RD) into an instructional discourse (ID), pedagogic discourse regulates the production and reproduction of consciousness and does so differentially to different groups of children. Bernstein further differentiates two interrelated spheres of reproduction: the official recontextualizing field (ORF), consisting of the regulatory function of the state and its Department of Education, and the pedagogic recontextualizing field (PRF), which consists of relatively autonomous educational professionals within higher education and within primary and secondary education. Both of these recontextualizing fields are relatively autonomous, but interrelated to the field of production within the economy. Finally, the recontextualizing fields are interrelated to the local pedagogic field (LPF) within the community and the family, where children acquire their initial communication codes. It is the complex and often conflictual relationship between the ORF, the PRF and the LPF that is at the heart of the reproduction of social class differences in education and educational change.

Thus, from his early work on code theory to the more recent works in *Class, Codes and Control, Volumes 4 and 5*, pedagogic discourse (1990 Ch. 5) and pedagogic practices (1990 Ch. 2; 1996), Bernstein's project sought to link microprocesses (language, transmission and pedagogy) to macroforms – to how cultural and educational codes and the content and process of education are related to social class and power relations.

Bernstein and 'No Child Left Behind'

In his final paper, written shortly before his death, for the first Bernstein research symposium in Lisbon in 2000, Bernstein analyzed the transformation of the UK into a totally pedagogized society (TPS), the first one since the dominance of the Church during the medieval period (Morais *et al.* 2001: 365–6). Responding to the shift from a manufacturing economy to an information economy, New Labour continued the Conservative domination of the official recontextualizing field through the extension and elaboration of a national curriculum and testing and the emphasis of 'life-long learning' in order to prepare citizens for an ongoing redefinition of jobs in an increasingly globalized society, where time and space have become increasingly irrelevant. With the elimination of the traditional avenues of employment for working-class children in an industrial and manufacturing economy, the old forms of social-class-based educational differentiation were no longer functional. The new global information economy required all students to have a common toolbox of official knowledge that would prepare them how to learn throughout their lives. The installation of a common academic curriculum, however, was less a product of the needs of a global economy and more related to the relative power of the pedagogic recontextualizing field of professional educators, who continued to dominate both the official and recontextualizing fields. Although the proponents of a national curriculum and the supporters of school-based evaluations by the ORF through Ofsted inspectors argued that such a common curriculum and testing process was essential to reducing class-based inequalities of educational provision and achievement, Bernstein argued that such powerful educational reforms continued to reproduce educational inequalities under different forms of pedagogic practice and discourse.

In the US, a similar evolution of standards-based reforms emerged in the 1980s, but given the lack of a national system of education, it took on a slightly different and more complicated process. As a response to the *Nation at Risk* report (1983), which argued that US economic superiority was threatened by its mediocre educational system for a majority of its students, educational reformers developed higher state curriculum standards for all students. Beginning in the 1990s with the presidencies of G.H.W. Bush and Bill Clinton, the federal role in education increased dramatically. Although control of education still resided in states and local school boards, Bush's *America 2000* and Clinton's *Goals 2000* set national goals for all children and incentives for states to implement standards to reach these goals. Although the social class and particularly the racial gap in achievement had been a concern of educational policy since the first Education and Secondary Education Act (ESEA) in 1965, the gap which had declined until the late 1980s began to widen considerably in the 1990s. As part of the reauthorization of the ESEA in 2001, No Child Left Behind married the standards and equity movements by demanding that all children achieve proficiency in reading and mathematics by 2014, that schools achieve adequate yearly progress toward that goal, and that states implement a system of annual testing to hold all schools accountable; and if schools failed to achieve such progress they would be subject to serious sanctions, including reconstitution or closure and their students eligible to transfer to successful schools. On the face of it, G.W. Bush managed to marry a conservative standards movement with a progressive equity movement by arguing that NCLB was necessary to ensure that all children regardless of race or social class background would achieve the proficiencies required in the new information global society, where such literacy would be required for the life-long learning necessary for a lifetime of occupational change.

No Child Left Behind, then, was the marriage of two movements that had coexisted often in opposition to one another from the 1960s: the equity and standards movements. In fact, with Ted Kennedy, one of the most liberal Democrats, co-sponsoring the legislation and with G.W. Bush, a conservative president, signing it, NCLB was heralded as a truly bipartisan effort. Further, the Education Trust, a progressive non-profit organization that had lobbied relentlessly for the elimination of the achievement gap, continues to be one of the staunchest supporters of the bill.

From a Bernsteinian perspective, NCLB represented two interrelated educational movements: the first, emphasizing the relationship between the economy and education, spoke to the need to change the official pedagogic discourse to one that prepared all students for an information economy requiring life-long learning; the other, emphasizing the unequal outcomes of pedagogic discourse and practice for low-income students and students of color, spoke to the need to close the achievement gap. With respect to the relationship between the economy and education, NCLB emphasized literacy in terms of mathematics and reading, without specifying other aspects of the curriculum. With respect to the unequal outcomes of education, NCLB mandated that all students be proficient in reading and mathematics, but did not specify how schools would meet these standards. Given the autonomy of state departments of education and the absence of a constitutional federal mandate for a national curriculum and testing regime, unlike the UK's national curriculum and testing, NCLB left it to individual states to determine the levels of proficiency and the tests used to measure proficiency. As critics have pointed out, this has resulted in many states lowering the cutoffs for proficiency in order to avoid sanctions.

From a Bernsteinian perspective, NCLB strengthened the power of the official recontextualizing field of the federal government and weakened the relative autonomy of states and local educational authorities. Further, the increased reliance on agents of the pedagogic recontextualizing field of professional educators, especially in the realms of testing and assessment experts, has resulted in the further domination of experts other than teachers and administrators in defining official pedagogic discourse.

No Child Left Behind, despite its stated intention of reducing the achievement gap, has done nothing to change the inner working of schools, that is, the pedagogic practices that have historically resulted in the achievement gap. Although there have been considerable efforts to replicate successful schools in lower-income communities, the law does not provide any mechanisms to change pedagogic practices, especially those that reproduce educational inequalities. In fact, the law provides a stick rather than a carrot to prod unsuccessful schools to improve through negative sanctions and punishments, albeit it does provide some Title I funds to implement scientifically proven pedagogic reforms, including phonic-based reading programs and successful comprehensive school reform models.

One of the most controversial aspects of the law is its school choice provisions, which allow children in schools in need of improvement to transfer to successful schools. However, given the concentration of low-performing schools in low-income communities, the lack of capacity in successful schools in these communities, and the reluctance of neighboring higher-income communities to accept students from schools in need of improvement, critics have argued that this is the first step to school vouchers and the privatization of public education. For example, if there are no places in successful schools, states such as Florida have already permitted the use of vouchers by students in failing schools to go to private and religious schools. Second, many localities such as Philadelphia have turned the management of failing public schools to private education management companies such as Edison, or to local universities. In addition, NCLB mandates that students in need of improvement receive supplemental tutoring, with the majority of approved providers in cities consisting of private companies such as Sylvan Learning Centers, Kaplan Learning Centers and Huntington Learning Centers. From a Bernsteinian perspective, NCLB has the potential of radically changing the composition of the official recontextualizing field and the pedagogic recontextualizing field, with publicly supported private schools becoming major players in schooling. Further, the law has the potential of weakening the classification between state and religious education, as the Supreme Court in the Zelman decision ruled that the Cleveland voucher program does not violate the constitutional separation of Church and state, thus weakening the boundaries between public and private and state and religious education.

Thus, from a market perspective, NCLB sets up the conditions for the ongoing entry of private educational corporations into the market of official pedagogic discourse. In the US, where education is a multi-billion dollar business and growing due to the profitability of assessments and school improvement programs, the longstanding monopoly of the state and its agents in public schools has been ideologically threatened by an anti-teacher (and teacher union) and anti-public-school movement that argues that private school choice is the remedy for failing schools and the new Civil Rights movement of the twenty-first century. Arguing that fifty years after the landmark Brown v. Board[2] decision US schools are more segregated and unequal than ever, both conservatives and liberals look to innovative ways to improve the quality of schooling for low-income children and especially children of color. NCLB requires that public schools reduce the achievement gap, but provide spaces for privatization to occur. Critics of Bush argue that, since his reelection, the reauthorization of NCLB in 2006 may well include his original intent of a private school voucher component for children in failing schools, funded publicly.

From a sociological perspective, the major shortcoming of NCLB is its entirely school-based solutions to problems of educational inequality. As Bernstein argued in 'Education Cannot Compensate for Society' (1970), schools are limited institutions in reducing educational and social inequality as the origins of inequality are outside the educational system in social and economic structures. Although schools reproduce inequality through social-class-based pedagogic discourse and practices, they do so in conjunction with the primary contextualizing context of the community and family, as well as in conjunction with available economic opportunities for different groups. Although NCLB provides some funds for increasing parental involvement in low-income communities, it does nothing to improve the economic opportunities for low-income families or their children. As Jean Anyon argues in her recent book *Radical Possibilities: Public Policy, School Reform, and a New Social Movement* (2005), without corresponding employment opportunities in cities and changes in federal employment, housing and transportation policies that for forty years have advantaged suburbs and disadvantaged cities, low-income children will have little incentive to be successful in schools. In fact, given the continuing outsourcing of technical jobs to India and China, if NCLB is truly successful it is not clear where all the proficient students will work. However, if NCLB is successful it might, as Bowles and Gintis argued in *Schooling in Capitalist America* (1976), delegitimate the educational rationale for inequality, that poor people are poor because they do not take advantage of a meritocratic educational system, and place the blame where it belongs, as Bernstein, although not a Marxist, understood, on the economic system that does not produce sufficient opportunities.

In 'Social Class and Pedagogic Practice' (1990 Ch. 2) Bernstein argued that the reproduction of educational inequalities is in part based on different educational codes within schools that house students from different social classes. Numerous studies of schooling in the US (Anyon 1980, 1997, 2005; Sadovnik 1991; Semel 1995; Semel and Sadovnik 1999) argue that social class differences in pedagogic practices and discourse are at the heart of how schools produce unequal results despite their ideological commitment to eradicating these differences. Over the past twenty years, since the important work on effective schools by Ronald Edmonds, there have been significant gains in our understanding of what works for low-income children, and examples of effective schools for low-income children and states that have lowered the achievement gap (Education Trust 2004; Just4kids 2004). This literature supports the Bernsteinian argument that school improvement requires changes in pedagogic discourse and practices; however, NCLB provides little guidance or funding for the replication of successful schools for low-income children, nor the funding to build local capacity to do this. A recent study of state takeover of failing school districts in New Jersey has indicated that the type of punitive, command-and-control methods of school improvement similar to those in NCLB did little to improve the schools in Jersey City (taken over in 1989), Paterson (taken over in 1991) and Newark (taken over in 1995), all of which are still state-operated (Tractenberg *et al.* 2002). There is little reason to believe the punitive measures in NCLB will lead to large-scale improvement of the schools attended mostly by low-income children.

NCLB has resulted in the reemergence of a strongly classified curriculum, with reading and mathematics dominating instruction, both as separate subjects. The progressive notion of a weakly classified curriculum with reading, and to a lesser extent mathematics, integrated into teaching other interdisciplinary subjects is impossible when high-stakes tests are constantly measuring literacy and numeracy. Other disciplines, such as literature, history, music and the arts, and even the sciences have taken a back seat to skills-based instruction, especially in low-income schools. Teaching to the test has replaced critical-inquiry-based learning and verbal and mathematical intelligences have become dominant at the expense of other forms of Gardner's multiple intelligences.[3] Although the law does not specify how the curriculum should be taught and framing rules continue to differ by social class composition of the school, with low-income schools continuing to have stronger framing rules, pedagogic practices are increasingly dictated by comprehensive school reform models (CSRM), some of which like Success for All provide teachers with a highly classified and framed scripted curriculum. Although the law does not require any one CSRM model, it may result in funding only those that are supported by scientific evidence (what constitutes scientific evidence is a controversial aspect of the law, as the Department of Education has privileged randomized controlled experiments as the 'gold standard').

The standards movement in general, and NCLB in particular, are incompatible with the principles of successful progressive urban school reform described by Sadovnik and Semel (2000). At a time when New York City is breaking up its large comprehensive high schools and replacing them with small progressive learning communities like the successful ones at Urban Academy and Central Park East Secondary school (Semel and Sadovnik 1999), New York State high-stakes high-school graduation requirements and strongly classified assessments for NCLB make the type of weakly classified and weakly framed processes at these schools highly problematic. Anti-high-stakes testing groups led by Ann Cook of Urban Academy[4] wonder why New York State and the federal government insist on a uniform assessment regime, when schools like hers have a proven track record of near 100 per cent graduation and college attendance rates for low-income students and children of color. In June 2005, Cook's anti-testing group won a compromise victory, with New York State Commissioner of Education Richard Mills approving a partial exemption for schools like Urban Academy until 2010, with their students required to pass only three of five high-stakes Regents examinations.[5]

In *Social Class and Pedagogic Practice* (in 1990 Ch. 2) Bernstein distinguished between two forms of visible pedagogy: autonomous visible pedagogy (AVP), consisting of a traditional humanist arts and sciences curriculum, and market dependent visible pedagogy (MVP), which is more vocationally based. The standards movement in the US, of which NCLB is the latest incarnation, privileges the AVP for all students. Arguing that low-income students and students of color have been tracked into vocational tracks with lower expectations, advocates of NCLB insist that a rigorous AVP is now a requirement for all children in an economy that requires high levels of literacy and numeracy. Anyon (2005) argues that the number of jobs requiring such high-level skills is actually diminishing because of outsourcing and technological efficiency and the largest number of jobs are lower-level service positions that do not require these high-level skills. Although it is true that there are fewer high-level positions, it is also the case that large numbers of high-skilled technical positions are filled by immigrants to the US and that because of the dismal state of urban schools many low-income students and students of color do not have the skills for these positions. Therefore, while it is necessary for more low-income students and students of color to graduate high school with the high-level skills demanded by NCLB, the erosion of MVP programs that prepare students for entry into the workplace without college has resulted in students graduating from high school with neither the academic skills for college nor the vocational skills for work.

At New York City's Kennedy High School in the Bronx, a large failing comprehensive school of over 4000 students, small learning communities are being phased in, all with an academic theme. Its successful vocational program in auto-mechanics has been phased out to make room for these AVP-based academies. As an attempt to combine an AVP and an MVP curriculum, Newark has developed small career academies into all of its comprehensive high schools, which will give students the option of going to college or entering the workforce. As Anyon (2005) notes, however, unless the economic sector provides well-paid jobs for graduates of these programs, proficiency in high-school subjects will not translate into economic mobility.

No Child Left Behind places most of its emphasis on the evaluative rules of pedagogic discourse through the reliance on high-stakes testing. Such an assessment-driven educational system, according to its proponents, is supposed to alter the unequal distributive rules that have favored higher-income students. However, there is little evidence that such an evaluation-driven pedagogic practice can reduce the unequal distribution of knowledge and skills, since such inequalities are related to both within and outside school variables. Bernstein's theory of pedagogic discourse and practice argued that the social class base of inequality has its origins in the social and economic division of labor and the local pedagogic practices of families and communities. Differences in power and wealth lead to inequalities of cultural and social capital and are brought by children to schools. Rather than addressing such outside school factors or even the social class differences in pedagogic practices examined by Bernstein, NCLB leaves both of these unchanged and stresses the outcomes of these unequal factors through testing. NCLB provides an empirical verification of what Bernstein and other social reproduction theorists told us thirty years ago, that schooling helps reproduce economic and social inequality. The law, however, provides few mechanisms for reducing these inequalities because it fails to focus on their causes.

The educational changes in the US from the 1980s to the present represent an ongoing battle between conservatives and progressives over the role of education in American society. Conservatives began with a critique of progressive education of the type popularized by Diane Ravitch (1983, 2000), which argued that weak classification and weak framing resulted in the destruction of academic standards for all students. In the 1980s, the conservative standards movement had an explicitly economic base, arguing that the educational system was inadequately preparing students for the economy. By the 1990s with a booming economy, growing economic inequality and a widening achievement gap, conservatives co-opted the progressive critique of schooling to argue that differences in standards resulted in low-income students and students of color failing to receive an adequate education. In 'From pedagogies to knowledges' (2001a) Bernstein argues that the 'totally pedagogized society' is one where a performance model dominates the educational arena and where the classification between education and the economy becomes weaker. The history of the US standards movement and NCLB supports this argument as over the past decade the boundaries between the public sphere of education and the private spheres of business have been increasingly blurred, with educational corporations making claims that they can educate better than professional educators. We are now witnessing a major conflict between agents of the Economic Field and agents of the Pedagogic Recontextualizing Field, as corporate leaders and their experts challenge professional educators on how to improve schools for all children. Both groups attempt to influence the Official Recontextualizing Field of the state and its departments of education in a battle for who will control the schools and how new knowledge forms will be transmitted, acquired and assessed. Bernstein ends his final article with the following pessimistic comment about the reduction of inequalities in the TPS, one that repeats his equally cautionary prediction on the democratizing effects of both the AVP and MVP a decade earlier in *Social Class and Pedagogic Practice* (in 1990 Ch. 2):

How will this new diversity of knowledges map onto our present educational institutions? Which institutions are vulnerable to the new claims, to whom will the new knowledge forms be distributed? Will diversity more likely be found in the less privileging institutions, whereas the elite institutions will be more selective of their preferred knowledge, manner of transmission, and evaluation of staff and students? If this is the case then the diversity of knowledges with their target of weakening boundaries (social, intellectual, procedural) will not be distributed across institutions and students. On the contrary, the diversity will be filtered through existing reproductive structures and so the present hierarchy of privileging institutions will be maintained. Plus ça change ...

(Bernstein 2001a: 368)

The educational reforms initiated by NCLB, based on this Bernsteinian forecast, will result in the same old wine in new bottles, an educational system with much more private control, with much more assessment-driven instruction, and unfortunately, with the same old inequalities. Unless more attention is given to the relationship between schools and society, Bernstein's admonition in 1970 that education cannot compensate for society will continue to hold, with federal sanctions only amplifying this sociological dictum.

Notes

1 The Sociology of Education Section of the American Sociological Association has held two conferences at its Annual Meetings in 2004 and 2005 on NCLB and *Sociology of Education* devoted one of its Perspectives sections to NCLB in 2005 (*Sociology of Education*, 78 (2)).

2 *Brown* v. *Board of Education* of Topeka, Kansas (1954) was the landmark US Supreme Court decision that ruled that 'separate but equal' education was inherently unequal and thus school segregation was unconstitutional. The case consisted of separate cases in four states: *Briggs* v. *Elliot* in South Carolina; *Brown* v. *Board of Education of Topeka* (Kansas); *Davis* v. *School Board of Prince Edward County* (Virginia); *Belton* v. *Gebhart* and *Bulah* v. *Gebhart* (Delaware); and a fifth case, *Bolling* v. *Sharpe* in the District of Columbia.

3 See Howard Gardner (2005) for a discussion of multiple intelligence theory. This theory argues that unlike traditional theories of intelligence that measure verbal and quantitative areas, there are multiple measures of intelligence, including artistic, physical and social/emotional.

4 See Semel and Sadovnik (1999) for a full discussion of Ann Cook's leadership of Urban Academy, a successful, alternative, progressive urban high school in New York City.

5 New York State requires all students to pass at least five comprehensive subject examinations, called Regents examinations, in order to graduate high school. This 'one size fits all' high-stakes testing requirement has been the subject of litigation by a group of alternative high schools, led by Ann Cook.

13 Literacy, pedagogy and social change

Directions from Bernstein's sociology

Ruqaiya Hasan

The problem I want to explore in this paper is whether the pedagogic practices of literacy in the classroom can be co-opted for bringing about social change of a specific kind, which in turn will raise questions about what change and why. The obvious sociological theory to which such issues can be usefully brought is Bernstein's – but it needs to be added that I do so not as a *sociologist manqué* but as a linguist interested in understanding society because society is the condition for the maintenance and evolution of language.

On recognizing change

The first obvious question is: why the implied declaration of need for social change? Change is, after all, an inherent condition of society, just as it is of language: both are always in flux. However, it is one thing to affirm the constancy of ongoing change; it is quite another to recognize its manifestations (or 'displays'), and yet another to assess its impact, or to justify the need. So far as impact is concerned, the declaration of need for change is itself often a symptom of negative response to some change that has already become part of our social life. The call for change is neither because change is not occurring, nor because we as social agents have not contributed – consciously or unconsciously – to that change. The call is made because the caller has an agenda: s/he consciously desires to set in motion a specific kind of change. This in turn calls for an assessment of the declared need.

Though most change in society and in language occurs through our participation in social and semiotic processes,[1] we often need a time depth[2] to 'see' change as change. In real time, we typically become aware of change after it has already set in. With deeper relation to an arena and with the ability to reflect, one might be equipped to observe a change while it is still in progress; with greater understanding of the inner character of the arena, one might assess the consequences of even an ongoing change, as Bernstein did in the arena of symbolic control in the early 1980s, when he analysed the State's 'increasing control over its own agencies of symbolic control, especially education' (1990: 154). He spelt out its 'profound implications [for pedagogy] from the primary school to the university', and from ways of learning to ways of being:

> Today led by the U.S.A. and the U.K., there is a new principle guiding the latest transition of capitalism. The principles of the market and its managers are more and more the managers of the policy and practices of education. Market relevance is becoming the key orienting criterion for the selection of discourses, their relations to each other, their forms and their research. ... Knowledge, after nearly a thousand years is *divorced from inwardness and literally dehumanized.*
>
> (Bernstein 2000: 86; emphasis mine)

The State-manufactured ideological conjunction of the Official Recontextualising Field and the Pedagogic Recontextualising Field has meant that pedagogic practices in official pedagogic sites are undergoing a rapid change; the knower is being distanced from what is to be known; the concept of 'trainability' is fast replacing that of commitment to knowledge, separating it 'from the deep structure of the self'. As others have also observed (Apple 2002; Beck 2002), Bernstein's assessment of these market-driven changes in official pedagogy was markedly negative. His last public pronouncement forcefully expresses the strength of this negative assessment, and it will probably be conceded that at the same time it calls for a constructive response to the situation:

> I am against any kind of pedagogy which leaves the self empty, and this is what I fear most of all, the emptying of the self and the role of pedagogy in such *evacuation,* and I think we have to mount a critique ... But a critique which enables us to show how pedagogic discourse works. How it's produced, how it's distributed, and ... you see, its effectiveness is often assumed ... we have to ask ourselves when it is effective, what are the conditions that have made it effective, and what does effectiveness actually mean with respect to what has been acquired?
>
> (Bernstein 2001b: 380)

If we agree with Bernstein's assessment, then mounting a critique from a position of understanding as he advises is a necessary response to the conditions leading to the production of today's 'totally pedagogized society'. And, if we deplore the 'emptying of the self' as undesirable, and want education to play a 'crucial role in creating tomorrow's optimism from today's pessimism' (Bernstein 2000: xix), then beyond the first indispensable step of informed critique, some urgent action is also needed. My excuse for selectively recalling details of Bernstein's discourse on the formation of the 'totally pedagogized society' lies in its relevance to my call for social change through literacy pedagogy: they provide not only its motivation but also suggest the direction of the change.

The domination of market orientation and 'schizoid' language

To elaborate, my sense of a need for change through literacy pedagogy dates back to the last months of 1999, when media were saturated with news of the Seattle protest riots (the first public voice raised against the 'latest transition of capitalism', by now transformed into *globalization*. Clearly, globalization is a celebration of 'free market fundamentalism' (Hobsbawm 1999: 69), which counts as the central principle of capitalism and acts as the prime motivator of globalization. Whatever the naïve readings of the word 'globalization', the free market principle inheres in the global circulation of all goods and services, be they tourism and trade, or fashion and ethnic food, or entertainment and sports, or education and progress, or freedom and democracy.

What struck me most about the Seattle encounter was the contradiction emerging from the discourse of the protagonists. The rioters were protesting not against 'trade' but against *free* and *liberal* trade; against exercising the policy of *non-discrimination in recruiting labour;* against *putting poverty-stricken countries on the path to prosperity.* On the face of it, the protest appeared irrational: it went against the tenets of what the west knows as democracy. Now, everyone who knows anything about linguistics knows about 'ungrammaticality' as a crucial concept in language description. However, it is quite easy to find a so-called ungrammatical sentence making perfect sense, but, by contrast, something natural language greatly abhors is internal contradiction: there is no way of making sense of sentences which claim or imply that non-discrimination is discriminatory, that freedom should be replaced by restrictions. If, language announces, in all seriousness, that fair is foul and foul fair, this has to be interpreted as the symptom of some pathology. In his account of market dominated pedagogy, Bernstein talks about the likelihood of 'schizoid' identities, which he feared were being produced by market-oriented agencies of official pedagogy. What one was encountering in the discourse of rioters and their opponents was 'schizoid' language, created by market-oriented ideology: non-discrimination *was* discriminatory; free trade imposed restrictions. Language was being pathologized, as it had been once before in the Third Reich (Klemperer 2002).

But while the rioters were being talked of as violent and wild by the representatives of the World Trade Organization (WTO), whose meetings they had disrupted, they were quite obviously not mad hooligans. A reading of commentaries by writers such as Madely (1999), Hertz (2001) and Ellwood (2002) suggested that their behaviour might even be justified. So what exactly was going on?

Markets and meanings

Let me not tax your patience with a detailed analysis of the linguistic features of this schizoid language, but something does need to be said about the constitutive elements of this schizophrenia, as they help explain why a particular kind of pedagogic action appears necessary.

First, the normal condition of a living language is variation/heterogeneity – not even an individual speaks the same variety of language all the time. From this point of view, the schizoid language, which I have called *glib-speak* (Hasan 2003), is simply a variety of English; and its speakers/propagators are identified by their extensive control of communal resources for the production and distribution of material capital. But to understand the specific nature of this variety, we need more information about its nature as semiosis: the principle underlying the linguistic character of glib-speak is that of *resemanticization* (Hasan 2003). A word then about the concept.

If, as Bernstein argues, the market orientation of pedagogy is separating knowledge from a knower, *glib-speak is an attempt to separate a signifier from its legitimate signified* – i.e. that signified which is treated by the speech community in general as legitimate. Glib-speak replaces the communally legitimized signified with one that is friendly to the interests and ideologies of its speakers. To be sure, the separation of a particular signifier and its associated signified is part of the natural process of change in language; but under natural conditions, it occurs slowly, often over generations and typically with wide communal participation.[3] Which explains why it is not perceived as a 'separation'; in fact, it is to be doubted whether in the natural course of normal meaning change, ordinary speakers are even aware of the changes happening. By contrast, in glib-speak, it would be truer to say that change is not just happening; it is being actively *manufactured:* its pace is grossly accelerated. The technical term for the process in either case is 'resemanticization': a word and its meaning are being forcibly divorced from each other, so that a new meaning may be attached to the word. But how is this achieved, and what does it do by way of furthering the interests of its speakers? By way of an answer consider two strategies for resemanticization, referred to here as (1) exploiting evaluation; and (2) subverting meaning.[4]

The strategy of *exploiting evaluation* depends on the fact that the words (more accurately *lexical items/lexemes*) of a language can be ranged along a cline of desirability. We may think of the two end-points of the cline as 'positive' (= desirable) and 'negative' (= undesirable), with the mid-point treated as (relatively) 'neutral'. This applies to all categories of lexemes/content words. The natural use of language will typically display what one might call 'internal evaluation agreement': thus it would be odd to say, 'they *praised* him for his *meanness*'; or, 'most people *enjoy* being *deceived*'. Neutral lexical words often tend to refer to general categories: examples would be *group, neighbourhood, contract, design, plan, action,* and so on; these have neither positive nor negative evaluation, and refer to a relatively less specific category of experience. When, however, a neutral word is combined with an evaluative word, the whole construction acquires the evaluative nuance of the latter, which suffuses the whole construction. Thus we may talk of *a fair contract* or *an unfair one*, or of *a rough neighbourhood*, or *a good neighbourhood*. Typically, such constructions are formed with an evaluative adjective as here, but this is less important than the presence of at least one evaluative term in the construction, as for example in *the liberalization of trade* where *liberalization* is simply a noun with positive value. Glib-speak makes heavy use of this strategy, but with a twist, to appreciate which we need to look at the second strategy, namely, *subverting meaning.*

Putting it simply, the meaning of a word is the product of the relations into which a word enters, and since each word enters into a vast network of relations, word meaning is typically considerably extensive. In ordinary uses of language, only some of the meaning relations are uppermost in our consciousness, while the others are, as it were, present in their silence, and clamour for attention if the threat of internal contradiction arises. One might, thus, see the meaning of a word such as *man* as a two-part affair. The part lying on the surface of our consciousness has such elements as, say, 'animate, human, adult, male', while the second part consists of meanings inferentially related to these elements. So from 'animate' we infer such things as *mobility* and *mutability*, i.e. subject to processes of change such as birth, growth, death; from 'human' we infer *humanity, non-brutishness,* i.e. *civility, fairness,* etc. and intelligence of a particular kind; from 'adult' we infer *maturity, judgment, reasoning,* and from 'male', *courage, strength,* and other physical attributes, such as a certain order of height and weight, among other things; a single word might thus pack a significant quantum of our ideology. Traditionally, the first grouping of semantic elements has been called denotation;[5] the second, connotation, which according to Lyons consists of 'secondary implications' (1977: 278). It is the first grouping that is uppermost in speakers' consciousness, which is why when someone says, *Susan's husband is not a man,* we do not hear it as claiming that Susan's husband is a female, or a baby, or an animal or an object.[6] Rather, the utterance brings to the surface of our consciousness the implicational/connotative/inferred elements of meanings. Thus we interpret it as claiming that Susan's husband does not conduct himself as a man would normally be expected to by the speech community. One effective way of subverting meaning is to simply ignore a denotative and/or a connotative element of meaning. As an illustration, I will briefly discuss the construction *liberalization of trade.*

Using a positive evaluative term in a construction introduces a *feel-good* factor. The general view is that liberalization makes laws, attitudes, etc. 'less strict and allows people more freedom in their actions' (COBUILD Dictionary: 833); restriction is taken to be coercive, and liberalization helpful. A connotative meaning of *liberal* is *munificent, generous,* which implies sensitivity to the needs and attitudes of another. The direction of liberality is other-oriented; thus it is odd to say *I am being liberal to myself.* So if A initiates a liberal trade contract with B, B may legitimately infer that it would be to his/her benefit. It is thus reasonable to interpret *liberal trade* as trade oriented to the benefit of the person or institution being invited to trade. However, in actual practice, a simple subversion of meaning undercuts the positive evaluation of the semantics of *liberal trade* by simply resemanticizing *liberal* so that it turns out to mean *liberal* as in *I took a liberal/generous helping* – i.e. *a big helping.* A comment from Madely (2000) supports this reading:

The principle of non-discrimination is embodied in the 1999 Uruguay agreement on trade related investment measures. It means that *developing countries cannot give special treatment to their domestic companies.* Neither can they insist that foreign companies use local labour ... To many civil society groups *the principle of non-discrimination is unjust* ... and anti-economic development, because it ties the hands of poor countries, making development policy subservient to trade policy. *The WTO's 'free trade' philosophy effectively reduces the freedom of governments* to buy locally produced materials or to use local labour.

(Madely 2000, emphasis mine)

Like middle-class maternal control, the strategies employed in glib-speak for the control of material gain are 'invisible', which is an important condition of its success. My research has so far shown no other *principle* of variation in glib-speak than that of 'manipulating' word meaning. Its grammar conforms impeccably to the standard variety – at least in English – right across the various 'genres', such as technological exposition, reports, plans or argumentation. This grammatical conformity is significant: it maintains the appearance of normality, thus rendering the manipulations of resemanticization invisible, and *that* is a necessary requirement for the successful functioning of glib-speak. Its speakers need to present themselves as benefactors, while engaged in acts of ruthless profiteering: the language they speak weaves a perfect web of lexical camouflage by exploiting evaluation and subverting meaning. No wonder the speakers of glib-speak have been so keen to strike international agreements on *liberal trade* with poverty-stricken countries whom they profess to be putting on the path to prosperity, while the terms of the agreements, fashioned by their own agencies, are biased in their own favour, not those of the poor countries.

Is change really needed?

Glib-speak is quite wide in its reach. The expressions *non-discrimination policy* or *liberal trade* are not just two isolated cases picked out from one instance of confrontation. For example, from Pakistan to Florida,[7] and from Florida to Iraq, the word *democracy* has been subtly resemanticized as and when needed. All over the western world, *accountability* in State documents is no longer about responsibility to society; it is about conformity with and accommodation of the money-making enterprises and market pressures. *Career* is pretty much an obsolete concept; and the idea of *success* whether in education or in other spheres of society increasingly celebrates commodification. Everyday news must be interpreted with caution; being a native speaker is no longer enough; you need to be an insider to know who is being bolstered, who is misrepresented. One of Bernstein's chief concerns was the evacuation of self in the changing Totally Pedagogized Society (TPS). I suggest that the evacuation of self is an enormous project: it cannot be achieved by change in one single arena, be it as pervasive in its influence as official pedagogy. Language is being coerced into recategorizing experience, and language is a main means of communication, not simply of pedagogic mediation. If language becomes schizoid, then what used to be taken as an undisputed 'fact' becomes subject to doubt, or worse still it is subverted for the benefit of corporate bodies. A very important element of what we knew as 'language education' is changing to suit the caprice of this 'new transition of capitalism', the 're-organized capitalism of the twenty-first century' (Bernstein 1990: 153).

One might ask: so what? Enormous changes have occurred before in society. Indeed, one way of conceiving human history is simply as a series of related changes. For example, education itself has moved from theistic to humanistic; from the concern of the sixteenth to eighteenth centuries with producing the well-rounded renaissance man, to twentieth-century concern with producing specialists, invested in some minute fragment of some specific knowledge structure. In retrospect, we appreciate the enormity of such changes, but while bringing about the changes, we think of it as 'marching with time'. So what is wrong in marching with time once again by substituting specialism with specializing in trainability? Isn't one's response to current changes somewhat hysterical? I believe the answer must be 'no' because of what the advent of glib-speak implies. The acceleration in the resemanticization of language cannot be ignored, if only because it is a mode of forcibly making exploitation legal *by contract and by convention.* Like cunning old Fury in the Mouse's Tale in *Alice in Wonderland,* our captains of enterprise have appointed themselves both judge and jury to condemn and dominate. Because the majority of this exploitation – you only have to examine the 'sweat trade' in China – is offshore, its effects are invisible to the private sectors of so-called developed countries. This, however, does not mean that our 'progressive' societies are safe from the effects of the legalization of exploitation: in a globalized world, discontent, like pollution, can have a worldwide effect. Collusion in providing a hospitable environment for glib-speak cannot be in the interest of humanity. But such collusion is occurring in the name of 'teaching what is usable' without also teaching how to question the uses themselves. A substantial segment of the academic community believes that their job is to produce humans who can fit into the globalized world. To neutralize the effectiveness of glib-speak, it is necessary to unravel the web of lexical camouflage. Though the agents of symbolic control in the private sector could play a major role in this enterprise (Bernstein 1990: 133 ff), perhaps changes in literacy pedagogy would be most effective, especially if they could become the norm in literacy pedagogy. What are these planned changes, and how feasible is it to implement them?

Changing literacy pedagogy

Despite the universal nature of the pedagogic device, the instantiations of pedagogy in the classroom are often enormously varied, literacy pedagogy not excepted. Even if we were to ignore multimodal literacies (van Leeuwen and Humphrey 1996), kinds of literacies as identified by reference to some (segments of a) given culture (Street 1995), and critical literacies (Gee 1990), literacy remains a complex concept, its pedagogy less than capable of coping with the problems posed by the advent of glib-speak. Due to lack of space I reluctantly abstain from elaborating this claim, but simply present my own conception of literacy. This will enable me to locate the various manifestations of what passes as literacy pedagogy. I take literacy to be fundamentally the process of making sense by interpreting some signing system, whether actively or receptively. The process is thus inherently semiotic (Hasan 1996) and clearly not restricted to language alone. However, the discussion of literacy here will concern only the semiotic modality of language, because language seems to be the only modality of meaning relevant to glib-speak. To sum up, as used here, *literacy is the process of making sense of instantiations of some language system, whether in its transmission or its reception.*

Even restricting literacy this way, there remains a good deal of latitude for variation in the interpretation of the term. For example, if the notion of sign is limited to its visual manifestation, literacy becomes a 'translation device' for converting *graphemes* (letters) into *phonemes* (sounds), and vice versa. If the notion of meaning is limited to naming or to correspondence between signs and elements of extra-linguistic reality, and/or the system of language is isolated from its process in context, then literacy pedagogy is restricted to what I have called *recognition literacy* (Hasan 1996): it amounts to 'barking at print'. The instructional discourse in such literacy pedagogy is focused on recognizing what written shape corresponds to what sound, what word corresponds to what meaning; little or no attention is paid to discourse as an object of study. Such literacy pedagogy is divorced from allied fields such as 'comprehension', 'composition', and so on. Recognition literacy is still alive and well, especially in the (always) developing (i.e. technologically/industrially backward) countries. The teaching and evaluation in recognition literacy come cheap, so despite its limitations as a resource for democracy, it is often found attractive. I would go so far as to suggest that, whatever the framing of pedagogic discourse, this variety of literacy pedagogy cannot play a constructive part in unravelling the lexical web of obfuscation woven by glib-speak. Despite this, the internalization of the relationships between the written shape and the uttered sound is fundamental to literacy pedagogy of any kind (Halliday 1985a, 1996); and where apprenticeship to vertical knowledge structures is concerned, such internalization is entirely indispensable. However impressive non-literate societies may be, the fact remains that the two modalities of language – the written and the spoken – do display a division of labour in the kind of knowledge structures they are able to mediate (Olson 1977).

If the sign system is interpreted as a resource for the living of life, then its process in context would be treated as an essential aspect of literacy. If, in addition, linguistic meaning is seen not merely as a surrogate of language-external reality, but as a meaning-creating system, essential to shaping reality and internalizing experience (Halliday and Matthiessen 1999), then the goal of literacy pedagogy will have to go a good deal beyond that of recognition literacy: it will focus on various forms of social process, relating them to the contexts in which they are embedded, and techniques for the production of various registers/genres will become an important part of instruction. I have referred to this as *action literacy:* it is performance oriented,[8] aimed at enabling pupils to act with their language, i.e. making sense *of* and *with* language used in (some) contexts of living. The most extensive programme for the pedagogy of action literacy was developed by Martin (e.g. 1986) and his colleagues. Known as 'genre-based pedagogy', it turned the concept of literacy in education from an aspect of language education to 'instruction in language across the curriculum'. Literacy as the process of making sense became synonymous with the displays of instructional discourse of one kind or another. Essential features of this programme have been co-opted internationally, with or without acknowledgement, in the instructional discourse of language education. Action literacy certainly appears to have the potential of being extended into a model that could de-construct glib-speak successfully, since behind it lies the powerful grammar provided by systemic functional linguistics (Halliday 1994a; Matthiessen 1995). However, despite its many strengths, genre-based literacy has been, on the one hand, selective in the genres that it chooses to bring to the students' attention – these happen to be privileged and privileging in the context of educational success; and on the other hand, the reception of discourse types had until recently been limited to identifying the structural composition, i.e. generic stages. This consumed most of the instructional programme of genre-based literacy, turning it into something more akin to a technology of text production and reception without, as it were, confronting the texts (whether produced by the student, or brought from outside as exemplars) with the wider contexts of communal existence, by reference to which they receive their true social meaning. However, changes have recently occurred in the writing and reading methodologies of genre-based pedagogy (Martin and Rose 2003) which pulls it a good deal closer to literacy as making sense.

It is somewhat ironic that the so-called 'literacy as social practice' approaches have tended to focus more on the individual.[9] The name of the game is self-expression; and the attainment of uniqueness is the prized goal. While lip-service is paid to 'meaning-making', the instructional programmes remain blithely innocent of the necessarily social basis of meaning. Like many false dichotomies which appear from time to time in humanities and social sciences, the opposition between individual and social perspective appears profitless. Nor have I come across any modes of instructional discourse associated with social and/or critical literacy which appear to actually engage with the processes of making sense by means of a semiotic system; language, it appears, has to be 'neutralized' in these approaches, because apparently it has been too privileged (Bourdieu 1992)! A social orientation to literacy pedagogy is an absolute necessity; I doubt, however, that the existing pedagogies associated with these models would succeed in an informed critique/decon-struction of glib-speak.

Hasan (1996) proposed a literacy model called *reflection literacy,* suggesting that such a model would build on the strengths of existing literacy pedago-gies, taking on board the text-and-context-based aspect of action literacy, the writing/speaking distinction basic to recognition literacy, and the social con-cerns professed by social/critical literacies. Distinctively, and importantly, it would also include the perspective of confronting the texts with the wider contexts of communal existence, in and from which they receive their true social meaning. Glib-speak at that point was not visible to me but I sug-gested that basic to reflection literacy are the concepts of semantic orientation, and of interrogation: what orders of meaning are viewed as rele-vant by whom as evidenced in their discursive practices. The aim of reflection literacy is to create in the acquirers an understanding of linguistic action as social in motivation and consequence: texts are not simply bearers of informa-tion organized and arranged in specific sequences/stages; they are not simply expressions of 'me'; they are also, and more importantly, potent instruments of social formation. Literacy as a process of making sense should therefore take seriously the construing power of language, and this means paying attention to the meaning of grammar. The grammar of language is not simply dry stuff without any relation to the living of life: rather than seeing it as a catalogue of mindless categories such as 'gerundives' or 'subject raising', grammar should be seen as the theory of human experience (Halliday 1994b). It is through the deep lexicogrammatical analysis of language that we can appreci-ate the strategic mendacity whereby *democracy* 'becomes' a different sign, each time friendly to the interests of those who subvert its meaning (Hasan 2003). There are three basic principles of reflection literacy: (i) the study of the meaning-making potential of language should never be divorced from liter-acy pedagogy: this potential is also a potential for linguistic variation; (ii) all instances of meaning-making should be subject to interrogation: e.g. 'why this meaning?', 'why here?'; and (iii) the significance of what language refers to, what meanings it makes, should never be divorced from the social context from where the pressures for meaning-making arise. If literacy education could go this far, it would create in the acquirer a sensitivity to the meaning-making practices of large sections of a community; it will make clear the centrality of meanings to the living of life in society; and it would be a recog-nition of the co-genetic relations of language and society, whereby each depends on the other for its existence. I believe that a literacy education of this kind could contribute to the formation of the kind of consciousness that is able to see 'through' the lexical webs of camouflage, whatever their origin.

The pedagogic device and planned change through pedagogy

Imagine, for a moment, that everyone here agrees with the goals of reflection literacy – an outcome highly unlikely given that we trade in segmental knowledge structures, and are not going to pusillanimously buy anyone else's ideas! But imagine that for some reason we do so. This, instead of a grand resolution, would only be the beginning of a host of problems – problems that attend all planned change; problems that might arise with innovation from below as it encounters aspects of some specific instance of the pedagogic device.

Contemporary discourse in much of humanities shows great concern with change; witness the plethora of titles – my own included! – sporting the word *change,* with or without the qualifier *social.* But it is not customary to clarify what kind of change, for whose benefit, who might actually desire it, and why. Bernstein often remarked that between language system and speech lies social structure; the same is true about an existing state of culture and some planned change. Even where the agenda of planned change has been clarified, its desirability for the majority of the community well argued, it is still a fact that the working of social structure lies between the agenda and the outcome: to strive for a particular change is probably within one's control, but what the outcome of the striving might be is not entirely so. This does not mean that change should not be contemplated, but to increase the chances of achieving the desired outcome, we must heed Bernstein's advice: *critique must be from a position of understanding; action must be in awareness of the terrain on which it has to be tried out.* So what are the conditions for making a change such as that outlined above? I want to explore this question by reference to the concept of pedagogic device. But first note that the instructional discourse of reflection literacy – the way linguistic meaning enters actively into the living of life – is embedded in a regulative discourse which orients acquirers' consciousness toward the salient features of social life. In what follows below, I shall focus largely on issues in the linguistic component of the instructional discourse.

There can be no doubt that today the insulation between the arenas of production and education has been greatly weakened, nor that the 'dominant principles' of the political party of the State are blatantly market oriented. Here is a piece of advice given by the State to academics as reported on page 8 of the *Guardian Weekly,* May 20–26, 2004:

> Academics have been urged to spend a little less time on expanding human knowledge, and more on drumming up cash for their universities' endowment funds. A government-appointed task force has said that £600m could be raised if staff adopted US-style techniques to extract donations from former students and big commercial donors.

In this climate, it would be somewhat naïve to expect that the agents of official or pedagogic recontextualizing fields are likely to be favourably impressed by the 'pedagogeme' of reflection literacy. The existing distributive rules of the official pedagogic device in much of Europe and European-style educational systems are stacked against any such innovation.[10]

If the innovation is to surface at all, it will have to do so from below, through the actual practices of literacy pedagogy.

In one respect, the situation is more promising here: the primary context of the production of the discourse at issue has been strongly supported; the 'intellectual field' of a socially aware and semiotically competent linguistics already exists which would support a literacy pedagogy of the type under consideration. In other words, primary contextualization of the field has taken place and a specialized discourse has been developed which could be taken as a resource for the pedagogy of reflection literacy. So far as the reproduction of this kind of discourse is concerned, some relevant material exists at primary, secondary and tertiary levels. Williams (2000) reports on research in the pedagogy of grammar as a resource for meaning at the primary level of schooling. Here, through instruction in the meaning-making potential of certain grammatical categories, children were able to do 'reflective' reading of a children's story. They identified how the relations of the various participants were linguistically enacted, what grammatical patterns go into creating what kind of character, how a variation on such patterns would vary meanings; and what is the social significance of how the linguistically created characters behave in relation to others in the story. This kind of literacy would put the acquirers well on the path of developing sensitivities to the power of language turned into text. At the secondary level the model of genre-based pedagogy would provide a strong basis for continuing such enquiries, though it will be necessary to develop the stance of enquiry into the social significance of the discourses brought to the acquirers' attention. In this context the latest innovations in genre-based pedagogy by Martin in collaboration with Rose (Martin and Rose 2003) could be highly relevant, though teacher education materials would need to sensitize the teachers to the relation of semiosis to the sociopolitical organization. Similarly, the work on the analysis of verbal art (Halliday 1971; Hasan 1971, 1985; Butt 1983, 1988), some of it written specifically for teachers' use, could be employed at the tertiary level for the pedagogy of reflection literacy. A good deal of work is available on linguistic variation, providing an understanding of the relation of language to speakers' social positioning, including the work on semantic variation (Hasan 1989, 1992a; Cloran 1989, 1994, 1999; Williams 1995, 2001). But there still remains the problem of the third context, which 'structures the field or subset of fields whose positions, agents, and practices are concerned with the movements of texts/practices from the primary context of discursive production to the secondary context of discursive reproduction' (Bernstein 1990: 192). For this step in recontextualization, Bernstein makes the following thoughtful comment: 'at the level of the university or equivalent institutions those who produce the new knowledge are also their own contextualizers' (Bernstein 1990: 188); thus, the prophet has to induct the priest who may then be able to address the laity. In other words any innovation in pedagogy from below has to be a boot-strapping enterprise; if academics are convinced of the value of bringing to attention a literacy that enables the acquirer to see through linguistic chicanery, they will have to act for its promotion.

Changes of the kind we are witnessing do not remain encapsulated within one segment of the community: there is bound to be external pressure from parents, who want their children to 'succeed': forms of education not directly contributing to the market-oriented conception of success are likely to be criticized. In Australia, media often criticize the academics for 'wasting tax-payers' money' by teaching what nobody wants to know. As things stand, the higher we move in the educational scheme, the more success in examinations matters for pupils' future. Any programme of teaching which does not directly seek to enable the students to jump this hurdle is often seen as 'incompetent' and irresponsible. Further, there is the most serious issue of winning the students over so they willingly invest time and effort in learning what 'does not pay' in terms of grades: the importance of positive student identification for successful pedagogy (Singh 2001) and boot-strapped innovation cannot be ignored. However, despite these problems, what favours the introduction of reflection literacy pedagogy is its status as a 'pedagogeme' in a space that, though often beset with ill-informed curricula designers leading to poor education, still remains a recognized legitimate intellectual field, namely that of language education. On a positive note, recent developments in literacy education, both linguistic and social, favour reflection literacy: all its propagation involves now is simply a difference in orientation.

Concluding remarks

I am aware that many questions remain; but I hope that the need for the introduction of a literacy pedagogy which enables students to reflect on their own experiences of discourse will be granted. I am not against pedagogy which assists resistance to bias in education against class, gender, ethnicity, skin colour: but all of these phenomena are elements of, and attain their value in, specific kinds of social structures. To see these specific problems as part of the larger picture, and ultimately pertaining to the field of production, could prove beneficial. Moss has remarked (2002: 557):

> Within the academic community there is a considerable degree of dis-quiet over the loss of autonomy that the new pedagogic concordat represents. This is almost always told as a story of deep loss, without always owning up to the real strengths and weaknesses of what went before. But the new pedagogic economy produces new affordances as well as constraints.

I do not question that the current changes in the educational system, almost despite themselves, might have got something right. But broadening the context of Moss's remark from visible/invisible, competence/performance pedagogy, the issue would seem somewhat different. A British Marxist remarked in the 1940s that the problem for capitalist educational authorities was how to educate their citizens so that they could read and understand the

Bren gun manual but not the Communist Manifesto. By contrast, our hope has to be that the capitalist world never succeeds in resolving this problem. There is something very wrong with a system of education, no matter what its affordances, that on the one hand pays such close and almost invariably ill-informed attention to details of how students should be educated by laying down rules about skills, tests and the like, and on the other, persuades its employees that a literacy pedagogy of the type being recommended here is subversive, and that the job of the educator is to turn the educational institutions into profit-making purveyors of pre-packaged knowledge.[11] And there is something very wrong with a literacy pedagogy which does not cultivate in the acquirer the basic function of learning, namely to interrogate, rather than to remain a docile recipient of information. Educational systems can never be divorced from society, but all things being equal, to obtain the socially most desirable outcome, the classification between education and production needs to be balanced. If this classification is very strong, it could encourage the 'ivory tower' syndrome with academe pursuing its own agenda irrespective of what the aspirations or problems of the external community happen to be; such education becomes a state within a state, catering to a parasitic elitism. But equally, if the classification is very weak, as is happening now, the ability to question the official agencies and the agents of production might be severely threatened, because the external pressures might translate themselves into internal ones. If this happens, then we are dangerously close to some form of fundamentalism, and I doubt that the fundamentalism of capitalism is any more palatable than that of religion. Certainly, reflection literacy will not be an antidote to all social problems; what makes it desirable is its treatment of discourse as discourse needs to be treated, i.e. dialogic. Above all, it enables the literate to see through the hypocrisy of the progressive and the civilized.

Notes

1 The relationship between social and semiotic processes is not one of simple co-occurrence but of mutual reliance: social processes typically need semiotic action, and all semiotic actions have their roots in some social action (Hasan 1999).

2 See Halliday 1992 on 'time depth' in relation to language change and the *langue parole* dialectic.

3 Bourdieu's (1992) account of how linguistic meanings get shaped appears suspect. Precipitate meaning disjunction is typically an indication of violent ideological change.

4 For discussion, see Hasan 2003.

5 'by the denotation of a lexeme ... will be meant the relationship that holds between that lexeme and persons, things, properties, processes and activities external to the language system' (Lyons 1977: 207).

6 Such interpretations would involve internal contradiction since the denotative meaning of *man* is included in the meaning of *husband*.

7 I refer to the managed first election of George W. Bush as President of the most powerful 'democracy' in the world.

8 Pupils are judged by textual performance, but a successful pedagogy of modes of performance must create competence in the learner.

9 See Moss (2002) for a description of one such case.

10 After a seminar at an Eastern university on this topic, a colleague criticized the 'shockingly subversive' tone of the presentation, adding indignantly: 'here am I fund-raising for my university and there you go giving me such advice!' In her contribution at the third Bernstein symposium, Moss, not convinced that the present pedagogic climate permits resistance, expressed serious doubts that such 'utopian' changes would be possible. I would say, it is relevant to ask: Did the Nazis permit resistance?

11 Bourdieu's (1992) suggestion that denotation is *official* and connotation is *personal/individual* appears unjustified. The possibility of communication demands social recognition for both denotative and connotative meanings. The success of glib-speak depends on shared connotations.

Bibliography

Adams, C. (2000) Statement by Carol Adams, Chief Executive of the General Teachers' Council for England, in *The GTC: Listening to Teachers*, London: General Teaching Council for England.

Adonis, A. (2001) *High Challenge, High Support*, London: Policy Network.

Agassi, J. (2003) 'Comparability and incommensurability', *Social Epistemology*, 17 (2, 3): 93–94.

Agre, P. E. (1997) *Computation and Human Experiences*, Cambridge: Cambridge University Press.

Ahier, J., Beck, J. and Moore, R. (2003) *Graduate Citizens? Issues of Citizenship and Higher Education*, London: RoutledgeFalmer.

Ahl, V. and Allen T. F. H. (1996) *Hierarchy Theory: a Vision, Vocabulary and Epistemology*, New York: Columbia University Press.

Alexander, R. (2004) 'Still no pedagogy? Principle, pragmatism and compliance in primary education', *Cambridge Journal of Education*, 34 (1): 7–33.

Allen, N. J. (1994) 'Primitive classification: the argument and its validity', in W. S. F. Pickering and H. Martins (eds) *Debating Durkheim*, London: Routledge and Kegan Paul.

Allen, W. (1959) 'The two cultures', *Encounter*, XIII (2): 67–68.

Althusser, L. (1971) 'Ideology and ideological state apparatus', in *Lenin and Philosophy*, (trans. B. Brewster), New York: New Left Books.

Anyon, J. (1980) 'Social class and the hidden curriculum of work', *Journal of Education*, 162 (1): 67–92.

Anyon, J. (1997) *Ghetto Schooling: A Political Economy of Educational Reform*, New York: Teachers College Press.

Anyon, J. (2005) *Radical Possibilities: Public Policy, School Reform and a New Social Movement*. New York: Routledge.

Apple, M (1979) *Ideology and the Curriculum*. London: Routledge and Kegan Paul.

Apple, M. (2002) 'Does education have independent power? Bernstein and the picture of relative autonomy', *British Journal of Sociology of Education, Special Issue: Basil Bernstein's Theory of Social Class, Educational Codes and Social Control*, 23 (4): 607–616.

Arnot, M. (2002) *Reproducing Gender? Essays in Educational Theory and Feminist Politics*, London: RoutledgeFalmer.

Arnot, M., McIntyre, D., Peddar, D. and Reay, D. (2004) *Consultation in the Classroom: Developing Dialogue about Teaching And Learning*, Cambridge: Pearson.

Arnot, M. and Reay, D. (2004) 'The framing of pedagogic encounters: regulating the social order of classroom learning', in J. Muller, B. Davies and A. Morais (eds) *Reading Bernstein, Researching Bernstein*, London: RoutledgeFalmer.

Atkinson, P. (1985) *Language, Structure and Reproduction: An Introduction to the Sociology of Basil Bernstein*, London: Methuen.

Atkinson, P., Davies, B. and Delamont, S. (1995) *Discourse and Reproduction: Essays in Honor of Basil Bernstein*, Cresskill, NJ: Hampton Press.

Bailey, C. H. (1984) *Beyond the Present and the Particular: A Theory of Liberal Education*, London: Routledge & Kegan Paul.

Bakhtin, M. M. (1981) The *Dialogic Imagination: Four Essays by M. M. Bakhtin* (ed. M. Holquist, trans. C. Emerson and M. Holquist), Austin: University of Texas Press.

Ball, S. J. (1990) *Politics and Policy Making in Education: Explorations in Policy Sociology*, London: Routledge.

Barber, M. (2001) *Large-Scale Education Reform in England: A Work in Progress*, paper for Managing Education Reform Conference, Moscow, 29–30 October.

Barber, M. (2003) *The Framework For Continuous Improvement*, speech delivered at the National College of School Leadership, 11 June, Nottingham. Available online at http://www.ncsl.org.uk/index.cfm?pageid=ev_auth_barber

Beck, J. (2002) 'The sacred and the profane in recent struggles to promote official pedagogic identities', *British Journal of Sociology of Education*, 23 (4): 617–626.

Beck, J. (2003) 'The school curriculum, the National Curriculum and New Labour reforms', in J. Beck and M. Earl (eds) *Key Issues in Secondary Education* (2nd edn), London: Continuum.

Beck, J. and Young, M. F. D. (2005) 'The assault on the professions and the restructuring of academic and professional identities', *British Journal of Sociology of Education*, 26 (2): 183–197.

Beck, U. (2001) *What Is Globalization?*, Cambridge: Polity.

Berlin, I. (2000a) *Three Critics of the Enlightenment: Vico, Hammann, Herder*, Princeton: Princeton University Press.

Berlin, I. (2000b) 'The essence of European Romanticism', in I. Berlin, *The Power of Ideas*, London: Pimlico Press.

Bernstein, B. (1970) 'Education cannot compensate for society', *New Society*, 387: 344–347.

Bernstein, B. (1971) 'On the classification and framing of educational knowledge', in M. F. D. Young (ed.) *Knowledge and Control*, London: Collier Macmillan.

Bernstein, B. (1973a) *Class, Codes and Control: Vol. 1*. London: Routledge & Kegan Paul (Original published in 1971).

Bernstein, B. (1973b) *Class, Codes and Control: Vol. 2*. London: Routledge & Kegan Paul (Original published in 1971).

Bernstein, B. (1974) *Class, Codes and Control, Volume I: Theoretical Studies Towards a Sociology of Language*, (2nd (revised) ed), London: Routledge & Kegan Paul.

Bernstein, B. (1977) *Class, Codes and Control, Volume III: Towards a Theory of Educational Transmissions*, London: Routledge & Kegan Paul.

Bernstein, B. (1981) 'Codes, modalities and the process of cultural reproduction: a model', *Language in Society*, 10: 327–363.

Bernstein, B. (1990) *Class, Codes and Control, Volume IV: The Structuring of Pedagogic Discourse*, London: Routledge & Kegan Paul.

Bernstein, B. (1995) 'Response', in A. R. Sadovnick (ed.) *Pedagogy and Knowledge: The Sociology of Basil Bernstein*, Norwood, NJ: Ablex.

Bernstein, B. (1996) *Pedagogy, Symbolic Control and Identity: Theory, Research, Critique*, London and Bristol: Taylor & Francis.

Bernstein, B. (1999a) 'Official knowledge and pedagogic identities', in F. Christie (ed.) *Pedagogy and the Shaping of Consciousness: Linguistic and Social Processes*, London: Continuum.

Bernstein, B. (1999b) 'Vertical and horizontal discourse: an essay', *British Journal of Sociology of Education*, 20 (2): 157–173.

Bernstein, B. (2000) *Pedagogy, Symbolic Control and Identity: Theory, Research, Critique* (rev. ed), London: Rowman & Littlefield.

Bernstein, B. (2001a) 'From pedagogies to knowledges', in A. Morais, I. Neves, B. Davies and H. Daniels (eds) (2001) *Towards a Sociology of Pedagogy: The Contribution of Basil Bernstein to Research* (pp. 363–368), New York: Peter Lang.

Bernstein, B. (2001b) Video Conference with Basil Bernstein, in A. Morais *et al.* (eds) *Towards a Sociology of Pedagogy*, New York: Peter Lang.

Bernstein, B. and Cook-Gumperz, J. (1973) *The Coding Grid in Socialisation and Social Control*, in B. Bernstein, Class, Codes and Control Vol. 2, Routledge & Kegan Paul.

Bernstein, B. and Solomon, J. (1999) 'Pedagogy, identity and the construction of a theory of structure of pedagogic control: Basil Bernstein questioned by Joseph Solomon', *British Journal of Sociology of Education*, 20 (2): 265–279.

Bevir, M. (2003) 'Notes towards an analysis of conceptual change', *Social Epistemology*, 17 (1): 53–63.

Bird, A. (2003) 'What is scientific progress?' Mimeo. Unpublished manuscript.

Bisseret, N. (1979) *Class, Language and Ideology*. London: Routledge & Kegan Paul.

Bloom, B. (ed.) (1964) *Taxonomy of Educational Objectives: The Classification of Educational Goals* (2 volumes), New York: McKay.

Blunkett, D. (2000) *Radical Changes Will Prepare Higher Education for the 21st Century*, press notice of speech at University of Greenwich, 15 February.

Blunkett, D. (2001) 'We *are* winning', *Guardian Education*, 6 March.

Boudon, R. (1971) *The Uses of Structuralism*, London: Heinemann.

Bourdieu, P. (1992) *Language and Symbolic Power*, Cambridge: Polity.

Bourdieu, P. (1993) *The Field of Cultural Production*, Cambridge: Polity.

Bourne, J. (2000) 'New imaginings of reading for a new moral order: a review of the production, transmission and acquisition of a new pedagogic culture in the UK', *Linguistics and Education*, 11 (1): 31–45.

Bourne, J. (2003) 'Vertical discourse: the role of the teacher in the transmission and acquisition of decontextualised language', *European Educational Research Journal*, 2 (4): 496–520

Bourner, T., Bowden, R. and Laing, S. (2001) 'Professional doctorates in England', *Studies in Higher Education*, 26 (1), 65–83.

Bowles, S. and Gintis, H. (1976) *Schooling in Capitalist America*, New York: Basic Books.

Bray, D. (2000) 'An examination of GCSE music uptake rates', *British Journal of Music Education*, 17 (1): 79–89.

Briggs, A. (1956) 'History and its neighbours', *Universities Quarterly*, 11 (1): 55–63.

Bronowski, J. (1961) *Science and Human Values*, London: Hutchinson.

Brookes, B. C. (1959a) 'The difficulty of interpreting science', *The Listener*, LXII: 519–521.

Brookes, B. C. (1959b) Letter to the editor, *The Listener*, LXII: 783–784.

Brown, A. J. (1999) 'Parental participation, positioning and pedagogy: a sociological study of the IMPACT primary school mathematics project', *Collected Original Resources in Education*, 24 (3): 7/A02–11/C09.

Brown, A. J. (2001) 'Becoming a researcher: reflections on the pedagogic practices of Basil Bernstein' in S. Power, P. Aggleton, J. Brannen, A. Brown, L. Chisholm and J. Mace (eds) *A Tribute to Basil Bernstein 1924–2000*: 72–76, London: Institute of Education.

Brown, A. J. and Dowling, P. C. (1998) *Doing Research/Reading Research: A Mode of Interrogation for Education*, London: Falmer.

BSCS (1995) *Developing Biological Literacy: Guide to Developing Secondary and Post-Secondary Biology Curricula*, Dubuque: Kendall/Hunt.

Butt, D. (1983) 'Semantic drift in verbal art', *Australian Review of Applied Linguistics*, 6 (1): 38–48.

Butt, D. (1988) 'Randomness, order and the latent patterning of text', in D. Birch and M. O'Toole (eds) *Functions of Style*, London: Pinter.

Callinicos, A. (2001) *Against the Third Way: An Anti-Capitalist Critique*, Cambridge: Polity.

Câmara, M. J. and Morais, A. (1998). 'O desenvolvimento científico no jardim de infância: Influência de práticas pedagógicas', *Revista de Educação, VII* (2): 179–199.

Cartwright, N. (2001) *The Dappled World: A Study of the Boundaries of Science*, Cambridge: Cambridge University Press.

Cloran, C. (1989) 'Learning through language: the social construction of gender', in R. Hasan and J. R. Martin (eds) *Learning Language, Learning Culture*, Norwood, NJ: Ablex.

Cloran, C. (1994) *Rhetorical Units and Decontextualization: An Enquiry into Some Relations of Context, Meaning and Grammar*, Nottingham: Department of English Studies, Nottingham University.

Cloran, C. (1999) 'Contexts for learning', in F. Christie (ed.) *Pedagogy and the Shaping of Consciousness: Linguistic and Social Processes*, London: Cassell.

Cole, M. (1996) *Cultural Psychology: A Once and Future Discipline*, Cambridge, MA: Harvard University Press.

Cole, M. and Engeström, Y. (1993) 'A cultural-historical approach to distributed cognition', in G. Salomon (ed.), *Distributed Cognition: Psychological and Educational Considerations*, New York: Cambridge University Press.

Cole, M., Engeström, Y. and Vasquez, O. (eds) (1997) *Mind, Culture and Activity*, Cambridge: Cambridge University Press.

Cook-Gumperz, J. J. and Hymes, D. (1972) *Directions in Sociolinguistics*, Oxford: Blackwell.

Cooper, B. and Dunne, M. (2000) *Assessing Children's Mathematical Knowledge: Social Class, Sex and Problem-solving*, Buckingham, England: Open University Press.

Coulson, S. (2001) *Semantic Leaps: Frame-shifting and Conceptual Blending in Meaning Construction*, Cambridge: Cambridge University Press.

Cross, C. T. (2004) *Political Education: National Policy Comes of Age*, New York: Teachers College Press.

Crouch, C. (2003) *Commercialisation or Citizenship: Education Policy and the Future of Public Services*, Fabian Ideas 606, London: The Fabian Society.

Daniels, H. (1988) 'An enquiry into different forms of special school organization, pedagogic practice and pupil discrimination', *CORE*, 12 (2): 4–11.

Daniels, H. (1989) 'Visual displays as tacit relays of the structure of pedagogic practice', *British Journal of Sociology of Education*, 10 (2): 123–140.

Daniels, H. (1995) 'Pedagogic practices, tacit knowledge and discursive discrimination: Bernstein and post-Vygtotskian research', *British Journal of Sociology of Education*, 16 (4): 517–532.

Daniels, H. (2001) *Vygotsky and Pedagogy*, London: RoutledgeFalmer.

Daniels, H. and Creese, A. with Hey, V. and Leonard, D. (2004) 'Gendered learning in two modalities of pedagogic discourse', in J. Muller, B. Davies and A. Morais (eds) *Reading Bernstein, Researching Bernstein*, London: RoutledgeFalmer.

Davies, B. (1995) 'Bernstein on classrooms', in P. Atkinson, B. Davies and S. Delamont (eds) *Discourse and Reproduction: Essays in Honour of Basil Bernstein*, Cresskill, NJ: Hampton Press.

DEB (1999) *Gestão flexível do currículo*, Lisbon: Ministry of Education.

DEB (2001) *Currículo nacional do ensino básico: Competências essenciais*, Lisbon: Ministry of Education.

DEB (2002) *Orientações curriculares para o 3° ciclo do ensino básico: Ciências Físicas e Naturais*, Lisbon: Ministry of Education.

Department of Education (2000) *A South African Curriculum for the 21st Century: Report of the Review Committee on Curriculum 2005.* Pretoria.

DfEE (Department for Education and Employment) (1997a) *Excellence in Schools*, London: Stationery Office.

DfEE (1997b) *Excellence for All Children: Meeting Special Educational Needs – A Programme of Action*, London: Stationery Office.

DfEE (1999) *Excellence in Cities*, London: Stationery Office.

DfEE (2001) *Schools: Building on Success*, Cmnd 5060, London: Stationery Office.

DfES (Department for Education and Skills) (2002) *Time for Standards: Reforming the School Workforce*, London: DfES.

DfES (2003) *Excellence and Enjoyment: A Strategy for Primary Schools*, London: DfES.

DfES/QCA (1999) *The National Curriculum for England: Music*, London: HMSO.

Diaz, M. (1984) '*A model of pedagogic discourse with special application to Colombian primary education*', unpublished PhD thesis, University of London.

Diaz, M. (2001) 'Subject, power and pedagogical discourse', in A. Morais, I. Neves, B. Davies and H. Daniels (eds) *Towards a Sociology of Pedagogy: The Contribution of Basil Bernstein to Research*, New York: Peter Lang.

Dixon, W. M. (1938) *The Englishman*, London: Hodder & Stoughton.

Doherty, C. (2004) 'Student subsidy of the internationalized curriculum: knowing, voicing and producing the Other', paper presented at *Reclaiming Knowledge: Registers of discourse in the community and school* conference, University of Sydney, 13–15 December.

Domingos (now Morais), A. (1989) 'Conceptual demand of science courses and social class', in P. Adey (ed.) *Adolescent Development and School Science*, London: Falmer.

Dowling, P. (1998) 'The sociology of mathematics education: mathematical myths/pedagogic texts', London: Falmer.

Dowling, P. (1999) 'Basil Bernstein in frame: "Oh dear, is this a structuralist analysis?", at: http://www.ioe.ac.uk/ccs/dowling/kings1999/index.html.

Driel, J., Beijaard, D. and Verloop, N. (2001) 'Professional development and reform in science education role of teachers' practical knowledge', *Journal of Research in Science Teaching*, 38 (2): 137–158.

Durkheim, E. (1977) *The Evolution of Educational Thought: Lectures on the Formation and Development of Secondary Education in France* (trans. P. Collins), London: Routledge & Kegan Paul.

Durkheim, E. (1995) *The Elementary Forms of Religious Life* (trans. K. Fields), New York: The Free Press.

Dworkin, A. G. (2005) 'The No Child Left Behind Act: accountability, high-stakes testing, and roles for sociologists', *Sociology of Education*, 78 (2): 170–174.

ESRC (Economic and Social Research Council) (2005) *Postgraduate Research Training Guidelines* (4th ed), Swindon: ESRC.

Education Trust (2004) at: www.educationtrust.org.uk

Edwards, A. D. (1987) 'Language codes and classroom practice', *Oxford Review of Education*, 13 (3): 237–247.

Edwards, A. D. (1994) 'A reply to Basil Bernstein', *Oxford Review of Education*, 20 (2), 183–184.

Edwards, A. and Westgate, D. (1987) *Investigating Classroom Talk*, London: Falmer Press.

Edwards, T., Fitz, J. and Whitty, G. (1989) *The State and Private Education: An Evaluation of the Assisted Places Scheme*, Basingstoke: Falmer.

Elkonin, D. B. (1972) 'Toward the problem of stages in the mental development of the child', *Soviet Psychology*, No. 4: 6–20.

Elliott, J., Bridges, D., Ebbutt, D., Gibson, R. and Niass, J. (1981) *School Accountability*, London: Grant McIntyre.

Ellwood, W. (2002) *The No-Nonsense Guide to Globalization*, London: Verso.

Engeström, Y. (1993) 'Developmental studies on work as a test bench of activity theory', in S. Chaikin and J. Lave (eds) *Understanding Practice: Perspectives on Activity and Context*, Cambridge: Cambridge University Press.

Engeström, Y. (1996) *Perspectives on Activity Theory*, Cambridge: Cambridge University Press.

Engeström, Y. (1999) 'Innovative learning in work teams: analyzing cycles of knowledge creation in practice', in Y. Engeström, R. Miettinen and R.-L. Punamaki (eds) *Perspectives on Activity Theory*, Cambridge: Cambridge University Press.

Engeström, Y. and Middleton, D. (eds) (1996) *Cognition and Communication at Work*, Cambridge: Cambridge University Press.

Engeström, Y. and Miettinen, R. (1999) 'Introduction', in Y.Engeström, R. Miettinen and R.-L. Punamaki (eds), *Perspectives on Activity Theory*, Cambridge: Cambridge University Press.

Ensor, P. and Hoadley, U. (2004) 'Developing languages of description to research pedagogy', *Journal of Education*, 32: 82–103.

Fairclough, N. (1992) *Discourse and Social Change*, Cambridge: Polity.

Fairclough, N. (2000) 'Discourse, social theory and social research: the discourse of welfare reform', *Journal of Sociolinguistics*, 4 (2): 163–195.

Fairclough, N. (2004) 'The dialectics of discourse', at: http://www.geogr.ku.dk/courses/phd/glob-loc/papers/phdfairclough2.pdf (accessed 30 June 2004).

Fauconnier, G. and Turner, M. (2002) *The Way We Think: Conceptual Blending and the Mind's Hidden Complexities*, New York: Basic Books.

Freitas. C. V. (2000) 'O currículo em debate: Positivismo – pós-modernismo. Teoria – prática', *Revista de Educação*, IX (1): 39–52.

Furlong, J. (2003) 'BERA at 30: have we come of age?' Presidential address to the British Educational Research Association Annual Conference, Heriot-Watt University, Edinburgh.

Available online at http://www.bera.ac.uk/pdfs/BERApresidentialnopics.ppt (accessed 1 August 2005).

Gagné, R. M. (1985) *The Conditions of Learning, and Theory of Instruction* (4th ed), New York: Holt, Rinehart & Winston.

Gardner, H. (2005) *The Development and Education of the Mind: The Selected works of Howard Gardner*. New York: Routledge.

Gee, J. (1990) *Social Linguistics and Literacies: Ideology in Discourse*, Brighton: Falmer.

Gee, J. (2001) 'Learning in semiotic domains: a social and situated account', paper presented to the *International Literacy Conference*, Cape Town, 13–17 November.

Gellner, E. (1964) 'The crisis in the humanities and the mainstream of philosophy', in J. H. Plumb (ed.) *Crisis in the Humanities*, Harmondsworth: Penguin.

Gibbons, M., Limoges, C., Nowotny, H., Schwartzman, S., Scott, P. and Trow, M. (1994) *The New Production of Knowledge: The Dynamics of Science and Research in Contemporary Societies*, London: Sage.

Giddens, A. (1991) *Modernity and Self-Identity: Self and Society in the Late Modern Age*, Cambridge: Polity.

Goals 2000: Educate America Act (1994) PL 1804. Washington DC: United States Congress.

Goldman, A. (1999) *Knowledge in a Social World*, Oxford: Oxford University Press.

Gray, J. (1999) *False Dawn: The Delusions of Global Capitalism*, London: Granta Books.

Green, L. (2001) *How Popular Musicians Learn: A Way Ahead for Music Education*, Burlington: Ashgate.

Griffin, P. and Cole. M. (1984) 'Current activity for the future: the zo-ped', in B. Rogoff and J. V. Wertsch (eds) *Children's Learning in the Zone of Proximal Development*, San Francisco: Jossey-Bass.

Guardian Weekly, May 20–26, 2004.

Gutiérrez, K., Baquedano-López, P. and Tejeda, C. (1999) 'Re-thinking diversity: hybridity and hybrid language practices in the third space', *Mind, Culture and Activity*, 6 (4) 286–303.

Haack, S. (2003) *Defending Science – Within Reason*, New York: Prometheus.

Halliday, M. (1971) 'Linguistic function and literary style: an enquiry into the language of William Golding', in S. Chatman (ed.) *Literary Style: A Symposium*. London: Oxford University Press.

Halliday, M. (1985a) *Spoken and Written Language*, Geelong, Vic: Deakin University Press.

Halliday, M. (1985b) *An Introduction to Functional Grammar*, London: Edward Arnold.

Halliday, M. (1992) 'The act of meaning', in J. E. Alatis (ed.) *Communication and Social Meaning, Georgetown University Round Table 1992*, Georgetown: Georgetown University Press.

Halliday, M. (1994a) *Introduction to Functional Grammar*, (2nd ed), London: Edward Arnold.

Halliday, M. (1994b) 'On language in relation to the evolution of human consciousness', in Sture Allen (ed.) *Of Thoughts and Words (Proceedings of Nobel Symposium 92: The Relations between Language and Mind)*, London: Imperial College Press (also in J. Webster (ed.) (2003) *On Language and Linguistics*, Vol. 3, Collected Works of M. A. K. Halliday, London: Continuum.

Halliday, M. (1996) 'Literacy and linguistics: a functional perspective', R. Hasan and G. Williams (eds) *Literacy in Society*, London: Longman.

Halliday, M. and Matthiessen, M. I. M. (1999) *Construing Experience through Meaning*, London: Continuum.

Halsey, A. H. (1962) 'The responsibilities of universities', *Universities Quarterly*, 16 (2): 167–179.

Harland, J., Kinder, K., Lord, P., Stott, A., Schagen, I., Haynes, J. with Cusworth, L., White, R. and Paola, R. (2000) *Arts Education in Secondary Schools: Effects and Effectiveness*, Slough: National Foundation for Educational Research.

Harré, R. (1975) 'Rhetoric, Official and Unofficial, *Times Educational Supplement*, 18 July, 23a.

Hasan, R. (1971) 'Rime and reason in literature', in S. Chatman (ed.), *Literary Style: A Symposium*, London: Oxford University Press.

Hasan, R. (1985) *Linguistics, Language and Verbal Art*, Geelong, Vic: Deakin University Press.

Hasan, R. (1989) 'Semantic variation and sociolinguistics', *Australian Journal of Linguistics*, 9 (2): 221–275.

Hasan, R. (1992a) 'Speech genre, semiotic mediation and the development of higher mental functions', *Language Science*, 14 (4): 489–528.

Hasan, R. (1992b) 'Meaning in sociolinguistic theory', in K. Bolton and H. Kwok (eds), *Sociolinguistics Today: International Perspectives*, London: Routledge.

Hasan, R. (1995) 'On social conditions for semiotic mediation: the genesis of mind in society', in A. Sadovnik (ed.) *Knowledge and Pedagogy: The Sociology of Basil Bernstein*, Norwood, NJ: Ablex.

Hasan, R. (1996) 'Literacy, everyday talk and society', in R. Hasan and G. Williams (eds) *Literacy in Society*, London: Longman.

Hasan, R. (1999) 'The disempowerment game: Bourdieu and language in literacy', *Linguistics and Education*, 10 (1): 25–87.

Hasan, R. (2002a) 'Semiotic mediation and mental development in pluralistic societies: some implications for tomorrow's schooling', in *Learning for Life in the 21st Century: Sociocultural Perspectives on the Future of Education*, Malden, MA: Blackwell.

Hasan, R. (2002b) 'Ways of meaning, ways of learning: code as an explanatory concept', *British Journal of Sociology of Education*, 23 (4): 537–548.

Hasan, R. (2003) 'Globalization, literacy and ideology', *World Englishes*, 22 (4): 433–448.

Hasan, R. (2004) (manuscript) 'Semiotic mediation, language and society: three exotripic theories – Vygotsky, Halliday and Bernstein'.

Hasan, R., Fries, P. and Gregory, M. (eds) (1995) 'The conception of context in text', in *Discourse in Society: Systemic Functional Perspectives* (Meaning and Choice in Language: Studies for Michael Halliday) (ADPS50), Norwood: NJ: Ablex.

Hasan, R. and Williams, G. (1996) (eds) *Literacy in Society*, London: Longman.

Held, D. and McGrew, A. (2002) *Globalization/Anti-Globalization*, Cambridge: Polity.

Hertz, N. (2001) *The Silent Take-Over: Global Capitalism and the Death of Democracy*, London: Heinemann.

Hickox, M. and Moore, R. (1995) 'Liberal-humanist education: the vocationalist challenge', *Curriculum Studies*, 3 (1): 45–59.

Hirst, P. and Thompson, G. (1996) *Globalization in Question*, Cambridge: Polity.

Hobsbawm, E. (1994) *Age of Extremes: The Short Twentieth Century*, London: Michael Joseph.

Hobsbawm, E. (1999) *The New Century*, London: Abacus.

Holland, J. (1981) 'Social class and changes in orientations to meanings', *Sociology*, 15 (1): 1–18.

Ilyenkov, E. V. (1977) *Dialectical Logic. Essays on its History and Theory*, Moscow: Progress.

Ivinson, G. (1998a) 'The construction of the curriculum', unpublished PhD thesis, Cambridge University, England.

Ivinson, G. (1998b) 'The child's construction of the curriculum', *Papers on Social Representations: Threads and Discussions. Special Issue: The Development of Knowledge*, 7 (1–2): 21–40.

Ivinson, G. (2000). 'The child's construction of the primary school curriculum', in H. Cowie and D. Van der Aalsvoort (eds) *Social Interaction in Learning and Instruction: The Meaning of Discourse for the Construction of Knowledge*, Kidlington: Pergamon Press and EARLI.

Ivinson, G. (2002) 'Instructional and regulative discourses: a comparative case study of two classroom settings designed to ameliorate boys' underachievement in English', 2nd International Bernstein Conference, Cape Town.

Ivinson, G. and Duveen, G. (2005) 'Classroom structuration and the development of social representations of the curriculum', *British Journal of Sociology of Education*, 26 (5): 627–642.

Jayyusi, L. (1984) *Conversation and the Moral Order*, London: Routledge.

Jessop, B., Bonnett, K., Bromley, S. and Ling, T. (1984) 'Authoritarian populism: a tale of two nations and Thatcherism', *New Left Review*, 147 (Sept/Oct): 32–60.

Jones, K. (1989) *Right Turn – the Conservative Revolution in Education?* London: Hutchinson.

Jones, L. and Moore, R. (1995) 'Approaching competence: the competency movement, the New Right, and the "culture change" project', *British Journal of Education and Work*, 8 (2) 78–92.

Just4kids (2004) at: www.Just4kids.org.

Kelly, G. A. (1955) *The Psychology of Personal Constructs*, New York: W. N. Norton.

Kermode, F. (1966) *The Sense of an Ending: Studies in the Theory of Fiction*, Oxford: Oxford University Press.

Klemperer, V. (2002) *The Language of the Third Reich* (trans Martin Brady), London: Continuum.

Koestler, A. (1967) *The Ghost in the Machine*, New York: Macmillan.

Kuhn, T. (1962) *The Structure of Scientific Revolutions*, Chicago: Chicago University Press.

Labaree, D. (2004) *The Trouble with Ed Schools*, New Haven: Yale University Press.

Lamont, A. (2004) 'What are the possible reasons for the low take-up of music GCSE?' *Music in Key Stage 4: QCA Music Development Group working paper*, London: Qualifications and Curriculum Authority.

Lamont, A., Hargreaves, D. J., Marshall, N. A. and Tarrant, M. (2003) 'Young people's music in and out of school', *British Journal of Music Education*, 20 (3): 1–13.

Lave, J. (1988) *Cognition in Practice*, Cambridge: Cambridge University Press.

Lave, J. and Wenger, E. (1991) *Situated Learning: Legitimate Peripheral Participation*, Cambridge: Cambridge University Press.

Lea, M. and Nicoll, K. (eds) (2002) *Distributed Learning*, London: RoutledgeFalmer.

Leaton Gray, S. (2004) 'Defining the future: an interrogation of education and time', *British Journal of Sociology of Education*, 25 (3): 323–340.

Lee, H. D. P. (1955) 'The position of classics in schools', *Universities Quarterly*, 9 (2): 135–144.

Lemke, J. (1997) 'Cognition, context, and learning: a social semiotic perspective', in D. Kirshner (ed.) *Situated Cognition Theory: Social, Neurological, and Semiotic Perspectives*, New York: Erlbaum.

Leonard, A. (2000) 'Achieving progression from the GCSE to AS', *Teaching History*, 98: 30–34.

Leontiev, A. N. (1978) *Activity, Consciousness, and Personality*, Englewood Cliffs: Prentice-Hall.

Leontiev, A. N. (1981) 'The concept of activity in psychology', in J. V. Wertsch (ed.) *The Concept of Activity in Soviet Psychology*, Armonk, NY: M. E. Sharpe.

Lunt, I. (2002) 'Professional doctorates in education', paper commissioned by the Education Subject Centre (ESCalate). Available online at: http://www.escalate.ac.uk/1712 (accessed 1 August 2005.

Lyons, J. (1977) *Semantics, 1*, Cambridge: Cambridge University Press.

Mackerness, E. D. (1960) 'Ignorant Armies'. *The Universities Review*, 33 (1): 14–17.

Madely, J. (1999) *Big Business, Poor People*, London: Zed Books.

Madely, J. (2000) 'Putting people before principles', *Guardian Weekly*.

Makitalo, A. and Saljo, R. (2002) 'Talk in institutional contexts and institutional contexts in talk: categories as situated practice', *Text* 22(1), 57–82.

Markus, G. (2003) 'The paradoxical unity of culture: the Arts and the Sciences', *Thesis Eleven*, 75: 7–24.

Marquand, D. (1995) 'Flagging Fortunes', *The Guardian*, 3 July, p. 13.

Martin, J. R. (1986) 'Intervening in the process of writing development', in *Writing to Mean: Teaching Genres Across the Curriculum*, C. Painter and J. R. Martin (eds), Occasional Paper No 9: Applied Linguistics Association of Australia.

Martin, J. R. and Rose, D. (2003) *Working With Discourse: Meaning Beyond the Clause*, London: Continuum.

Maton, K. (2000) 'Recovering pedagogic discourse: a Bernsteinian approach to the sociology of educational knowledge', *Linguistics and Education*, 11 (1): 79–98.

Maton, K. (2002) 'Popes, kings and cultural studies: placing the commitment to non-disciplinarity in historical context', in S. Herbrechter (ed.) *Cultural Studies: Interdisciplinarity and Translation*, Amsterdam: Rodopi.

Maton, K. (2004) 'The wrong kind of knower: education, expansion and the epistemic device', in J. Muller, B. Davies and A. Morais (eds) *Reading Bernstein, Researching Bernstein*, London: RoutledgeFalmer.

Maton, K. (2005) 'The field of higher education: a sociology of reproduction, transformation, change and the conditions of emergence for cultural studies', unpublished PhD thesis, University of Cambridge.

Matos, M. and Morais, A. (2004). 'Trabalho experimental na aula de ciências físico-químicas do 3° ciclo do ensino básico: Teorias e práticas dos professores', *Revista de Educação*, XII (2), 75–93.

Matthews, M. R. (2004a) 'Editorial', *Science and Education*, 13 (1–2): 1–6.

Matthews, M. R. (2004b) 'Re-appraising positivism and education: the arguments of Philipp Frank and Herbert Feigl', *Science and Education*, 13 (1–2): 7–39.

Matthiessen, M. (1995) *Lexicogrammatical Cartography: English Systems*, Tokyo: International Language Science Publishers.

Merton, R. K. (1993) (1st pub. 1965) *On the Shoulders of Giants*, Chicago: University of Chicago Press.

Merttens, R. and Vass, J. (1990) *Sharing Maths Cultures: IMPACT – Inventing Maths for Parents and Children and Teachers*, London: Falmer.

Merttens, R. and Vass, J. (1993) (eds) *Partnerships in Maths: Parents and Schools*, London: Falmer.

Moore, R. (2004a) *Education and Society: Issues and Explanations in the Sociology of Education*, Cambridge: Polity.

Moore, R. (2004b) 'Cultural Capital: objective probability and cultural arbitrary', *British Journal of Sociology of Education*, 25 (4): 445–456.

Moore, R. and Maton, K. (2001) 'Founding the sociology of knowledge: Basil Bernstein, epistemic fields and the epistemic device', in A. Morais, I. Neves, B. Davies and H. Daniels (eds) *Towards a Sociology of Pedagogy: The Contribution of Basil Bernstein to Research*, New York: Peter Lang.

Moore, R. and Muller, J. (1999) 'The discourse of 'voice' and the problem of knowledge and identity in the sociology of education', *British Journal of Sociology of Education*, 20 (2): 189–206.

Moore, R. and Muller, J. (2002) 'The growth of knowledge and the discursive gap', *British Journal of Sociology of Education*, 23 (4): 627–637.

Morais, A. and Antunes, H. (1994) 'Students' differential text production in the regulative context of the classroom', *British Journal of Sociology of Education*, 15 (2): 243–263.

Morais, A., Fontinhas, F. and Neves, I. P. (1993) 'Recognition and realization rules in acquiring school science: contribution of pedagogy and social background of pupils', *British Journal of the Sociology of Education*, 13 (2): 247–70.

Morais, A. and Neves, I. (2001) 'Pedagogic social contexts: studies for a sociology of learning', in A. Morais, I. Neves, B. Davies and H. Daniels (eds) *Towards a Sociology of Pedagogy*, New York: Peter Lang.

Morais, A., Neves, I. and Afonso, M. (2005) 'Teacher training processes and teachers' competence: a sociological study in the primary school', *Teaching and Teacher Education*, 21:415–437.

Morais, A., Neves, I. P., Afonso, A. and Pires, D. (1997) *Caracterização da prática pedagógica do 1º Ciclo do Ensino Básico (Contexto instrucional e contexto regulador)*, ESSA Group, Department of Education, School of Science, University of Lisbon.

Morais, A., Neves, I. Davies, B. and Daniels, H. (2001) *Towards a Sociology of Pedagogy: The Contribution of Basil Bernstein to Research*, New York: Peter Lang.

Morais, A., Neves, I. P., Medeiros, A., Peneda, D., Fontinhas, F. and Antunes, H. (1993) *Socialização primária e prática pedagógica: Vol. 2, Análise de aprendizagens na família e na escola*, Lisbon: Gulbenkian Foundation.

Morais, A., Neves, I. and Pires, D. (2004) 'The *what* and the *how* of teaching and learning', in J. Muller, B. Davies and A. Morais (eds) *Reading Bernstein, Researching Bernstein*, London: RoutledgeFalmer.

Morais, A., Neves, I. P. *et al.* (2000) *Estudos para uma sociologia da aprendizagem*. Lisbon: Institute for Educational Innovation and Centre for Educational Research of SSUL.

Morais, A., Peneda, D., Neves, I. P. and Cardoso, L. (1992) *Socialização primária e prática pedagógica: Vol. 1*. Lisbon: Gulbenkian Foundation.

Morris, M. (1959) 'The two cultures and the scientific revolution', *Marxism Today*, 3 (12): 374–380.

Moss, G. (2001) 'Bernstein's languages of description: some generative principles', *International Journal of Social Research Methodology*, 4 (1), 17–19.

Moss, G. (2002) 'Literacy and pedagogy in flux: constructing the object of study from a Bernsteinian perspective', *British Journal of Sociology of Education*, Special Issue: Basil Bernstein's Theory of Social Class, Educational Codes and Social Control, 23 (4): 549–558.

Moss, G. (2004) 'Changing practice: the NLS and the politics of literacy policy', *Literacy*, 38 (3): 126–133.

Muller, J. (2000) *Reclaiming Knowledge: Social Theory, Curriculum and Education Policy*, London: RoutledgeFalmer.

Muller, J. (2002) 'Progressivism redux: ethos, policy, pathos', in A. Kraak and M. Young (eds) *Education in Retrospect: Policy and Implementation Since 1990*, Pretoria and London: HSRC Publishers and Institute of Education, University of London.

Muller, J., Davies, B. and Morais, A. (eds) (2004) *Reading Bernstein, Researching Bernstein*, London: RoutledgeFalmer.

Nagel, E. (1961) *The Structure of Science: Problems in the Logic of Scientific Explanation*, London: Routledge & Kegan Paul.

Nash, R. (2002) 'Numbers and narratives: further reflections in the sociology of education', *British Journal of Sociology of Education*, 23, (3): 397–412.

National Commission on Excellence in Education (NCEE) (1983) *A Nation at Risk*, Washington DC: U.S. Department of Education.

Neves, I. P. and Morais, A. (2001) 'Texts and contexts in educational systems: studies of recontextualising spaces', in A. Morais, I. Neves, B. Davies and H. Daniels (eds), *Towards a Sociology of Pedagogy: The Contribution of Basil Bernstein to Research*, New York: Peter Lang.

Niiniluoto, I. (2002) 'Scientific progress', *The Stanford Encyclopaedia of Philosophy*, (Winter 2002 edition), E. N. Zalta (ed.), at: http://plato.stanford.edu/archives/win2002/entries/scientific-progress/.

No Child Left Behind Act of 2001 [NCLB] (2002) P.L 107–110. Washington, DC: United States Congress.

Norman, E. R. (1977) 'The threat to religion', in C. B. Cox and R. Boyson (eds) *Black Paper 1977*, London: Temple Smith.

Olson, D. (1977) 'From utterance to text: the bias of language in speech and writing', *Harvard Educational Review*, 47 (3): 257–281.

Pakenham, T. (1963) 'The study of the university teacher: the Gulbenkian educational discussion 1962', *Universities Quarterly* 17 (2): 149–164.

Patterson, J. T. (2002). *Brown v. Board of Education: A Civil Rights milestone and its Troubled Legacy*, New York: Oxford University Press.

Pedro, E. R. (1981) *Social Stratification and Classroom Discourse: A Sociolinguistic Analysis of Classroom Practice*, Lund: liber laromedel.

Phillips, D. C. (2004) 'Two decades after "After the wake": postpositivistic educational thought', *Science and Education*, 13 (1–2): 67–84.

Pinker, S. (1999) *Words and Rules: The Ingredients of Language*, Cambridge: Cambridge University Press.

Pinker, S. (2002) *The Blank Slate: The Modern Denial of Human Nature*, London: Allen Lane.

Plato (1994) *Republic* (trans R. Waterfield), Oxford: Oxford University Press.

Plato (1994) *Symposium* (trans R. Waterfield), Oxford: Oxford University Press.

Plumb, J. H. (ed.) (1964) *Crisis in the Humanities*, Harmondsworth: Penguin.

Popper, K. (2002) (1st pub. 1963) *Conjectures and Refutations: The Growth of Scientific Knowledge*, London: Routledge Classics.

Porter, A. (2002) 'Measuring the content of instruction: uses in research and practice', *Educational Researcher*, 31 (7): 3–14.

Power, S. (2000) 'Missing: A sociology of educating the middle class', in J. Demaine (ed.) *Sociology of Education Today*, London: Macmillan.

Power, S., Edwards, T., Whitty, G. and Wigfall, V. (2003) *Education and the Middle Class*, Buckingham: Open University Press.

Power, S. and Whitty, G. (2002) 'Bernstein and the Middle Class', *British Journal of Sociology of Education*, 23 (4) 595–606.

Power, S., Whitty, G. and Edwards, T. (forthcoming) 'Success sustained?' A follow-up study of the 'Destined for Success?' cohort. *Research Papers in Education*.

QCA (Qualifications and Curriculum Authority) (2004) *Music in Key Stage 4: Developing Qualifications within the Vision of a Holistic and Progressive Music Education for All*, London: QCA. Music Development Working Paper.

Quicke, J. (1988) 'The 'New Right' and education', *British Journal of Educational Studies*, 36 (1): 5–20.

Ravtich, D. (1983) *The Troubled Crusade*, New York: Basic Books.

Ravtich, D. (2000) *Left Back: A Century of Battles over School Reform*, New York: Simon & Schuster.

Readings, B. (1996) *The University in Ruins*, Cambridge, MA: Harvard University Press.

Reay, D. and Arnot, M. (2004) 'Participation and control in learning: a pedagogic democratic right?', in L. Poulson and M. Walters (eds) *Learning to Read Critically in Teaching and Learning*, London: Sage.

Reeves, C. and Muller, J. (2005) 'Picking up the pace: variation in the structure and organization of learning school mathematics', Cape Town: School of Education, University of Cape Town.

Rocha, M. C., and Morais, A. (2000) 'A relação investigador-professor nos projectos de investigação-acção: Uma abordagem sociológica', in A. Morais, I. Neves *et al.*, *Estudos para uma sociologia da aprendizagem* (Chap. XVII), Lisbon: Institute for Educational Innovation and Centre for Educational Research (SSUL).

Rogoff, B. and Lave, J. (1984) (eds) *Everyday Cognition: Its Development in Social Context*, Cambridge, MA: Harvard University Press.

Rosa, C. (2002) 'Actividades em ciências no jardim de infância: Estudo sobre o desenvolvimento profissional dos educadores', unpublished Master's Dissertation, School of Science, University of Lisbon.

Rosen, H. (1972) *Language and Class: A Critical Look at the Theories of Basil Bernstein*, Bristol: Falling Wall Press.

Sacks, H. (1992) *Lectures on Conversation (Vol.1)*. Oxford: Blackwell.

Sadovnik, A. (1991) 'Basil Bernstein's theory of pedagogic practice: a structuralist approach', *Sociology of Education*, 64 (1): 48–63.

Sadovnik, A. (ed.) (1995) *Knowledge and Pedagogy: The Sociology of Basil Bernstein*, Norwood, NJ: Ablex.

Sadovnik, A. and Semel, S. (2000) 'Bernstein's theory of pedagogic practice: a sociological analysis of urban and suburban schools in the New York City Metropolitan Area', in A. Morais (ed.) *Towards a Sociology of Pedagogy: The Contribution of Basil Bernstein to Research* (pp. 189–207), New York: Peter Lang.

Sarangi, S. and Roberts, C. (1999) 'Introduction: discursive hybridity in medical work', in S. Sarangi and C. Roberts (eds) *Talk, Work and Institutional Order: Discourse in Medical, Mediation and Management Settings*, Berlin: Mouton de Gruyter.

Savage, M. (2000) *Class Analysis and Social Transformation*, Buckingham: Open University Press.

Savage, M., Barlow, J. and Fielding, T. (1992) *Property, Bureaucracy and Culture: Middle Class Formation in Contemporary Britain*. London: Routledge.

Scott, D., Brown, A. J., Lunt, I. and Thorne, L. (2003) 'Integrating academic and professional knowledge: constructing the practitioner-researcher', in E. McWilliam, (ed.) *Research Training for the Knowledge Economy* (pp. 15–24), Brisbane: Queensland University of Technology.

Scott, D., Brown, A. J., Lunt, I. and Thorne, L. (2004) *Professional Doctorates: Integrating Professional and Academic Knowledge*, Buckingham: Open University Press.

Semel, S. (1995) 'Bernstein's theory of pedagogic practice: applications to the history of progressive education in the United States', in A. Sadovnik (ed.), *Knowledge and Pedagogy: The Sociology of Basil Bernstein*, Norwood, NJ: Ablex.

Semel, S. and Sadovnik, A. (eds) (1999) *Schools of Tomorrow, Schools of Today: What Happened to Progressive Education?*, New York: Peter Lang.

Shapin, S. (1996) *The Scientific Revolution*, Chicago: University of Chicago Press.

Sharp, R. and Green, R. (1975) *Education and Social Control*, London: Routledge & Kegan Paul.

Silva, P., Morais, A. and Neves, I. P. (2003) *Caracterização da prática pedagógica do 1º Ciclo do Ensino Básico (Contexto instrucional e contexto regulador)*, ESSA Group, Department of Education, School of Science, University of Lisbon.

Silverman, D. and Torode, B. (1980) *The Material World*, London: Routledge.

Singh, P. (1993) 'Institutional discourse: a case study of the social construction of technical competence in the primary classroom', *British Journal of Sociology of Education*, 13 (1): 189–206.

Singh, P. (2001) 'Pedagogic discourse and student resistance in Australian secondary schools', in A. Morais, I. Neves, B. Davies, and H. Daniels (eds) *Towards a Sociology of Pedagogy: The Contribution of Basil Bernstein to Research*, New York: Peter Lang.

Singh, P. (2002) 'Pedagogising knowledge: Bernstein's theory of the pedagogic device', *British Journal of Sociology of Education*, 23 (4): 571–582.

Sloboda, J. A. (2001) 'Conference keynote: emotion, functionality and the everyday experience of music', *Music Education Research*, 3 (2): 243–253.

Snow, C. P. (1959) *The Two Cultures and the Scientific Revolution*, Cambridge: Cambridge University Press.

Snow, C. P. (1964) *The Two Cultures and a Second Look*, Cambridge: Cambridge University Press.

Strathern, M. (1992) *After Nature: English Kinship in the Late Twentieth Century*, Cambridge: Cambridge University Press.

Street, B. (1995) *Social Literacies: Critical Approaches to Literacy Development, Ethnography and Education*, Harlow, UK: Longman.

Tashakkori, A. and Teddlie, C. (2003) 'Issues and dilemmas in teaching research methods courses in social and behavioural sciences: US perspective', *International Journal of Social Research Methodology*, 6 (1), 61–77.

Taylor, C. (2002) *The RCBN Consultation Exercise: Stakeholder Report*, Research Capacity Building Network Occasional Paper 50, Cardiff: Cardiff University School of Social Sciences.

Tomlinson, J. (1993) *The Control of Education*, London: Cassell.

Tractenberg, P., Holzer, M., Miller, J., Sadovnik, A. and Liss, B. (2002) *Reestablishing Local Control in New Jersey's Takeover Districts*, Trenton: New Jersey Department of Education.

Tyler, W. (1988) *School Organization: A Sociological Perspective*, London: Croom Helm.

UK Council for Graduate Education (1998) *The Status of Published Work in Submissions for Doctoral Degrees in European Universities*, Warwick: UKCGE.

Valsiner, J. (1997) *Culture and the Development of Children's Action: A Theory of Human Development* (2nd edition), New York: John Wiley and Sons.

van Leeuwen, T. and Humphrey, S. 1996. 'On learning to look through a geographer's eyes', in R. Hasan and G. Williams (eds) Literacy in Society (Applied Linguistics and Language Study), London: Longman.

Vygotsky, L. S. (1978) *Mind in Society: The Development of Higher Psychological Processes*, M. Cole, John-Steiner, S. Scribner and E. Souberman (eds and trans), Cambridge MA: Harvard University Press.

Walford, G. and Pickering, W. S. F. (1998) *Durkheim and Modern Education*, London: Routledge.

Walkerdine, V. (1988) *The Mastery of Reason*, London, New York: Routledge.

Walkerdine, V. (1989) *Counting Girls Out*, London: Virago.

Weinberg, S. (1993) *Dreams of a Final Theory*, New York: Vintage.

Wenger, E. (1998) *Communities of Practice: Learning, Meaning and Identity*, Cambridge: Cambridge University Press.

Wenger, E., McDermott, R. and Snyder, W. (2002) *Cultivating Communities of Practice*, Harvard Business School Press.

Wertsch, J. V. (1991) *Voices of the Mind: A Socio-Cultural Approach to Mediated Action*, Cambridge, MA: Harvard University Press.

Wertsch, J. V. (1985) *Vygotsky and the Social Formation of Mind*, Cambridge, MA: Harvard University Press.

Wexler, P. and Grabiner, G. (1986) 'America during the crisis', in R. Sharp (ed.) *Capitalism, Crisis and Schooling*, South Melbourne: Macmillan.

Wheelahan, L. (2005) 'Comparing realist and rationalist defences of propositional knowledge in the curriculum'. Paper presented at: *Engaging Realist Alternatives: IACR Conference*, Sydney, 10–12 July.

Whitty, G. (1990) 'The New Right and the National Curriculum: state control or market forces?', in M. Flude and M. Hammer (eds) *The Education Reform Act 1988: Its Origins and Implications*, London: Falmer.

Whitty, G. (2001) 'Education, social class and social exclusion', *Journal of Education Policy*, 16 (4) 287–295.

Whitty, G. with Power, S. (2002) 'The overt and hidden curricula of quasi-markets', in G. Whitty, *Making Sense of Education Policy*, London: Paul Chapman.

Whitty, G., Rowe, G. and Aggleton, P. (1994) 'Discourse in cross-curricular contexts: limits to empowerment', *International Studies in the Sociology of Education*, 4 (1): 25–41.

Wilber, K. (1995) *Sex, Ecology, Spirituality: The Spirit of Evolution*, Boston: Shambhala.

Williams, G. (1995) 'Joint book-reading and literacy pedagogy: a socio-semantic examination', unpublished doctoral dissertation, Macquarie University, North Ryde, Australia.

Williams, G. (2000) 'Children's literature, children and uses of language description', in L. Unsworth (ed.) *Research Language in Schools and Communities: Functional Linguistic Perspectives*, London: Cassell.

Williams, G. (2001) 'Literacy pedagogy prior to schooling: relations between social and semantic variation', in A. Morais, I. Neves, B. Davies, and H. Daniels (eds) *Towards a Sociology of Pedagogy: The Contribution of Basil Bernstein to Research*, New York: Peter Lang.

Wilson, S. and Berne, J. (1999) 'Teacher learning and the acquisition of professional knowledge: an examination of research on contemporary professional development', in A.

Iran-Nejad and P. Pearson (eds), *Review of Research in Education*, Washington DC: American Educational Research Association.

Young, M. F. D. (1971) *Knowledge and Control: New Directions for the Sociology of Education*, London, Collier Macmillan.

Young, M. F. D. (2000) 'Rescuing the sociology of educational knowledge from the extremes of voice discourse: towards a new theoretical basis for the sociology of the curriculum', *British Journal of Sociology of Education*, 21 (4): 523–536.

Zelman v. Simmons-Harris, 122 S. Ct. 2460 (2002).

Index

Abbott, Peter 98–101
abstraction, as educative aim 66
activity theory 163–7, 165*t*, 166*t*, 168, 170, 172–7, 176*t*; future directions 178; joint 166; situated analysis 176–7
Adie, Kate 105
Adonis, Andrew 190
Agrippa 19
Ahl, Valerie 72*n*
Alcibiades 62–3, 65
Alexander, Robin 188, 190, 195*n*
Allan, Sian 104–5
Allen, T.H.F. 72*n*
Althusser, Louis 79
American Sociological Association 210*n*
Antunes, Helena 85
Anyon, Jean 206, 208
Arnot, Madeleine 4, 5, 43*n*
art: pupils' perceptions of 121–2; teaching methods 117
Attenborough, Richard 104
Australia 223
authoritarianism (within classroom) 115–17, 125
AVP (autonomous visible pedagogy) 197, 208, 209–10

Bacon, Francis 18
Bailey, C.H. 188
Banks, Tony 104
Barber, Michael 187, 190–2
beauty 60–3; 'ladder of' 64, 65, 67, 68, 71
Beck, John 7
Berlin, Isaiah 17–18
Bernard of Chartres 20
Berne, J. 146
Bernstein, Basil 1–8; on activity theory 173–4, 176; on code theory 200–1, 202; on 'discursive gap' 36–8; features of

theoretical mode 34–5; on 'grammar' 39–42; on knowledge structures 12–14, 15, 21–2, 27*n*, 44–5, 46–8, 58, 72*n*; on language codes 84; on market-dominated education 211–12, 213, 214; objections to 35–6, 106–7; on (pedagogic) discourse 109–10, 146, 148, 171–2, 178, 212; on pedagogic hierarchy 67–71; on pedagogic identities 95–8, 99, 102, 103, 105–8, 118, 213; on pedagogic structures 23–4; on politics and education 181, 182–3, 185, 192–3, 194, 195*n*; on recontextualization 109, 124, 222; on research 129–30, 132, 134, 137, 138, 144–5; on the self 212, 216–17; on social change 221; on social class 94, 106–7, 108*n*, 143, 200, 201–2, 203–10, 208; on social formation of mind 163; on social practice/positioning 167–70; on sociology of education 28–9, 30–1, 33–6, 41, 42, 77–8, 141, 197, 206, 211; teaching methods 136; on UK system 203; on 'voice' 76–7, 86, 88–9, 91–23
Blair, Tony 104
Bloom, Benjamin 72*n*
Blunkett, David 190, 191
Boot, Louise 101–2
Bottomley, Virginia 105
Boudon, Raymond 36, 43*n*
boundaries (between categories) 78–9
Bourdieu, Pierre 11*t*, 13, 34, 37, 43*n*, 79, 138, 171, 219, 224*n*, 225*n*
Bourne, Jill 92
Bowles, Samuel 29, 206
Brahe, Tycho 19
Branson, Richard 101, 104
Briggs, Asa 52
Brookes, B.C. 51